PLAYFAIR WORLD CUP MEXICO 1986

D1392408

Queen Anne Press

A *Queen Anne Press* Book

© Queen Anne Press 1986

Cover photograph: Zico of Brazil and Bertoni of Argentina,
World Cup 1982 by Colorsport

First published in Great Britain in 1986 by
Queen Anne Press, Macdonald & Co (Publishers) Ltd,
Greater London House, Hampstead Road, London NW1 7QX
A BPCC plc company

British Library Cataloguing in Publication data

Playfair World Cup 1986.
    1. World Cup *(Football championship)* — History
I. Dunk, Peter
796.334'66   GV943.49

    ISBN 0-356-10636-5

Filmset by The Eastern Press Ltd of London & Reading
Printed and bound in Great Britain by
Hazell Watson & Viney Limited,
Member of the BPCC Group,
Aylesbury, Bucks

CONTENTS

Introduction 4
The History of the World Cup 5
The Qualifying Competition 117
The Game Plan for Mexico 160
The Stadia 170
The British Stars 173
Form Guide to the Finalists 187
Quiz 213
Miscellany 229
Merit Table 238
Final Tournament Results 241

INTRODUCTION

'The Germans have stopped playing – they think it's all over!' *(Hurst scores)* 'It is now!'

So ended Kenneth Wolstenholme's commentary on the World Cup final of 1966. The country that gave the game to the world had finally won the biggest prize in football, but it had been a long time coming. Now another twenty years have passed, and the World Cup, a competition which started in uncertain style between the wars, wracked by petty jealousies and recriminations, has developed into the greatest and most popular sporting festival in the world. In the Azteca Stadium, Mexico City, on 31 May 1986, Italy and Bulgaria will kick off the thirteenth championships watched by a world-wide television audience of billions.

How long ago it was when a mere four European nations sent their soccer stars on a gruelling two-and-a-half week sea voyage to Montevideo, where the newly-built Centenary Stadium hosted the first championship, and a dazzling Uruguayan team showed us how the game could be played. To be more accurate, of course, they didn't show us at all – there was no television then, few Europeans bothered to make the journey, and word spread only slowly – but some very important seeds had been sown in 1930.

The next two tournaments were held in a Europe lurching inevitably towards another terrible war, and it has really been in the nine post-war World Cups that this competition has matured into the marvellous and magnetic spectacle that we all look forward to so avidly every four years.

For the second time, the tournament has been awarded to Mexico. In many senses this was a strange, if not poor choice, especially for the Europeans and others not used to coping with the combination of heat and rarified atmosphere which will be encountered there, but the 1970 tournament managed to produce some of the most thrilling and brilliant football entertainment of recent years, and if Mexico '86 comes anywhere near that standard, we're in for another real football treat.

This book sets the scene with the history of the World Cup, full details of the qualifying tournament, the Mexico '86 game plan and much more besides. Here's hoping you enjoy it, but, more importantly, here's hoping for another World Cup to remember!

PETER DUNK   December 1985

CHAPTER ONE

THE HISTORY OF
THE WORLD CUP

Introduction

The birth of modern football can be dated precisely on 26 October 1863, the day on which the Football Association was formed at a meeting in the Freemason's Tavern in Great Queen Street in London's Holborn. Within a decade, international football was started with the first fixture between England and Scotland ending in a goalless draw at Hampden Park on 30 November 1872.

These were the days, in the middle of Victoria's reign, when Great Britain was the foremost world power in everything from economics to sport – especially football – and the game soon spread to every corner of the globe. But hand in hand with this pre-eminence went an almost unbelievable insularity, and so the seeds of the World Cup were not sown in the game's homeland.

Probably the oldest association to be formed outside the United Kingdom was Denmark's *Boldspil Union*, which was established in 1889, and by the turn of the century football associations had sprung up in many other countries, but it was to Britain that they looked for leadership. British football was regarded by foreigners as something from another world, and the Football Association was seen as the obvious choice to lead the world in the international administration of the game. Indeed, this awestruck admiration of the British game was justified – it would not be until 15 May 1929 that England suffered defeat at the hands of a team from outside the British Isles, losing 3-4 against Spain in Madrid. Even then, beating England in England was virtually unthinkable, and would not be achieved until 1953 when Puskas and the other Marvellous Magyars inflicted a humiliating 6-3 defeat on the English in the hitherto impregnable fortress of Wembley.

So the English were wanted, but the English didn't want to know. As far back as the early 1890s feelers were put forward by the *Union Belge des Societes des Sports,* but to the Football Association the idea of an international soccer authority extending beyond the British Isles seemed at least superfluous, if not downright presumptuous. A classic illustration of the attitude of the Football Association towards these foreign upstarts can be seen in something which happened in 1902.

Early that year, C.A.W.Hirschman, on behalf of the Dutch Football Association, wrote to the Football Association in London urging them to sponsor an international football championship (the idea is ascribed to Count van der Straten Ponthoy), and to help in the formation of an international body which could organise the event and at the same time safeguard and guarantee uniform international rules. Here can be seen the seed of the World Cup, though the seed did not mature for more than a quarter of a century.

Frederick J.Wall, Secretary of the Football Association, replied to Mr Hirschman on 4 June 1902:

Dear Sir,
    In reply to your letter, your proposals were considered by my Council . . . our representatives to the International Board were asked to bring the letter before the Board at its meeting on the 16th inst . . . our representatives will of course make a full report to the Council after which I will again communicate with you.
    I may say, however, that my Council will not meet again until August next.

Despite the promise to 'again communicate with' Hirschman after the FA Council meeting of August 1902, it was not until 8 April 1903 that we find Wall's next letter to the hapless Dutch official. The International board of the FA Council had, Hirschman was informed, decided to pass his proposals on to the four British Associations, and further consideration would be given to the ideas at the next Board meeting, due to take place in June 1903.

It was at this point that Robert Guerin of the *Union des Sociétés Françaises des Sports Athletiques* appeared on the

6

scene and suggested to the Football Association in the person of Frederick Wall that a federation of the European soccer nations should be founded. Wall's reply was described, even in the official *History of the FA*, as a 'monumental example of British insularity'. It stated, tersely:

> The Council of the Football Association cannot see the advantages of such a Federation, but on all matters upon which joint action was desirable they would be prepared to confer.

Neither Guerin nor Hirschman could understand why the English so persistently refused to undertake the world leadership which was being offered to them. The truth was that the British associations were so isolationist that they simply had no idea how fast soccer was progressing on the Continent, nor did they even want to know. Football was a British game, and whilst we were quite happy, perhaps even a little flattered, that our foreign friends had adopted it, there was no way in which we were actually going to condescend to co-operate with them in any sort of official manner.

Guerin reluctantly abandoned his struggle with the Football Association, and undertook to invite delegates from various countries himself. So it was that on 21 May 1904, in Paris, the *Fédération Internationale de Football Association* (FIFA) was formed, without the benefit of British participation. The founder nations were Belgium, Denmark, France, Holland, Spain, Sweden and Switzerland. Three of them (France, Spain and Sweden) had no national association, while Denmark, Spain and Switzerland had never even played an international.

It was at this very first meeting that the idea of a World Championship was first discussed, and a clause was inserted in the constitution of FIFA which said that they alone had the right to organise any such tournament. This right would not be exercised for a further twenty-six years.

It was fitting that FIFA was created in France, for two Frenchmen, Jules Rimet and Henri Delaunay, were to be the real architects of the World Cup. Rimet, after whom the first World Cup trophy would be named, was President of the French Federation from 1919 until 1949 and President of FIFA from 1920 until 1954, while Delaunay, after whom the European Championship trophy would be named, was Secre-

7

tary of the French Federation from its beginning in 1919 until his death in 1956, shortly before the death of the eighty-three-year-old Rimet.

Meanwhile, the English were beginning to see the light, although their relationships with FIFA were destined to be fraught with difficulties until after the Second World War. In April 1905 the promised conference finally took place in England and within a year England at last joined the Federation. Four FA Council members had been sent to an international conference in Berne in early June 1905, where they discovered exactly how soccer had flourished on the Continent. This was reported back to the full Council, who decided, belatedly, to take part in proceedings from now on.

Even after Britain's insufferable pomposity in the period leading up to the formation of FIFA, she was still held in sufficiently high regard in football circles overseas for one D.B.Woolfall of the FA to be elected President of FIFA in 1906, succeeding Robert Guerin. Woolfall remained in office until his death in 1918.

The year of Woolfall's death saw the end of hostilities in the Great War of 1914-18, but it also heralded the beginning of serious problems between the British Football Associations and their European neighbours, problems which would lead to Britain being left out in the cold when the World Cup actually started twelve years later. At first, the British refused to play against countries which had fought against them in the war or had remained neutral. It took six years for that little problem to be sorted out, and the British Associations re-affiliated in 1924.

There followed four years of argument about the definition of the amateur. As far as the British were concerned, an amateur was only entitled to enough money to cover necessary hotel and travelling expenses. Anything more, for whatever reason, and he should be regarded as a professional. Many Europeans did not agree, taking the view that compensation for loss of wages was perfectly acceptable within the definition of amateurism.

The matter came to a head in 1928 when, at the Olympic Games in Amsterdam, 'broken time' payments were allowed. The British withdrew from both the Olympic movement and FIFA, not rejoining the latter body until 1946. How the English or the Scots would have fared in the three World Cup tournaments they missed is a matter for speculation, but

8

certainly by the time the English did take part for the first time in 1950, they were no longer the dominant force that they had been a half-century before, and it would not be until 1966, on their home ground, that they would claim the title which Frederick Wall and his Council would have considered to be rightfully theirs.

Meanwhile, FIFA got on without the British, and the World Cup – for so long the dream of people like Rimet and Delaunay – came into being. FIFA held a congress in 1920 in Antwerp, concurrent with the Olympic Games, and the often-discussed idea of a World Championship was accepted in principle. Rimet was now President, but still things moved relatively slowly and it was not until the 1924 meeting, during the Paris Olympics, that really detailed planning began in earnest. It was significant that the Uruguayan football team, about which little was known, carried off the Olympic title that year with a brilliant display, beating Switzerland 3-0 in the final.

By the time of the FIFA congress two years later, Rimet and Delaunay recognized that because only amateurs were allowed to take part in the Olympic Games, the Olympic soccer tournament could no longer be regarded as a true World Championship. Delaunay was quoted as saying: 'Today international football can no longer be held within the confines of the Olympics…many countries where professionalism is now recognized and organised cannot any longer be represented there by their best players.'

This was especially true in the game's homeland – the Football Association had accepted professionalism as early as 1885 – and now some of mainland Europe's best sides were being kept out of the Olympics for the same reasons, notably Austria and Hungary, who in October 1902 had staged the first international match involving non-British sides. The World Cup was finally on its way, and in 1928 Henri Delaunay and Hugo Meisl, the Secretary of the Austrian FA, were charged with making the preparations for the first tournament. That same year, in Amsterdam, the wonderful Uruguayans once more carried off the Olympic title, this time beating Argentina 2-1 in the final. South American soccer was already a real force and that continent was destined to stage the first World Championship of the sport which had been born in Britain and, in an international sense, raised in France.

So, in 1929, FIFA met in Barcelona to decide where the first World Cup finals should be held. There were four European candidates – Spain, Holland, Italy and Sweden – plus Uruguay. The latter, a country with a great football tradition but a population of only two million, made a surprising offer which was to clinch the vote for them. They would pay the travelling and hotel costs for all the visiting teams and would also build a new stadium for the finals in central Montevideo. This stadium would be named the Centenary Stadium in honour of the fact that in 1930 Uruguay would be celebrating one hundred years of independence and would, FIFA were assured, be completed in only eight months.

Upon hearing this the four European aspirants withdrew, not only in their attempts to stage the championship, but, sadly, from the championships themselves. Hurt but undaunted, Uruguay went ahead with her plans.

Uruguay 1930

Unlike their modern counterparts, the European footballers of 1930 could not simply board a jetliner at their local airport and arrive in Uruguay a few hours later. No such facilities existed then, and European teams were faced instead with a gruelling sea voyage which took the best part of three weeks. Faced with this prospect, there was not much enthusiasm on the part of the Europeans, and with only eight weeks left before the start of the 1930 tournament there was not one single European entry, despite the generosity of the Uruguayan offer to defray all expenses.

As well as the four candidates who withdrew when they failed to secure the nomination for staging the tournament, the Austrians, Swiss, Czechs, Germans and Hungarians all said no. The four British associations were in any event out of FIFA, and the Belgians, French, Rumanians and Yugoslavians were all undecided. Eventually, these last four named agreed to go. Jules Rimet, a Frenchman, was now FIFA President and the French Association, who had played hosts to the Uruguayans in the 1924 Paris Olympics, were unable to withstand Rimet's pressure. The Rumanians for their part succumbed to the pressure of King Carol himself. He wasn't one of the great monarchs of European history and was in fact generally unpopular in his realm for being a German-speaking king, but he was very keen on sport. He picked the team personally and brought pressure to bear on the players' employers to allow the squad the necessary time off work.

Even so, the four European entrants were hardly representative of the best of European football at the time, and there was much bitterness in Montevideo, bitterness which could still be tasted four years later. However, Uruguay's arch rivals, the Argentinians, would be there. Since 1902 they had been traditional rivals for the Lipton Cup, a trophy presented by the tea millionaire Sir Thomas Lipton for international competition, and the South American neighbours had also fought out the Olympic final in 1928.

The United States sent a team consisting largely of Scottish and English professionals, and the Brazilians also took part, although in those days black players had only just been accepted in the national team and it would be some time before they blended in to produce perhaps the most formidable team in the history of the game. The other entrants, all from South and Central America, were Chile, Mexico, Bolivia, Peru and Paraguay.

Thus thirteen nations were represented, and as it was clearly too small a number to make a knock-out competition feasible, the teams were arranged in four qualifying pools, each headed by a seeded team. Pool 1 consisted of Argentina (seeded), Chile, France and Mexico; Brazil led Pool 2 and were joined there by Yugoslavia and Bolivia; the host nation headed Pool 3, which was completed by Rumania and Peru; the United States were seeded in Pool 4, ahead of Paraguay and Belgium. Thus there was one European team in each pool, and the four pool winners would go forward to the semi-finals.

Three of the European teams – France, Belgium and Rumania – made the crossing on one boat, the Yugoslavs having departed two days earlier. Among the passengers were the FIFA party, who carried with them the valuable trophy. Weighing almost nine pounds, including four pounds of solid gold, it was the work of the French sculptor Abel Lafleur. One of the boats picked up the Brazilians en route, and when they docked in Montevideo they were all given the most tremendous welcome by the waiting crowds. The cordial nature of relations between the hosts and those Europeans who had bothered to turn up is perhaps best illustrated by the visitors who surprised Jules Rimet in his hotel one day. The President of Uruguay, accompanied by his Prime Minister and several other notables, had arrived to serve the FIFA President with the *assado*, a typical Uruguayan lunch!

Unfortunately, a particularly heavy rainy season had delayed progress on the Centenary Stadium, which was not quite ready, and the Peñarol and Nacional club stadiums had to be used for some of the early matches. But before Uruguay's opening fixture with Peru on 18 July Raoul Jude, President of the Uruguayan Football Association and Chairman of the organising committee, declared the stadium and, belatedly, the tournament open.

Five days earlier, on 13 July, the tournament had in fact started with the game between France and Mexico. The French won 4-1, even though their superb goalkeeper, Alex Thepot, had to be replaced by full-back Chantrel after ten minutes, having sustained a nasty kick on the jaw. Substitutes were not to arrive on the scene until 1970. The French captain that day, right-half Alex Villaplane, was ultimately shot by the French Resistance because he had allegedly collaborated with the Nazis.

Two days later France faced Argentina in what was to be one of the most controversial matches of the tournament. Early in the game the hard-tackling Argentinian, Monti, tackled the French inside-left, Lucien Laurent, so ferociously that Laurent was reduced to the role of right-wing passenger. Still the Argentinians could not break down the French defence until nine minutes before the end when Monti took a free kick which had been awarded twenty yards from goal. As he kicked the ball his team-mate Pinel stepped across to unsight Thepot in the French goal and the ball found the back of the net before Thepot could recover.

Then, with only four minutes remaining and the French centre-forward limping after yet another of Monti's crunching tackles, Marcel Langiller raced the length of the pitch and looked certain to score the equaliser, but the Brazilian referee, Almeido Rego, inexplicably blew for time. The Argentinian Cherro was so overcome with joy that he collapsed and had to be carried off. Similarly joyful Argentinian supporters invaded the pitch in a mood of celebration, but the French players surrounded Señor Rego, who suddenly realised his error. Mounted police were called in to clear the pitch and the remaining four minutes were duly played, but the French failed to level the scores.

Argentina won their next match, against Mexico, 6-3, although the score could easily have been higher had not three of the five penalties awarded by Bolivian referee Ulysses Saucedo been missed. A young Argentinian called Guillermo Stabile made his debut in this game, and went on to become the competition's leading scorer with eight goals. In later years he was appointed manager of the Argentine national team.

Having scored a hat-trick against Mexico, Stabile kept his place for the last Pool 1 match, against Chile. Monti, who had missed the game against Mexico, was back for this fixture and made his presence felt shortly before half-time when he kicked Torres, the Chilean left-half, as the latter was attempting to head the ball. Torres was not slow to react, and within moments there was a dreadful brawl involving all the players which took the police some time to break up. Argentina had been 2-1 up at the time, and finished the match as 3-1 winners, with Stabile getting two of them.

Meanwhile Chile, who had started by beating Mexico 3-0, had surprisingly beaten France by the only goal of a game in which the French looked dispirited from the start, and so it was that Argentina, with maximum points, went through to the semi-finals.

In Pool 3, Uruguay, as expected, qualified. Their preparations had been meticulous, with the players confined to training camps for several weeks prior to the tournament. Discipline had been strict, so much so that when the star goalkeeper, Mazzali, a hero with two Olympic gold medals, was caught by a member of the coaching staff returning to camp from a late-night visit to his family, he was immediately dropped from the squad. This was not only a tremendous blow to his prestige and earning capacity, but could have affected the team's performances. In the event, his successor Ballesteros proved adequate.

Uruguay's opening match in the new Centenary Stadium was, however, somewhat disappointing – a precedent which host countries have seemed to follow ever since. Their opponents from Peru had let in three goals against Rumania in the opening game in Pool 3, but held out well against the Uruguayans until Castro – a player who had lost half of one arm – managed to score a late winner. The final match in the pool, between Uruguay and Rumania, was therefore vital to both teams and took on the status of a quarter-final, but the Uruguayans dropped Castro and Petrone and brought in Scarone and a new star, Pelegrin Anselmo. They won comfortably by 4-0.

In Pool 2, the first result was a surprise, with Yugoslavia beating Brazil 2-1. The Brazilians displayed much of the individual skill which was to be their hallmark in later years, but the Yugoslavs demonstrated the value of superior teamwork. Two of the Yugoslavs, Beck and Stefanovic, had been playing in France, where they had just helped Sete to win the French Cup, and Beck and Tirnanic scored early goals. Another effort was judged to be offside, and although the Brazilian captain Neto pulled one back after half-time, Yugoslavia got the points. Both Yugoslavia and Brazil beat Bolivia 4-0, Yugoslavia's effort being the more remarkable as one of their players suffered a broken leg in the first few minutes, and so the Yugoslavs were Europe's sole representatives in the semi-finals.

14

The United States, with their liberal sprinkling of expatriot Brits, sailed through their Pool 4 matches, beating both Belgium and Paraguay 3-0. The hapless Belgians lost the inconsequential third game 1-0 against Paraguay. The performance of the United States, especially against a Paraguayan side which had trounced Uruguay 3-0 in the last international before the tournament began, made such a great impression that were immediately made favourites for the championship! For the record, the six Britons who had become naturalised American citizens in order to qualify for the team were Alec Wood, James Gallacher, Andrew Auld, James Brown and Bart McGhee from Scotland, plus George Moorhouse from England.

The semi-finals proved to be a different story. The United States found themselves facing Argentina, and although they went in at half-time trailing by only one goal – goalkeeper Douglas misjudged a ball and the effervescent Monti was on hand to snap up the chance – they were outclassed in the second half, when they conceded five more and managed only one in reply, scored by Brown. Stabile added two more to his personal tally in the process.

The other semi-final was to end in the same 6-1 scoreline, but in this case the figures are misleading. Yugoslavia shocked the home crowd by taking the lead through Seculic as early as the fourth minute, and although Uruguay soon replied, their first goal was widely reported to be yards offside. Anselmo made it 2-1, but although Yugoslavia appeared to equalise soon after, their 'goal' was disallowed by an extremely dubious offside decision. Then, to make matters worse for the Yugoslavs, a third Uruguayan goal was allowed although the ball had quite clearly gone out of play moments earlier. This seemed to knock the spirit out of the Europeans, who conceded a further three goals after the interval.

So the stage was set for the first World Cup final, and if the conservative Old World had not been convinced when these same two teams met in the thrilling Olympic final of 1928, they were about to have their eyes opened. Already in Britain the so-called 'third back' had been evolved in a domestic game which was becoming ever more defensive and safety-conscious, but the South Americans didn't care about such things. They seemed intent only on playing fine, fast attacking football, and so it proved on 30 July 1930 in the Centenary Stadium, Montevideo.

Across the River Plate in Buenos Aires, the atmosphere was extraordinary. Ten packet boats were chartered to take the fans across to Montevideo, but they weren't enough, as thousands more clamoured for some way to cross the water and see their team. On arrival in Montevideo, each Argentinian was searched for concealed weapons, but in the event the huge crowd – limited to 90,000 in the 100,000-capacity stadium – behaved in a sporting manner.

John Langenus of Belgium was chosen to referee the final, but such was the atmosphere of tension in Montevideo that morning that Langenus insisted on guarantees of safety for himself and his linesmen, and it was only a couple of hours before the kick-off that his fellow referees agreed that he should go ahead. Both teams were under constant armed guard, and outside the stadium soldiers with fixed bayonets kept the crowds moving.

Meanwhile, inside the stadium, an argument had developed about the match ball. Each of the two national associations insisted that a ball manufactured in their own country should be used, and FIFA officials were horrified to learn that this had not been covered in the regulations. In the end a compromise was agreed and two balls were used – one in each half!

Uruguay were now favourites to win the title, but Anselmo was unfit and was replaced by Castro, and Petrone seemed to be past his best. For their part, Argentina had been playing well and had found a truly world-class striker in Stabile. Unfortunately for the visitors from Buenos Aires, they had no really good goalkeepers. Angelo Bossio had been dropped for being unreliable, but his replacement, Juan Botasso, wasn't much better.

Uruguay started well, taking the lead after only ten minutes through their right-winger, Dorado. Peucelle soon equalised, and then, after thirty-five minutes, Stabile scored a goal for Argentina which was allowed to stand despite bitter protests from the home side that the whistle should have gone for offside. To their credit, the home supporters in the crowd accepted the decision with a stony silence.

Soon after the interval the Uruguayan section of the crowd were cheered up by a goal from Cea, who tucked the ball home after a dazzling solo run. Ten minutes later Iriarte put Uruguay ahead, and then, with play still finely balanced, Stabile crashed a shot against the crossbar. It proved to be

16

Argentina's final chance, and Castro, who had scored Uruguay's first goal of the tournament against Peru twelve days earlier, scored his side's fourth goal with only seconds remaining.

Montevideo went mad. The following day was declared a national holiday, and the tournament was widely considered to be a major success. Four times the big new stadium had been filled to capacity, and those European countries who had made the trip went home with their coffers swelled. For Uruguay, two Olympic victories had been capped by the World Cup, and who could argue that they were not the greatest team of their day? Argentina, perhaps. In Buenos Aires the Uruguayan Consulate was stoned by an infuriated mob, which was eventually dispersed when the police decided to open fire on them. Soon afterwards, the two football associations broke off relations. The story of the World Cup had begun.

Uruguay 1930 – Results

Pool 1
France (3)4, Mexico (0)1
Argentina (0)1, France (0)0
Chile (1)3, Mexico (0)0
Chile (0)1, France (0)0
Argentina (3)6, Mexico (0)3
Argentina (2)3, Chile (1)1

	P	W	D	L	F	A	Pts
Argentina	3	3	0	0	10	4	6
Chile	3	2	0	1	5	3	4
France	3	1	0	2	4	3	2
Mexico	3	0	0	3	4	13	0

Pool 2
Yugoslavia (2)2, Brazil (0)1
Yugoslavia (0)4, Bolivia (0)0
Brazil (1)4, Bolivia (0)0

	P	W	D	L	F	A	Pts
Yugoslavia	2	2	0	0	6	1	4
Brazil	2	1	0	1	5	2	2
Bolivia	2	0	0	2	0	8	0

Pool 3
Rumania (1)3, Peru (0)1
Uruguay (0)1, Peru (0)0
Uruguay (4)4, Rumania (0)0

	P	W	D	L	F	A	Pts
Uruguay	2	2	0	0	5	0	4
Rumania	2	1	0	1	3	5	2
Peru	2	0	0	2	1	4	0

Pool 4
United States (2)3, Belgium (0)0
United States (2)3, Paraguay (0)0
Paraguay (1)1, Belgium (0)0

	P	W	D	L	F	A	Pts
United States	2	2	0	0	6	0	4
Paraguay	2	1	0	1	1	3	2
Belgium	2	0	0	2	0	4	0

Semi-finals
Argentina (1)6 *(Monti, Scopelli, Stabile 2, Peucelle 2)*
United States (0)1 *(Brown)*
Argentina: Botasso; Della Torre, Paternoster, Evaristo J.,
Monti, Orlandini, Peucelle, Scopelli, Stabile, Ferreira,
Evaristo M.
United States: Douglas; Wood, Moorhouse, Gallacher,
Tracey, Auld, Brown, Gonsalvez, Patenaude, Florie,
McGhee.

Uruguay (3)6 *(Cea 3, Anselmo 2, Iriarte)*
Yugoslavia (1)1 *(Seculic)*
Uruguay: Ballesteros; Nasazzi, Mascheroni, Andrade,
Fernandez, Gestido, Dorado, Scarone, Anselmo, Cea,

Iriarte.
Yugoslavia: Yavocic; Ivkovic, Milhailovic, Arsenievic,
Stefanovic, Djokic, Tirnanic, Marianovic, Beck,
Vujadinovic, Seculic.

Final   Montevideo, 30 July 1930
Uruguay (1)4 *(Dorado, Cea, Iriarte, Castro)*
Argentina (2)2 *(Peucelle, Stabile)*
Uruguay: Ballesteros; Nasazzi, Mascheroni, Andrade,
Fernandez, Gestido, Dorado, Scarone, Castro, Cea, Iriarte.
Argentina: Botasso; Della Torre, Paternoster, Evaristo J.,
Monti, Suarez, Peucelle, Varallo, Stabile, Ferreira, Evaristo
M.

Italy 1934

Benito Mussolini saw the World Cup as a way of generating useful propoganda for his fascist regime, but FIFA were also pleased with the choice of venue, because in Italy several games could be played at once in different venues. Unfortunately, none of those games would involve World Champions Uruguay. Still upset at the lack of European participation four years earlier, still furious with Argentina and plagued both by a players' strike and the refusal of clubs to release star players to the national squad in a nation where professionalism had only recently been recognised, they stayed away – the only time in the history of the tournament that the Champions have declined to defend their title.

The tournament had been awarded to Italy at FIFA's Stockholm congress of 1932. Although the scale of the competition was growing – there would be sixteen finalists this time – the Italian Football Association promised to bear the financial burden. Uruguay had, after all, made a profit, and in any case the fascist government was standing in the wings, only too happy to pick up the bill.

There were thirty-two entrants for the 1934 World Cup, and so it was decided to hold a qualifying tournament. The teams were split into twelve groups as follows:

Group 1: USA, Cuba, Mexico, Haiti.
Group 2: Brazil, Peru.
Group 3: Argentina, Chile.
Group 4: Egypt, Palestine, Turkey.
Group 5: Sweden, Estonia, Lithuania.
Group 6: Spain, Portugal.
Group 7: Italy, Greece.
Group 8: Austria, Hungary, Bulgaria.
Group 9: Czechoslovakia, Poland.
Group 10: Yugoslavia, Switzerland, Rumania.
Group 11: Netherlands, Belgium, Ireland.
Group 12: Germany, France, Luxembourg.

It was intended that the winner of each Group would qualify, plus the runners-up from Groups 8, 10, 11 and 12, but there were problems in Group 1, where the travelling distances were enormous for those days. It was therefore decided that the winner of a triangular tournament between Cuba,

Mexico and Haiti would play off against the USA in Rome on 24 May, three days before the First Round Proper was due to begin. In the event, the USA beat Mexico 4-2. The sixteen finalists were therefore Austria, Argentina, Belgium, Brazil, Czechoslovakia, Egypt, France, Germany, Hungary, Italy, the Netherlands, Rumania, Spain, Sweden, Switzerland and the United States.

This time, the tournament was to be on a knock-out basis throughout – which proved to be a great pity for the only South American finalists – and eight stadia were to be used: Bologna, Florence, Genoa, Milan, Naples, Rome, Trieste and Turin. These stadiums would all be used for the first round matches, Bologna, Naples, Milan and Turin would stage the second round ties, the semi-finals went to Milan and Rome, and the final would be in Rome on 10 June, the match for third place being staged in Naples three days earlier.

Conscious of the pulling power of certain teams, it was decided to seed the 'best' eight in the first round matches to avoid the early demise of any teams which could pull in big money. The chosen ones were Italy, Czechoslovakia, Hungary, Argentina, Austria, Germany, Brazil and the Netherlands. The choice of the last two was surprising, most people being of the opinion that Spain and Switzerland were stronger teams, and it was therefore ironic that Spain defeated Brazil 3-1 in the first round, while the Swiss disposed of the Dutch 3-2. Meanwhile, Argentina, with not a single survivor of the 1930 final in their side, went down 3-2 against Sweden, and thus the entire South American contingent went home after only one game. The reason for the complete change in the Argentinian line-up was that three Italian nationals who had represented Argentina four years earlier – Guaita, Orsi and the infamous Monti – had been recalled to Italy, so Argentina sent a weakened team in protest and to discourage further poaching of their players.

The United States, fresh from their final eliminating match against Mexico, were thrashed 7-1 by Italy in Rome's Stadio Torino. Meanwhile in Turin, the French surprised everyone by making life very difficult for the acclaimed Austrians. Extra time was needed before the Austrians scraped through by the odd goal in five, and controversy surrounded the winning effort. The Germans, who were taking things very seriously, beat Belgium 5-2 with the help of a hat-trick from their centre-forward Conen, although they had been frightened by two quick Belgian goals in the first half, and had trailed 2-1 at the interval.

Czechoslovakia, another of the fancied teams, trailed to an early Rumanian goal scored by Dobai, but in the second half Puc and Nejedly scored to take the Czechs through to the quarter-finals. In Naples, Egypt put up a good display against Hungary but were eventually beaten 4-2. The quarter-finals would therefore be a wholly European affair.

It is interesting that even half a century ago, the Italians were using 'foreign' players. The three Argentinians reclaimed for this tournament had Italian fathers, and were an important element in the Italian squad. Indeed, few Italian clubs at the time had any really local players in their sides, and when one of the United States' players, Donelli, was discovered to have been born in Naples and taken to the States by his parents when only a baby, he was persuaded to sign for Napoli. This prompted one witty Italian newspaper journalist to report the signing under the headline 'At last – a genuine Napolitano in Naples' eleven'. None of his team-mates had been born in the region.

There were two intriguing matches in prospect among the quarter-finals – Italy v Spain and Austria v Hungary – but both were spoiled by rough play. The worst was the clash between the hosts and Spain in Florence, where the brave Spaniards were unlucky to be held to a 1-1 draw. No fewer than seven of their players, including the legendary veteran goalkeeper Ricardo Zamora, were unfit for the replay as a result of the attentions of their opponents. Even the Italians had to replace four of their number.

The replay took place the following day, and Italy won by virtue of a single goal, headed in the first half by Meazza from a cross by Orsi. For their part, Spain got the ball into the Italian net twice, but both efforts were ruled offside by the Swiss referee Mercet. Both decisions were dubious, and Mercet's own national association were so displeased by his performance that they suspended him forthwith.

The Austro-Hungarian quarter-final in Bologna was described by Austrian manager Hugo Meisl as a brawl. Seven minutes into the game, Horwarth scored from a cross by Zischek, and the Hungarians were always struggling to get back into the game. Early in the second half Zischek himself made it 2-0 and that's when things started to get rough. Sarosi scored from the penalty spot to make it 2-1, and soon afterwards, with Hungary threatening to equalise, their right-winger Markos was sent off. With him went any chance that the Hungarians might have had, and Austria were through.

A large crowd, liberally sprinkled with swastika flags, stood under a forest of umbrellas in pouring rain in Milan to see the quarter-final between Germany and Sweden. Both teams were strong rather than skilful, and Germany's inside-right, Hohmann, scored twice – the second a truly spectacular effort. Soon after the second goal Sweden lost their left-half, Andersson, through injury, and although Dunker got a goal back for the Swedes towards the end, it was never likely to be any more than a consolation.

In Turin the Czechs, helped immeasurably by their fine goalkeeper Planicka, overcame the Swiss 3-2 in what most observers regarded as the best of the four ties, and learned that they would face Germany in Rome in the semi-finals. In Milan the home side would line up against Hugo Meisl's Austria.

Mussolini turned up to watch his erstwhile allies from Germany outclassed by the Czechs in Rome. The Germans were well disciplined but lacking in flair, and most of the chances they created were wasted by poor finishing. Hohmann, their gifted but injured inside-right, was sorely missed, and the Czechs soon established their superiority. Nejedly scored in the twenty-first minute after Junek's shot had been beaten away by Kress, but soon after the interval they suffered a temporary set-back. Planicka made a rare error of judgement when he simply watched a speculative long shot from Noack float over his head and into the goal.

The equaliser woke the Czechs up, and ten minutes later Krcil scored their second. Germany seemed to give up, and it was Nejedly who scored his second and Czechoslovakia's third to clinch a place in the final.

In Milan, the Italians were favoured by a torrential rainstorm shortly before the kick-off. The resulting heavy conditions were far from suitable for the delicately skilful Austrians, but even so they conceded only one goal, scored after eighteen minutes by the Argentinian winger Guaita. Indeed, Austria should have equalised in the final minute when Zischek picked up a long clearance from goalkeeper Platzer and ripped through the Italian defence, but with only the goalkeeper to beat he shot wide. The sigh of relief was audible in the home crowd, and Italy were through.

This was the moment for which two men in particular had been waiting. The smirking Mussolini, who had been publicly referring to the Italian team as his '*azzurri*' wanted the home victory to boost his own image; the Italian manager Vittorio Pozzo, reknowned for his authoritarian style, could not bear the thought of defeat. The eyes of the world were not exactly on Italy, as they would be in today's televised times, but the match would be widely broadcast on radio throughout Europe and the astonishing number of two hundred and seventy-seven sports journalists were among the 55,000 spectators in the Stadio Torino that afternoon.

Amazingly, the people of Rome seemed less than enraptured by the occasion, and the stadium was not quite full, but *Il Duce* was in attendance and had no doubt not even considered the opinion of many observers that perhaps the match should have been played in the north.

Most of the final was disappointing, no doubt partly because both teams must have been so keyed up, and twenty minutes from the end it was still scoreless. Then the Czechs took the lead. Puc tried a long shot, the Italian goalkeeper Combi dived too late. Soon afterwards Sobotka and Svoboda both missed good chances which would certainly have sealed the fate of the host nation.

With eight minutes to go, and the crowd starting to resign themselves to defeat, a freak goal levelled the scores. Orsi shaped up to shoot with his left foot, but then fired one in with his right. The ball swerved viciously to defeat the despairing Planicka. The next day Orsi tried to swerve the ball again for the benefit of photographers, but couldn't do it!

For the first time, the World Cup final went to extra time. Pozzo wanted his two front-runners, Schiavio and Guaita, to keep switching positions, but such was the noise from the Italians in the stadium that he had to rush half-way round the pitch to get the message to Guaita. After seven minutes of extra time, the ploy worked. Meazza crossed to Guaita, who in turn got the ball through to Schiavio. Though desperately tired, Schiavio managed to go past one defender before scoring the winner.

Pozzo and Mussolini celebrated the triumph. The Italians were given win bonuses of 10,000 lire each as well as the national gold medal for sport and art; the losing Czechs were welcomed at Prague railway station by more than 20,000 fans, and each player received the republic's gold medal from

President Masaryk to mark their achievement; even the Germans, who had taken third place by beating Austria 3-2, were given any number of civic receptions. Already, success on the soccer field was considered to be national property, and the heroes were suitably rewarded.

The second World Cup had been an even bigger financial success than the first. Overall gate receipts were published as 3,683,000 lire, more than a million of which was clear profit. Cynics were wondering if home advantage was all-important, but four years later Pozzo would prove them wrong.

Italy 1934 – Results

First Round
Italy (3)7, United States (0)1
Czechoslovakia (0)2, Rumania (1)1
Germany (1)5, Belgium (2)2
Austria (1)3, France (1)2 *(after extra time, 90 mins 1-1)*
Spain (3)3, Brazil (1)1
Switzerland (2)3, Holland (1)2
Sweden (1)3, Argentina (1)2
Hungary (2)4, Egypt (1)2

Second Round
Germany (1)2, Sweden (0)1
Austria (1)2, Hungary (0)1
Italy (1)1, Spain (1)1 *(after extra time)*
Italy (1)1, Spain (0)0 *(replay)*
Czechoslovakia (1)3, Switzerland (1)2

Semi-finals
Rome
Czechoslovakia (1)3 *(Nejedly 2, Krcil)*
Germany (0)1 *(Noack)*
Czechoslovakia: Planicka; Burger, Ctyroky, Kostalek, Cambal, Krcil, Junek, Svoboda, Sobotka, Nejedly, Puc.
Germany: Kress; Haringer, Busch, Zielinski, Szepan, Bender, Lehner, Siffling, Conen, Noack, Kobierski.

Milan
Italy (1)1 *(Guaita)*
Austria (0)0
Italy: Combi; Monzeglio, Allemandi, Ferraris IV, Monti,
Bertolini, Guaita, Meazza, Schiavio, Ferrari, Orsi.
Austria: Platzer; Cisar, Seszta, Wagner, Smistik, Urbanek,
Zischek, Bican, Sindelar, Schall, Viertel.

Third Place Play-off
Naples
Germany (3)3 *(Lehner 2, Conen)*
Austria (1)2 *(Seszta 2)*
Germany: Jakob; Janes, Busch, Zielinski, Muenzenberg,
Bender, Lehner, Siffling, Conen, Szepan, Heidemann.
Austria: Platzer; Cisar, Seszta, Wagner, Smistik, Urbanek,
Zischek, Braun, Bican, Horwath, Viertel.

Final   Rome, 10 June 1934
Italy (0)2 *(Orsi, Schiavio)*
Czechoslovakia (0)1 *(Puc)*
(after extra time, 90 mins 1-1)
Italy: Combi; Monzeglio, Allemandi, Ferraris IV, Monti,
Bertolini, Guaita, Meazza, Schiavio, Ferrari, Orsi.
Czechoslovakia: Planicka; Zenisek, Ctyroky, Kostalek,
Cambal, Krcil, Junek, Svoboda, Sobotka, Nejedly, Puc.

France 1938

The third World Cup was overshadowed by the menacing clouds of war. The Austrians had qualified but had then been overrun by Hitler's armies and on 12 April the organisers were officially informed that owing to the *anschluss* Austria were no longer an independent soccer nation and were therefore withdrawn. England were invited by FIFA to take the place of Austria, but declined. Spain, wracked by Civil War, were unable to mobilise a national team. Argentina entered the tournament, and their entry was accepted even though it was late, but they eventually withdrew, upset that the tournament had been awarded to France, instead of them, as a compliment to Jules Rimet, the French President of FIFA. When the withdrawl was announced in Buenos Aires it provoked a fierce riot which the police suppressed with some difficulty.

Uruguay once more refused to participate, although on this occasion their refusal was more difficult to understand because France had at least made the trip to Montevideo eight years earlier. For the first time it was decided that neither the reigning champions nor the host nation needed to qualify for the final tournament, measures which were widely approved and still in force today.

A record thirty-six countries entered the competition, and the qualifying tournament was arranged in the following groupings:

Europe
Group 1: Germany, Sweden, Finland, Estonia.
Group 2: Norway, Eire, Poland, Yugoslavia.
Group 3: Egypt, Rumania.
Group 4: Switzerland, Portugal.
Group 5: Hungary, Palestine, Greece.
Group 6: Czechoslovakia, Bulgaria.
Group 7: Austria, Lithuania, Latvia.
Group 8: Netherlands, Belgium, Luxembourg.
North and Central America: USA, Mexico, Costa Rica, Cuba, El Salvador.
South America: Brazil, Argentina, Colombia, Dutch Guiana.
Asia: Dutch Indonesia, Japan.

European Groups 1, 2 and 8 were to send two finalists, all other groups one each, and once again, despite the enormous travelling distances involved and the prospect of early elimination, the entire final tournament was to be on a knock-out basis. The following eight teams from the sixteen finalists were seeded: Germany, France, Brazil, Czechoslovakia, Cuba, Hungary, Austria and Italy. However, Austria's late withdrawl meant that Sweden were awarded a walk-over into the quarter-finals. The venues for the finals were Paris, Strasbourg, Le Havre, Toulouse, Reims, Lyons and Marseilles.

The tournament began on 4 June at the Parc des Princes with the tie between Germany and Switzerland. The Germans were clear favourites, but the Swiss rose to the occasion and the match finished in a 1-1 draw. For the replay five days later, the Germans included three Austrians in their line-up, while the Swiss fielded an unchanged side, and the tactic seemed to be paying off as the Germans went in at half-time leading 2-0. But the second half produced the first major shock of the competition as first Wallaschek and then Aebi pulled goals back for the Swiss before the popular Abegglen, who played in the French League with Sochaux, scored twice to give victory to the Swiss.

In Marseilles, the champions very nearly went out at the first hurdle by virtue of a splendid performance from the Norwegian amateurs. Italy took the lead in the second minute, but were unable to consolidate their position and faced relentless Norwegian pressure which culminated in an equaliser from Brustad in the second half. On three other occasions in the second half the Norwegians were foiled by post or bar and Brustad got the ball into the net again, only to be judged offside. Italy were mightily relieved when Piola scored the winner in the first period of extra time.

The Brazilians were drawn against Poland, and for the first time European audiences were treated to a spectacular and vastly entertaining exhibition which, unlike their first round match four years before, the Brazilians won – but only by the odd goal in eleven! Particularly outstanding was the black centre-forward Leonidas, who, like his Polish counterpart Willimowski, scored four times. Leonidas went on to become the tournament's leading scorer with eight.

Cuba, in the finals as a replacement for Mexico, who had withdrawn, provided another shock, holding the Rumanians to a 3-3 draw in Toulouse and then won the replay 2-1 despite the strange decision to drop their goalkeeper Carvajales, who had attracted widespread praise in the first match. Yet another upset was nearly caused by the Dutch amateurs, who took the formidable Czechs to extra time before, having lost van der Veen through injury, they were sunk by three goals.

The host nation had been drawn against their old rivals, the Belgians, and were 1-0 up after only forty seconds through Veinante. Ten minutes later Nicolas scored a second, but Isemborghs pulled one back for Belgium and it was half-way through the second half before Nicolas scored his second goal of the match to clinch a quarter-final place. Meanwhile, at Reims, Hungary disposed of Dutch Indonesia 6-0, with Sarosi and Zsengeller scoring two apiece.

The quarter-finals saw the hosts facing the holders in Paris, and Pozzo's *azzurri* were never in serious trouble. After only six minutes they took the lead through Colaussi, and though the French equalised within a minute, the second half belonged to the Italian Piola, who scored twice.

The Cubans, still rank outsiders despite their surprise win over Rumania, were swept aside 8-0 by Sweden, who were managed by the Hungarian Joseph Nagy. Meanwhile Hungary themselves overcame Switzerland 2-0 in an uninspiring match in Lille.

The last quarter-final, in Bordeaux, needed a replay to decide whether Brazil or Czechoslovakia would go through to the semi-finals, and unfortunately degenerated into a brutal battle. The brilliant Czech forward Nejedly suffered a broken leg, and veteran goalkeeper Planicki – still in the national side – had an arm broken. There were several other less serious injuries, including one to Leonidas – now dubbed the 'Black Diamond' – and three players were sent off. They were Machados and Zeze of Brazil and Czech right-winger Riha. For the record, Leonidas scored first for Brazil, and Nejedly equalised from the penalty spot.

The replay featured a new referee – Capdeville of France succeeding the Hungarian Hertzka – and the match was peaceful throughout. Perhaps the new referee was an influence, perhaps the fact that the Czechs fielded six new players, the Brazilians nine! In any event, the Brazilians were so confident of victory in the replay that the main body of their contingent left for the semi-final venue in Marseilles before the replay had even kicked off! Had they heard the half-time score during their journey, they might have been less confident, because Kopecky, the replacement for Nejedly, gave the Czechs a 1-0 lead, but in the second half the Brazilians got going and won with goals from Leonidas and Roberto.

It was, perhaps, over-confidence which proved the undoing of Brazil in their semi-final against Italy. Eight further changes were made to the side, and they even rested Leonidas. They soon realised that they had made a mistake when Colaussi streaked past Da Guia to open the scoring in the first half. Minutes later the sparkling Piola went past him, not for the first time, and Da Guia resorted to hacking him down. Piola made a meal of it, and the penalty was duly awarded. Meazza converted it, and as he turned to receive the congratulations of his team-mates, his ripped shorts fell down! It was all too much for Brazil. Peracio, standing in for Leonidas but nowhere near his class, missed two reasonable chances to score, and although Romeo pulled one back after eighty-seven minutes, it was too little and too late to worry the champions.

Sweden's semi-final against Hungary coincided with the eightieth birthday of their popular monarch Gustav V, and the Swedish players wanted to present him with a victory. Within a minute, Sweden were 1-0 up, but the Hungarians were unfazed and by half-time were leading 3-1. They scored twice more in the second half and such was their superiority that they could probably have scored twice as many as they did, but that did not concern them as they left the pitch with the World Cup final in their sights.

The Swedes suffered a further disappointment three days before the final when they lost the third-place play-off 4-2 to Brazil, after having led the colourful South Americans 2-1 at half-time. Leonidas, restored to the team and made captain for the day, scored twice, and the damage was completed by Romeo and Peracio. Jonasson and Nyberg were the Swedish scorers.

The final was a classic. The Italians, just as they still seem to do today, had been improving from match to match, and in the twenty-five-year-old Silvio Piola had a forward of quite exceptional ability. His skill flourished all the more for the fact that he was playing between the two excellent inside-forwards, Meazza and Ferrari – the only survivors of the World Cup-winning team of 1934. For their part Hungary had the dangerous Sarosi in their forward line, and a team full of individual skill. The encounter was eagerly awaited by the capacity crowd at the specially enlarged Stade Colombes.

After six minutes the Italians took the lead. Meazza slid the ball through for Colaussi to pounce and score, but the cheers had scarcely died away when the Hungarians equalised through Titkos. Unfortunately, the Hungarians were a little less well-organised than the Italians, and seemed to have just that bit less commitment. The inside-forwards, Meazza and Ferrari, were given a shade too much space and time, and after a quarter of an hour it was Meazza who provided Piola with the chance to restore Italy's lead. He did not pass the chance up, and the lead was increased when, ten minutes before the interval Meazza fed Colaussi with the opportunity which made the half-time score 3-1 to Italy.

After twenty minutes of the second half, Sarosi reduced the score to 3-2 with a scrappy goal after a mix-up in the Italian goal-mouth, but the Italians kept their nerve and absorbed further Hungarian pressure quite superbly until ten minutes from the end, when Biavati and Piola interpassed their way through the Hungarian defence for Piola to score his second goal and clinch the title for Italy once again.

Financially, the tournament had been another great success, and after all expenses and taxes had been paid, and FIFA had pocketed their ten per cent, there was still around 1.4 million francs to be distributed among the national associations in proportion to their gate figures during the final tournament. There had, perhaps, been a greater number of unpleasant incidents than in the previous two competitions, but the final had been played in fine spirit. At a time when tension between France and Italy was mounting, the French press were generous in their praise for the champions, and this was appropriate. Surely this was the golden age of Italian soccer. Not only had they won two successive World Cups, but they had taken the Olympic title at the 1936 Berlin Olympics. In a sense this was a greater achievement than Uruguay's two Olympic titles and one World Cup, but the Uruguayans had not been in Italy or France to argue about it, and when the World Cup resumed twelve years later, they would get their chance. Meanwhile, the world had more important battles to fight.

France 1938 – Results

First Round
Switzerland (1)1, Germany (1)1 *(after extra time)*
Switzerland (0)4, Germany (2)2 *(replay)*
Cuba (0)3, Rumania (1)3 *(after extra time, 90 mins 3-3)*
Cuba (0)2, Rumania (1)1 *(replay)*
Hungary (4)6, Dutch East Indies (0)0
France (2)3, Belgium (1)1
Czechoslovakia (0)3, Holland (0)0 *(after extra time, 90 mins 0-0)*
Brazil (3)6, Poland (1)5 *(after extra time, 90 mins 4-4)*
Italy (1)2, Norway (0)1 *(after extra time, 90 mins 1-1)*

Second Round
Sweden (4)8, Cuba (0)0
Hungary (1)2, Switzerland (0)0
Italy (1)3, France (1)1
Brazil (1)1, Czechoslovakia (1)1 *(after extra time)*
Brazil (0)2, Czechoslovakia (1)1 *(replay)*

Semi-finals
Marseilles
Italy (2)2 *(Colaussi, Meazza pen.)*
Brazil (0)1 *(Romeo)*
Italy: Olivieri; Foni, Rava, Serantoni, Andreolo, Locatelli, Biavati, Meazza, Piola, Ferrari, Colaussi.
Brazil: Walter; Domingas Da Guia, Machados, Zeze, Martin, Alfonsinho, Lopez, Luisinho, Peracio, Romeo, Patesko.

Paris
Hungary (3)5 *(Szengeller 3, Titkos, Sarosi)*
Sweden (1)1 *(Nyberg)*
Hungary: Szabo; Koranyi, Biro, Szalay, Turai, Lazar, Sas, Szengeller, Sarosi, Toldi, Titkos.
Sweden: Abrahamson; Eriksson, Kjellgren, Almgren, Jacobsson, Svanstroem, Wetterstroem, Keller, Andersson H., Jonasson, Nyberg.

Third Place Play-off
Bordeaux

Brazil (1)4 *(Romeo, Leonidas 2, Peracio)*
Sweden (2)2 *(Jonasson, Nyberg)*
Brazil: Batatoes; Domingas Da Guia, Machados, Zeze, Brandao, Alfonsinho, Roberto, Romeo, Leonidas, Peracio, Patesko.
Sweden: Abrahamson; Eriksson, Nilssen, Almgren, Linderholm, Svanstroem, Berssen, Andersson H., Jonasson, Andersson A., Nyberg.

Final   Paris, 19 June 1938
Italy (3)4 *(Colaussi 2, Piola 2)*
Hungary (1)2 *(Titkos, Sarosi)*
Italy: Olivieri; Foni, Rava, Serantoni, Andreolo, Locatelli, Biavati, Meazza, Piola, Ferrari, Colaussi.
Hungary: Szabo; Polgar, Biro, Szalay, Szucs, Lazar, Sas, Vincze, Sarosi, Szengeller, Titkos.

Brazil 1950

On the first day of the 1938 tournament, in the assembly hall of the French Automobile Club overlooking the Place de la Concorde, the FIFA Congress had gathered. High on the agenda was the fourth World Cup, scheduled for 1942. Brazil and Germany both laid claim to the right to stage the tournament, and a little later they were joined by Argentina, but the delegates, possibly feeling that plans for a 1942 World Cup were likely to be frustrated, postponed the discussions until the 1940 Congress in Luxembourg.

In the event, Britain declared war on Germany on 3 September 1939, but during the six years of conflict FIFA Secretary Dr Ivo Schricker kept the office going in Zurich, and although the 1940 Luxembourg congress was postponed indefinitely, the Executive Committee of FIFA met several times. One important decision taken during that period was the one which safeguarded the trophy itself. At the outbreak of hostilities, the precious gold statuette was locked in a safe at Italian FA headquarters in Rome, and it was known that the Germans wanted it. Although the Germans occupied Rome, it was one more ambition which they failed to fulfil. Officials secretly took the trophy from the safe and deposited it in the vault of a Swiss bank in Rome. Later it was spirited away to France, where it spent the bulk of the war years hidden under Jules Rimet's bed in German-occupied Paris!

On 1 July 1946, the Luxembourg congress finally opened. There was only one candidate for the championship, Argentina having withdrawn in deference to Brazil while a now divided Germany had been suspended *sine die* by FIFA, so the tournament was duly awarded to Brazil. At the same time, Switzerland put in a bid to stage the following championship, and that, too, was agreed.

By this time, the British associations had rejoined FIFA, and it was agreed by the organising committee that the British Championship should constitute one of the qualifying groups. As if this wasn't indulgent enough, it was also decided that the top two teams from the 'British zone' should qualify for the finals. There is an old saying that one should not look a gift horse in the mouth, but the Scottish Football Association managed to shove the gift straight back down FIFA's throat by announcing that they would not compete in the finals unless they actually won the British Championship. This decision – not the most popular ever made by the SFA – gave even more importance than usual to the traditional end-of-season clash between the 'auld enemies', which in 1950 took place at Hampden Park. England won 1-0 with a goal from Chelsea's Roy Bentley, but despite Billy Wright practically begging Scottish captain George Young to appeal to the SFA to change their mind, Scotland were adamant. Most members of FIFA thought it inexcusable that one of the oldest foot-balling nations in the world should refuse to take part in the game's showpiece tournament, and so it was no surprise to anybody when, at the next FIFA Congress in Brazil, the Scottish vice-president of FIFA was not re-elected.

The competition was still plagued with petty dissensions. Argentina withdrew again after an argument with their Brazilian neighbours; Czechoslovakia, in some disarray after the war, pulled out; Turkey, having beaten Syria 7-0 to qualify, refused to take part; Belgium withdrew; India, having been told that their normally barefooted players must be shod, also pulled out; perhaps most important of all, Henri Delaunay resigned from the organising committee in 1948 when it was decided to depart from the knock-out principle of previous tournaments and arrange the sixteen finalists in four mini-leagues of four teams each. This League idea, which avoided the difficulties of teams travelling long distances and then having to go home again and also ensured that there would be more matches (and therefore more gate money), was to be extended right through the tournament, with no final as such. Delaunay hated the idea, but he rejoined the committee a year later.

The withdrawal of Turkey and Scotland (the other dissidents either failed to qualify or did not attempt to do so) meant that the final tournament was reduced to fourteen teams. To make up the shortage, France and Portugal were invited to take part. The French accepted the invitation, but the Portuguese, despite their strong cultural links with Brazil, declined. Uruguay was seeded instead of Argentina, who were the last team to pull out. At this point, the final tournament League groupings looked like this:

Group 1: Brazil, Yugoslavia, Mexico, Switzerland.
Group 2: England, Spain, USA, Chile.
Group 3: Italy, Sweden, Paraguay, India.
Group 4: Uruguay, France, Bolivia.

Then came the Indian withdrawal, which was suddenly followed by that of France, thus reducing the field to thirteen – exactly the same number as had participated in the first competition twenty years earlier. The French took their decision partly because the national team had started stringing together some remarkably poor results and partly because they were unhappy with the arrangements they would face in Brazil. They would be expected to play their first match, against Uruguay, in Porto Alegre and then travel about two thousand miles to Recife for the match with Bolivia. The French federation sent a cable asking for the arrangements to be changed and, perhaps foolishly, threatening to boycott the tournament if they were not accommodated. The organisers refused, and so the French stayed at home.

Meanwhile in Rio, work was proceeding apace to try and finish the new showpiece Maracana stadium on time. Things were getting so far behind schedule that thousands of workmen had to be taken off important road construction work, and for more than two weeks before the tournament was due to begin work went ahead all round the clock. The job was finished just in time, and the proud Brazilians could justifiably boast that they now had the biggest and, in some senses, the most beautiful football stadium in the world. Situated on the banks of the little Maracana river, the immense, three-tiered edifice could seat 200,000 people, with practically all seats covered – against the sun, not the rain.

At last, everything was ready. There can be no doubt that the fixture lists favoured the home side, who played five of their six matches in Rio while other teams had to undertake exhausting journeys across the vast land mass which is Brazil. It doesn't seem to have occurred to anybody that the teams in each group should play their games in one centre. Furthermore, anybody other than the hosts were at a distinct disadvantage playing in Rio, where the heat and humidity were almost unbearable for those unaccustomed to it.

With only thirteen teams left, the Uruguayans only had to beat lowly Bolivia in order to progress to the next phase, and this they duly did, by a score of 8-0. Why the organisers were unable to move one of the teams from a four-strong group into Group 4 is anybody's guess, particularly as the groups were not arranged in any sort of geographical pattern.

In the opening game in the new Maracana stadium, Brazil

beat Mexico 4-0, and this was followed on the same day by England's opening match, against Chile, also in the Maracana. England won 2-0 with goals from Mortensen and Mannion, but it would have been interesting had Jackie Milburn been fit to lead the attack, for the Chilean forward line was led by George (Jorge) Robledo, Milburn's Newcastle team-mate. England, with such talents as Matthews, Finney, Wright, Ramsey, Milburn, Mannion and Mortensen, were among the favourites for the World Cup, and this opening game against Chile did nothing to alter that.

In São Paulo on the following day, the tournament threw up its first major surprise. Champions Italy were due to play all their games in this fast-growing city south of Rio, and there was the added benefit that a large section of the population was either Italian or of Italian extraction. However, a Swedish side coached by the Englishman George Raynor beat the World Champions 3-2, and even the partisan crowd admitted by their prolonged applause at the end that the win was on merit. Sweden now only needed a draw against Paraguay to clinch the group, and this they achieved. The subsequent Italian victory over Paraguay was of no consequence – the champions were out.

Back in Group 2, Spain beat the USA 3-1 at Curitiba. The States were captained by Eddie McIlvenny, who had been given a free transfer by Wrexham eighteen months earlier, but despite the team's lack of pedigree, they frightened the Spaniards by taking the lead after seven minutes with a goal from Souza and then hanging on until ten minutes from the end. At this point Basora scored twice in two minutes and centre-forward Zarra completed the job with the third goal.

England then travelled to Belo Horizonte for their match against the USA, little knowing that they were about to experience the most humiliating and inexplicable defeat in English football history. In those days the stadium at Belo Horizonte was not the great stadium that is there today, and the pitch in particular was atrocious, a fact more likely to suit the football 'primitives' of the USA, who relied largely on kick and run tactics. Apart from that, England had nothing to complain about. The cool mountain air was a welcome relief after Rio and the England selector, Arthur Drewry, resisted the temptation of treating the match as a run-out for the reserves. He picked the same team which had so competently disposed of Chile, and although this meant that Matthews was not playing, there was still sufficient talent in the side to take care of the United States, or so everybody thought. Even Bill Jeffrey, the Scottish manager of the USA, gave his side no chance, and several of the Americans were so resigned to what was going to happen to them that they stayed up half the night before enjoying themselves.

The match started, and England quickly established territorial advantage, spending most of their time in the American half. They hit the post, they hit the bar, they missed by fractions of an inch, and the crowd, although generally supporting the underdogs from the north, waited for the inevitable England goal to come. They waited in vain, and eight minutes before half-time the unbelievable happened when the American centre-forward, Larry Gaetjens, deflected a shot from Bahr past the England goalkeeper Bert Williams. Twenty years later Gaetjens, a native of Haiti, disappeared mysteriously in that sinister place', but for now he was a hero.

In the second half, England missed a penalty and there was a moment when the ball appeared to cross the goal line before being cleared by the American defence, but it didn't matter, and England went quietly back to Rio, where they needed to beat Spain to stand a chance of winning the Group. Indeed, it would have been enough, for Spain had already beaten Chile 2-0 and Chile went on to beat the USA 5-2 in the final match in the group.

But it was not to be. England made a good start, and after fourteen minutes Finney centred for Milburn, now back in the side after injury, to head past the Spanish goalkeeper Ramallets. The Italian referee, Galeati, disallowed the effort for offside, and it was no consolation that film of the match showed that a Spanish defender had put Milburn onside. Five minutes after half-time, Zarra headed what was to be the only goal of the game, and Spain were through.

Back in Group 1, the Brazilians were up against it, having dropped a point against Switzerland while the impressive Yugoslavs cruised through 3-0 against the Swiss and 4-1 against Mexico. The match between Brazil and Yugoslavia was therefore the one which would decide the group winner, and Yugoslavia needed only a draw. However, the Brazilians chose this match to unveil the legendary inside-forward trio of Zizinho, Ademir and Jair, while the Yugoslavs started the game without their superb inside-forward Rajko Mitic, who had unluckily gashed his head open on a girder shortly before the game. Welsh referee Mervyn Griffiths refused to delay the start while Mitic received treatment.

Within three minutes the Swiss fell behind to a goal by Ademir, and although they were revitalised when Mitic finally made an appearance with his head heavily bandaged, Zizinho scored Brazil's second goal after half-time and the hosts were through to the final stages. In 1950, as neither before nor since, the final stages consisted of the strange idea of yet another mini-league, in which the four teams played each other once, with the league champions being declared World Cup winners. This was a strange idea for what was essentially supposed to be a 'cup' competition, but luckily the final match in the series turned out to be the decider, and so in a sense there was a World Cup final in 1950 after all.

As the final pool matches got under way, the Brazilians started turning on the sort of magical performances for which they have been famous ever since. Only three British journalists stayed on in Brazil after England were eliminated, but those who did were treated to what was virtually perfect football. Sweden were the first victims.

The Brazilians have often been accused of being unsound in defence, but they clearly believe that attack is the best form of defence, and attack they did. By half-time they were 3-0 up, and in the second half, when they added four more against a solitary penalty by the Swedes, they were playing as no Europeans had ever really thought the game could be played.

Next in line for the treatment were the Spanish, who had just come from a gruelling 2-2 draw against Uruguay, and were devasted by a 6-1 Brazilian victory. Meanwhile the Uruguayans just managed to beat the Swedes by 3-2, and so the Brazilians, with four points, needed only a draw against Uruguay to take the trophy that most observers were firmly convinced was as good as theirs.

Throughout the first half Brazil attacked vigorously, but could not score, and towards the end of the half there were signs that the patient and calm Uruguayans were beginning to get into the game. If the vast and mostly Brazilian crowd of 200,000 sensed this change in the pattern of the game, they were mightily relieved when, two minutes after the restart, Brazil went ahead.

Ademir and Zizinho, two of the feared trio at the head of the Brazilian attack, drew the defence with a series of typically accurate and mesmerising passes before pushing the ball though to Friaca on the right. He ran through, shot first time, and scored. The crowd went wild, but the Uruguayans stayed calm, and half-way through the second half they got their reward. Ghiggia went tearing down the right wing, and his lovely cross found Schiaffino, who thundered the ball past the despairing Barbosa in the Brazilian goal.

The Brazilians seemed to lose heart with this equaliser, even though they needed only a draw to win the cup, and inside the last ten minutes it was Ghiggia who did the final damage. After an exchange of passes with Perez he scored Uruguay's second, after which the Brazilians were out of it. The English referee, George Reader, duly blew his whistle and the World Cup was back in Montevideo after twenty years.

Although the Brazilian public were stunned by the defeat (several suicides were reported and nearly all the Brazilian players were in tears) the 150,000 or so who stayed behind in the stadium to watch the presentation of the trophy were generous in their applause. On reflection, the Brazilians had nothing to be ashamed of. They had thrilled the public with a brand of football that would one day win that same trophy for them outright, and the tournament had been a huge financial success, making a profit of more than half-a-million pounds.

Brazil 1950 – Results

Pool 1
Brazil (1)4, Mexico (0)0
Yugoslavia (3)3, Switzerland (0)0
Yugoslavia (2)4, Mexico (0)1
Brazil (2)2, Switzerland (1)2
Brazil (1)2, Yugoslavia (0)0
Switzerland (2)2, Mexico (0)1

	P	W	D	L	F	A	Pts
Brazil	3	2	1	0	8	2	5
Yugoslavia	3	2	0	1	7	3	4
Switzerland	3	1	1	1	4	6	3
Mexico	3	0	0	3	2	10	0

Pool 2
Spain (0)3, United States (1)1
England (1)2, Chile (0)0
United States (1)1, England (0)0
Spain (2)2, Chile (0)0
Spain (0)1, England (0)0
Chile (2)5, United States (0)2

	P	W	D	L	F	A	Pts
Spain	3	3	0	0	6	1	6
England	3	1	0	2	2	2	2
Chile	3	1	0	2	5	6	2
United States	3	1	0	2	4	8	2

Pool 3
Sweden (2)3, Italy (1)2
Sweden (2)2, Paraguay (1)2
Italy (1)2, Paraguay (0)0

	P	W	D	L	F	A	Pts
Sweden	2	1	1	0	5	4	3
Italy	2	1	0	1	4	3	2
Paraguay	2	0	1	1	2	4	1

Pool 4
Uruguay (4)8, Bolivia (0)0

	P	W	D	L	F	A	Pts
Uruguay	1	1	0	0	8	0	2
Bolivia	1	0	0	1	0	8	0

Final Pool
Sao Paulo
Uruguay (1)2 *(Ghiggia, Varela)*
Spain (2)2 *(Basora 2)*
Uruguay: Maspoli; Gonzales M., Tejera, Gonzales W.,
Varela, Andrade, Ghiggia, Perez, Miguez, Schiaffino, Vidal.
Spain: Ramallets; Alonzo, Gonzalvo II, Gonzalvo III, Parra,
Puchades, Basora, Igoa, Zarra, Molowny, Gainza.

Rio de Janeiro
Brazil (3)7 *(Ademir 4, Chico 2, Maneca)*
Sweden (0)1 *(Andersson)*
Brazil: Barbosa; Augusto, Juvenal, Bauer, Danilo, Bigode,
Maneca, Zizinho, Ademir, Jair, Chico.
Sweden: Svensson; Samuelsson, Nilsson E., Andersson,
Nordahl K., Gard, Sundqvist, Palmer, Jeppson, Skoglund,
Nilsson S.

Sao Paulo
Uruguay (1)3 *(Ghiggia, Miguez 2)*
Sweden (2)2 *(Palmer, Sundqvist)*
Uruguay: Paz; Gonzales M., Tejera, Gambetta, Varela,
Andrade, Ghiggia, Perez, Miguez, Schiaffino, Vidal.
Sweden: Svensson; Samuelsson, Nilsson E., Andersson,
Johansson, Gard, Johnsson, Palmer, Mellberg, Skoglund,
Sundqvist.

Rio de Janeiro
Brazil (3)6 *(Jair 2, Chico 2, Zizinho, Parra o.g.)*
Spain (0)1 *(Igoa)*
Brazil: Barbosa; Augusto, Juvenal, Bauer, Danilo, Bigode,
Friaca, Zizinho, Ademir, Jair, Chico.
Spain: Eizaguirre; Alonza, Gonzalvo II, Gonzalvo III, Parra,
Puchades, Basora, Igoa, Zarra, Panizo, Gainza.

Sao Paulo
Sweden (2)3 *(Johansson, Mellberg, Palmer)*
Spain (0)1 *(Zarra)*
Sweden: Svensson; Samuelsson, Nilsson E., Andersson,
Johansson, Gard, Sundqvist, Mellberg, Rydell, Palmer,
Johnsson.
Spain: Eizaguirre; Asensi, Alonzo, Silva, Parra, Puchades,
Basora, Fernandez, Zarra, Panizo, Juncosa.

Rio de Janeiro
Uruguay (0)2 *(Schiaffino, Ghiggia)*
Brazil (0)1 *(Friaca)*
Uruguay: Maspoli; Gonzales M., Tejera, Gambetta, Varela,
Andrade, Ghiggia, Perez, Miguez, Schiaffino, Moran.
Brazil: Barbosa; Augusto, Juvenal, Bauer, Danilo, Bigode,
Friaca, Zizinho, Ademir, Jair, Chico.

Final Table

	P	W	D	L	F	A	Pts
Uruguay	3	2	1	0	7	5	5
Brazil	3	2	0	1	14	4	4
Sweden	3	1	0	2	6	11	2
Spain	3	0	1	2	4	11	1

Switzerland 1954

As in 1950, the 1954 World Cup finals were thought to be a foregone conclusion, and this time it was the Hungarians who were the hot favourites. In 1952 they had emerged from behind the iron curtain for the first time since the war, and carried off the Helsinki Olympic title with a brand of football which seemed to combine supreme artistry and skill with robust strength. Since 1952 they had been unbeatable, and had even, on 25 November 1953, breached the citadel of Wembley – the first non-British side to do so.

Once more, the organisation of the finals was changed, but the changes were hardly for the better, being almost staggeringly illogical. There were sixteen finalists, who would be arranged in four groups of four to play the first phase matches on a league basis. Thereafter the competition would be on a knock-out basis. The problem was that two teams in each group of four would be seeded, and seeded teams would not play against each other until the quarter-final stages. With equality on points between the second and third-placed teams in each group therefore being a distinct possibility, provision was made for play-offs, and the most ridiculous aspect of this arrangement was seen when Spain, who had been seeded before the qualifying competition had finished, failed to qualify.

Turkey, who had qualified ahead of Spain, were seeded in her place, but were clearly easy meat for one of the unseeded teams in that group – West Germany. Therefore when West Germany played the other seeded team, Hungary, they didn't bother to try too hard, knowing that they would surely beat Turkey, who they had already overcome 4-1, in the inevitable play-off. The world was therefore treated (this was the first World Cup to be televised) to the spectacle of a first round match in which Hungary beat West Germany 8-3. The Germans duly beat Turkey 7-2 in the play-off, and turned in a very different standard of performance in the eventual final against Hungary.

Once again, the British Championship had been designated as a qualifying zone, and once again the Scots finished as runners-up to England, but this time they deigned to take part. Unfortunately they did not have a very strong squad, although it did include a fair-haired and powerful wing-half from Preston North End by the name of Tommy Docherty.

England, seeded along with Italy in a group which also included Belgium and Switzerland, still had Stanley Matthews and Tom Finney, and there was a squat, powerful new centre-forward called Nat Lofthouse.

But the names on everybody's lips were mostly Hungarian. Puskas, Kocsis, Hidegkuti, Bozsik were all too well-known in England, still smarting not only from the 6-3 defeat at Wembley but also from an even more humiliating 7-1 trouncing in Budapest only weeks before the finals got under way.

Everybody's fears about the Hungarians were confirmed when they scored seventeen goals in their first two matches, but the eight against West Germany were more or less conceded and in retrospect it was an injury sustained by Puskas in that game which probably proved to be more significant. It kept him out until the final, and he later claimed bitterly that Leibrich, the German centre-half, had kicked him deliberately. Most observers thought he might have been right.

England's campaign began with a 4-4 draw against Belgium. The Belgians had qualified by eliminating Sweden, who had lost most of her stars to Italian clubs, and for the first time a British television audience was able to watch England in a World Cup final tournament match. They were disappointed by the way in which England surrendered what should have been an unassailable lead. Although the Belgians scored first through Anoul, England got two before half-time and in the second half they increased their lead to 3-1, but then they seemed to collapse, with Luton's Sid Owen having a particularly shaky game at centre-half, and Belgium equalised. Nat Lofthouse restored England's lead early in extra time, but the hapless Jimmy Dickinson headed Dries' free kick into his own goal to make it 4-4. Significantly Billy Wright, hitherto a wing half, spent the latter part of the match at centre-half, while Owen, suffering with cramp, limped on the wing. Wright was not an obvious choice for the position because of his lack of height, but it was a position in which he played out the remaining five years of his international career with distinction.

The unseeded Scots started their programme with a defeat by 1-0 at the hands of Austria. The Scottish press thought the Austrians had been lucky, and indeed they were lucky on one occasion when Happel brought Mochan down heavily inside the penalty area and the Belgian referee Franken gave the kick just outside, but Scotland's forwards were never any great threat, and before their next game the squad received a shock.

The Scots had, prior to the tournament, appointed a team manager – still a novelty in British international football in those – days and the man they chose was Andrew Beattie, a former Scottish left-back and by then manager of Huddersfield Town. Now Beattie resigned. He announced that he would leave the job after Scotland's second game, versus champions Uruguay. Although the reasons for his decision were not made public at the the time, it's a fair assumption that the SFA, having appointed a manager, were unable to let him manage. The immediate consequences were disastrous.

On the hottest day of the year the Scots faced the hottest opposition – champions Uruguay. Although the South Americans had started their campaign with a fairly undistinguished 2-0 defeat of Czechoslovakia, they now proceeded to tear the Scots apart. To give due credit to the Scots that day, they accepted their defeat with a remarkably sportsmanlike grace. They were good losers, which must have been hard for them as they were not only soundly beaten, but also humiliated. After establishing a 2-0 half-time lead, the Uruguayans ran riot in the second half, scoring five more without reply, and the Scots just didn't know what to do about the bewildering, bewitching and truly beautiful football with which they were destroyed. The Scottish forwards were as impotent as they had been against Austria, and the defence, according to one English observer, 'stood around like Highland cattle'. Scotland's first World Cup campaign was over:

The seeded Austrians and Uruguayans having duly qualified in Scotland's group, attention was now turned to whether Italy would fail at the first hurdle for the second World Cup in succession. England added a 2-0 victory over Switzerland to their 4-4 draw with Belgium to make certain of being in the quarter-finals, but Italy contrived to lose to the same Swiss team in a bad-tempered match which was somewhat spoiled by the erratic refereeing of the Brazilian Viana. The *azzurri* then picked themselves up to whack the Belgians 4-1 and thus ensure the play-off which would give them not only the opportunity of qualifying for the quarter-finals, but also of revenge against the Swiss.

Sadly for the Italians, it was not to be. There were stories of anarchy coming from the squad's mountain retreat, and a reshuffled Italian team went down 4-1 to the Swiss, who thus joined England in the quarter-finals.

In Group 1, Brazil and France had been seeded ahead of Mexico and Yugoslavia, and although the Mexicans justified their ranking by promptly losing both of their fixtures, the Yugoslavs were surprising everybody. Firstly they beat France 1-0, but it was their second game, against Brazil, which was widely regarded as the best of the opening phase matches. Yugoslavia took the lead shortly before half-time through Zebec, and it was a fair reward for a first half in which the Yugoslav midfield had dominated. In the second half, the roles were reversed, the Brazilians turned on their magical brand of football and equalised with an exquisite goal by Didi. Thus the score at ninety minutes was 1-1, both Brazil and Yugoslavia had three points (Brazil had crushed Mexico 5-0), all the fixtures in the group had been played, Brazil and Yugoslavia had both qualified for the quarter-finals, and yet the stupid rules of the tournament meant that extra time had to be played. Naturally, neither team took those last thirty minutes very seriously.

England's quarter-final opponents were the world champions, Uruguay, and on the day the South Americans proved just too strong, although the English played their best match of the tournament and in some senses were unlucky to lose. Unfortunately Gil Merrick in goal played a stinker and should have saved two, if not three, of the shots that went past him. The rest of the English defence, inspired by Billy Wright in his new position at centre-half, played well and had good reason to feel let down.

Abbadie opened the scoring after five minutes, but England responded quickly when, after a quarter of an hour, Matthews got past his marker and the ball went through to Lofthouse via Wilshaw. The Bolton centre-forward beat Maspoli to equalise and for the next twenty minutes England took control. Then, just before the interval, Varela tried a speculative long shot which was misjudged by Merrick and so the champions led 2-1 at half-time.

Shortly after the restart Uruguay went further ahead with a goal that was clearly unfair. Varela picked the ball up for a free kick and proceeded to drop kick it. The English defence stood still in astonishment, Schiaffino ran through and netted, and the goal was allowed to stand! Still the English didn't give up, and after sixty-seven minutes a shot from Finney was only half parried by Maspoli and the score was 3-2. Then, with thirteen minutes remaining, Ambrois scored Uruguay's fourth. Merrick should have saved it, but he didn't, and England were out.

The quarter-final between Brazil and Hungary went down in history as the Battle of Berne. Only the superb refereeing of Arthur Ellis enabled the match to be completed at all, although he was obliged to dismiss three players. Puskas was still out with injury, but the Hungarians started strongly, and were two goals up within eight minutes. At this point they seemed to relax, and the Brazilians came more into the game, displaying their abundant gifts in attack. Santos converted a penalty after Indio had been chopped down by Buzansky, and by half-time the match was open.

Toth I was a passenger on the Hungarian wing in the second half, and the match soon degenerated with the pro-liferation of a series of cynical fouls leading, inevitably, to another penalty. This time Pinheiro handled Czibor's cross and Lantos put Hungary 3-1 up from the spot. Soon after-wards the Brazilians clawed their way back into the game with a brilliant goal from Julinho, but then things really started to get out of hand.

First Bozsik and Santos were sent off after coming to blows when Bozsik retaliated to a bad tackle from Santos and then, after the Hungarians had increased their lead again through Kocsis, the young Brazilian inside-left Tozzi was despatched to the dressing room for kicking Lorant. Begging and weeping on his knees, he was unable to change Ellis's mind.

It was after the final whistle that some of the worst violence was seen, and unseen. As the players were making their way down the tunnel Puskas, who had been watching from the bench, smashed a bottle into Pinheiro's face, causing a three-inch gash, and this was followed by a Brazilian invasion of the Hungarian dressing room, where there was the most dreadful brawl. To its shame, the World Cup Disciplinary Committee took no action, and both national associations refused to punish their players.

The quarter-final between Austria and Switzerland pro-duced one of the highest scoring matches in World Cup history, the Austrians winning 7-5. The sequence of scoring was astonishing. The home side scored three in the first twenty minutes, then the Austrians responded with three in three minutes. It was later learned than the Swiss captain and centre-half, Roger Bocquet, was in need of an operation for a tumour behind one of his eyes, and had been advised not to play. Certainly this contributed to his poor performance, although the operation was later completed successfully.

By half-time the Austrians led 5-4. In the second half they went further ahead at 6-4, were pegged back to 6-5 and then Probst dribbled through to score the best goal of the game and make the final score 7-5.

The fourth quarter-final produced the least likely result of all, with the Germans beating Yugoslavia 2-0, but as they were helped by an early own goal and a later injury to the Yugoslav goalkeeper Vladimir Beara which left him virtually unable to move, most observers still didn't rate ultimate German chances all that highly.

They started to change their minds when, in the semi-finals, the West Germans overran the Austrians 6-1. The Austrians started the game as favourites, but for some unaccountable reason they dropped the efficient Schmied and replaced him in goal with Zeman, who was clearly out of form. Even so, the Germans led only 1-0 at half-time, but in the second half they ran amok, Zeman completely lost his nerve, and the record crowd of 58,000 in Basel were treated to an eye-opening display of incisive football from the Germans. The Austrians gained some small compensation by beating Uruguay 3-1 in the third place play-off, but the team which the Hungarians professed to fear more than any other was out.

In Lausánne those Hungarians faced Uruguay in the other semi-final, and had promised everyone that there would be no repeat of the disgraceful scenes at Berne. They kept their word, and the match was highly entertaining. Puskas was still missing, but so was Varela for Uruguay. The South Americans looked faster and more threatening early on, but were 1-0 down at half-time. Soon after the restart they went further behind, but fifteen minutes from the end they pulled one back through Hohberg, who had been fed by Schiaffino. With a couple of minutes remaining that same pair went through again and Hohberg equalised. So many of his team-mates jumped on him in delight that he was knocked out!

In extra time, the deadly Uruguayan duo almost did it again, but this time Hohberg's shot crashed against the post. Soon after they lost Andrade for a few minutes, and while he was off receiving treatment Kocsis headed Hungary into the lead. Near the end Kocsis repeated the trick and the pre-tournament favourites were comfortably through to the final.

Speculation was rife as to whether or not Puskas would play in the final. In the end he did, and it looked like a sound decision when he opened the scoring after six minutes, but in truth the Hungarians committed the same deadly sin as the Brazilians had done four years earlier – they were over-confident. The Germans, after all, were an unseeded team, and the Magyars took victory for granted.

Most of final day the rain bucketed down, and the pitch in Berne's Wankdorf stadium was soaked, as were most of the 60,000 crowd, but this didn't seem to make any difference to Hungary. Not only did Puskas score after six minutes, but two minutes later they were two up after the German goalkeeper, Turek, dropped the ball after a misjudged back pass from Kohlmeyer and Czibor was on hand to drive it home.

Far from being demoralised, the Germans hit back within three minutes when Morlock deflected the ball past Grosics to make it 2-1. It now became clear that it had been a mistake to play Puskas, who was obviously not running smoothly. Five minutes later the Germans were level, Rahn scoring from a corner by Walter.

Still the Hungarians were a force to be reckoned with. At half-time the match was anybody's, and in the early part of the second half the Hungarians mounted a sustained attack on the German defences. Turek in the German goal was brilliant, and the Hungarians were denied. Then, five minutes from the end, the Germans hit back to clinch victory. Schaefer crossed, Lantos only half cleared, and Rahn trapped the ball, paused for a tantalising moment, then drove the ball home left-footed.

Two minutes later Puskas was controversially given off-side when it seemed he had equalised, and three minutes later it was all over. Jules Rimet, the retiring FIFA President, handed the trophy which bore his name to the German captain Fritz Walter. The team not thought worthy of seeding had carried off the game's greatest trophy, and the apparently unbeatable Hungarians had been conquered.

Switzerland 1954 – Results

Pool 1
Yugoslavia (1)1, France (0)0
Brazil (4)5, Mexico (0)0
France (1)3, Mexico (0)2
Brazil (0)1, Yugoslavia (1)1 *(after extra time)*

	P	W	D	L	F	A	Pts
Brazil	2	1	1	0	6	1	3
Yugoslavia	2	1	1	0	2	1	3
France	2	1	0	1	3	3	2
Mexico	2	0	0	2	2	8	0

Pool 2
Hungary (4)9, Korea (0)0
West Germany (1)4, Turkey (1)1
Hungary (3)8, West Germany (1)3
Turkey (4)7, Korea (0)0

	P	W	D	L	F	A	Pts
Hungary	2	2	0	0	17	3	4
West Germany	2	1	0	1	7	9	2
Turkey	2	1	0	1	8	4	2
Korea	2	0	0	2	0	16	0

Play-off: West Germany (3)7, Turkey (1)2

Pool 3
Austria (1)1, Scotland (0)0
Uruguay (0)2, Czechoslovakia (0)0
Austria (4)5, Czechoslovakia (0)0
Uruguay (2)7, Scotland (0)0

	P	W	D	L	F	A	Pts
Uruguay	2	2	0	0	9	0	4
Austria	2	2	0	0	6	0	4
Czechoslovakia	2	0	0	2	0	7	0
Scotland	2	0	0	2	0	8	0

Pool 4
England (2)4, Belgium (1)4
England (1)2, Switzerland (0)0
Switzerland (1)2, Italy (1)1
Italy (1)4, Belgium (0)1

	P	W	D	L	F	A	Pts
England.......................	2	1	1	0	6	4	3
Italy...........................	2	1	0	1	5	3	2
Switzerland	2	1	0	1	2	3	2
Belgium......................	2	0	1	1	5	8	1

Play-off: Switzerland (1)4, Italy (0)1

Quarter-finals
Geneva
West Germany (1)2 *(Horvat o.g., Rahn)*
Yugoslavia (0)0
West Germany: Turek; Laband, Kohlmeyer, Eckel, Liebrich, Mai, Rahn, Morlock, Walter O., Walter F., Schaefer.
Yugoslavia: Beara; Stankovic, Crnkovic, Cjaicowski I., Horvat, Boskov, Milutinovic, Mitic, Vukas, Bobek, Zebec.

Berne
Hungary (2)4 *(Hidegkuti 2, Kocsis, Lantos pen.)*
Brazil (1)2 *(Santos D. pen., Julinho)*
Hungary: Grosics; Buzansky, Lantos, Bozsik, Lorant, Zakarias, Toth M., Kocsis, Hidegkuti, Czibor, Toth J.
Brazil: Castilho; Santos D., Santos N., Brandaozinho, Pinheiro, Bauer, Julinho, Didi, Indio, Tozzi, Maurinho.

Lausanne
Austria (2)7 *(Koerner A. 2, Ocwirk, Wagner 3, Probst)*
Switzerland (4)5 *(Ballaman 2, Hugi 2, Hanappi o.g.)*
Austria: Schmied; Hanappi, Barschandt, Ocwirk, Happel, Koller, Koerner R., Wagner, Stojaspal, Probst, Koerner A.
Switzerland: Parlier; Neury, Kernen, Eggimann, Bocquet, Casali, Antenen, Vonlanthen, Hugi, Ballaman, Fatton.

Basle
Uruguay (2)4 *(Borges, Varela, Schiaffino, Ambrois)*
England (1)2 *(Lofthouse, Finney)*
Uruguay: Maspoli; Santamaria, Martinez, Andrade, Varela, Cruz, Abbadie, Ambrois, Miguez, Schiaffino, Borges.
England: Merrick; Staniforth, Byrne, McGarry, Wright, Dickinson, Matthews, Broadis, Lofthouse, Wilshaw, Finney.

Semi-finals
Basle
West Germany (1)6 *(Schaefer, Morlock, Walter F. 2 pens, Walter O. 2)*
Austria (0)1 *(Probst)*
West Germany: Turek; Posipal, Kohlmeyer, Eckel, Leibrich, Mai, Rahn, Morlock, Walter O., Walter F., Schaefer.
Austria: Zeman; Hanappi, Schleger, Ocwirk, Happel, Koller, Koerner R., Wagner, Stojaspal, Probst, Koerner A,

Lausanne
Hungary (1)4 *(Czibor, Hidegkuti, Kocsis 2)*
Uruguay (0)2 *(Hohberg 2)*
Hungary: Grosics; Buzansky, Lantos, Boszik, Lorant, Zakarias, Budai, Kocsis, Palotas, Hidegkuti, Czibor.
Uruguay: Maspoli; Santamaria, Martinez, Andrade, Carballo, Cruz, Souto, Ambrois, Schiaffino, Hohberg, Borges.

Third Place Play-off
Zurich
Austria (1)3 *(Stojaspal pen., Cruz o.g., Ocwirk)*
Uruguay (1)1 *(Hohberg)*
Austria: Schmied; Hanappi, Barschandt, Ocwirk, Kollmann, Koller, Koerner R., Wagner, Dienst, Stojaspal, Probst.
Uruguay: Maspoli; Santamaria, Martinez, Andrade, Carballo, Cruz, Abbadie, Hohberg, Mendez, Schiaffino, Borges.

Final   Berne, 4 July 1954
West Germany (2)3 *(Morlock, Rahn 2)*
Hungary (2)2 *(Puskas, Czibor)*
West Germany: Turek; Posipal, Kohlmeyer, Eckel, Liebrich, Mai, Rahn, Morlock, Walter O., Walter F., Schaefer.
Hungary: Grosics; Buzansky, Lantos, Bozsik, Lorant, Zakarias, Czibor, Kocsis, Hidegkuti, Puskas, Toth J.

Sweden 1958

The World Cup of 1958 was notable for several reasons: the emergence of a precocious seventeen-year-old Brazilian named Pele, the participation of the Soviet Union for the first time, the qualification of all four British teams for the first and only time so far, and the coming of age of commercialism linked to the extended television coverage. In many senses these were the first modern finals, but they were not particularly distinguished.

The idea of treating the British Championship as a qualifying competition was finally abandoned, and the four British teams were separated into different qualifying groups. Ironically, they rose to the challenge and all four qualified, although Wales made it by the back door. England didn't have too much to do in overcoming the Republic of Ireland and the amateurs of Denmark; Scotland, helped by an unexpected draw gained by Switzerland against Spain, headed their group; Northern Ireland surprisingly qualified in a group which also contained Portugal and Italy; Wales came second to Czechoslovakia, with East Germany third in the group, and thought they were out.

That Wales appeared in the finals was really thanks to Turkey. Turkey had been drawn in the Asia/Africa Group 2 to play against Israel, but did not want to play against the Israelis and so withdrew. FIFA decided that Israel should not be allowed to qualify without playing against somebody, and so there was a lottery to decide which of the runners-up from the other groups should provide the opposition. Wales came out of the hat and went on to beat the Israeli amateurs 2-0 in both matches.

The qualification of Northern Ireland also had an interesting aspect. The Italians, twice former World Champions, declared themselves quite happy at the prospect of having to play Portugal and the Irish in order to qualify, but their confidence was not justified. Ireland drew 1-1 in Lisbon and were unlucky to lose by a single goal in Rome, against the run of play. The Portuguese, as expected, lost in Belfast (3-0) but then, sensationally, the Italians crashed 3-0 in Lisbon, which opened up the group and gave Northern Ireland a chance, should they manage to get a result against the Italians in Belfast.

On the day of the match, with the Italians already in

Belfast, a thick fog in England prevented the Hungarian referee and his two linesmen from completing their journey to the game, and so it was decided to turn the match into a friendly. The result was a 2-2 draw, which would have been enough for the Italians to qualify, but it had been the Italians who had insisted on changing the status of the fixture, and when they eventually returned to Belfast to play the real tie, they were deservedly beaten 2-1 by an Irish team inspired by Danny Blanchflower. Once the Irish had qualified there was an outcry from hard-line Protestants in the province over the fact that their team would be required to play some matches on Sunday once they reached Sweden.

The Hungarians were no longer the great team they had been four years earlier. After the 1956 uprising, the authorities forced most of the best players to join Honved, the army team, and then made the mistake of sending them off on a foreign tour. Some of the stars, including Puskas and Kocsis, promptly took the opportunity to defect and were welcomed into the Spanish League.

The Swedes were back with a stronger team, now that the Swedish authorities had relented on the question of professionalism and so paved the way for the return of those stars who had gone abroad, principly to Italy, to seek their fortune.

Nobody gave much thought to the French, but they had a Moroccan-born striker named Just Fontaine, who would finish as the tournament's leading scorer with thirteen goals – still a record. West Germany were not the team they had been four years before, but they did have a young player in their squad called Uwe Seeler, and their formidable winger, Rahn, had recovered from a serious drink problem. He would play some of the best soccer of his life in these finals.

From South America came Argentina, Brazil and Paraguay. Argentina's strength had been sadly depleted by the lure of the Italian lira, the Paraguayans had qualified sensationally at the expense of the great Uruguay – they had beaten the former champions 5-0 – and Brazil arrived with the best South American side ever to visit Europe.

Apart from Pele, who was injured at first, Brazil had the likes of Garrincha, the 'Little Bird', crippled since childhood, but dangerous and unpredictable; Vava, the sturdy Vasco da Gama centre-forward; Didi, whose 'falling leaf' free kicks would cause havoc; Zagalo, the Flamenco winger. It was a marvellous team. The world would be enchanted by them.

Three of the next four World Cups would be theirs.

England qualified comfortably, but they were still reeling from the cruel blow of the Munich air disaster in February of 1958. The Manchester United team were on their way home from a 3-3 draw against Red Star in Belgrade, and the aircraft had stopped at Munich. In filthy weather, the twin-engined Elizabethan could not gain any height on take-off and smashed into a building beyond the end of the runway. Eight of the famous Busby Babes were killed, as well as several other passengers, including former England goalkeeper-turned-journalist Frank Swift. Instant death came to England players Roger Byrne and Tommy Taylor, while the twenty-one-year-old Duncan Edwards, the finest England left-half in living memory, died some days later in hospital.

Strangely, in view of this loss, England travelled to Sweden with only twenty players, two short of their entitlement, and it was astonishing that they omitted Lofthouse, who had just scored both Bolton goals in the FA Cup final against Manchester United, and Matthews, who was still, at forty-three, in imposing form.

In England's first game, against the USSR in Gothenburg, Tom Finney was injured, and this was, in a sense, the final nail in the coffin. There simply wasn't enough world class left in the squad any more, and although England went through the first phase matches undefeated, drawing with the USSR (2-0), Brazil (0-0) and Austria (2-2) they lost the necessary play-off 0-1 to the Soviets and were on their way home. The Soviets went through to the quarter-finals with Brazil.

In Group 1, the West Germans started with the expected 3-1 win over Argentina, but it was the Northern Irish who began what was to be an astonishing World Cup for them by beating the fancied Czechs 1-0 with a goal from Wilbur Cush. Meanwhile in Group 2 France started at a gallop, beating Paraguay 7-3, while Scotland did well to hold Yugoslavia to a 1-1 draw. Wales also started with a draw, 1-1 against the weakened Hungarians, while Sweden overcame Mexico 3-0 in the tournament's opening game.

In the next batch of games, the Irish came unstuck against the Argentinians, losing 3-1, while West Germany and Czechoslovakia played out a 2-2 draw in which the Czechs were unlucky not to win. In Group 2 Yugoslavia unexpectedly beat the French 3-2, with Fontaine scoring both goals for his side, and Scotland lost a disappointing game 3-2 against Paraguay. Wales dropped a point in playing badly against Mexico and getting only a 1-1 draw, while the Swedes made further progress towards the quarter-finals by beating Hungary 2-1.

In the final round of group matches the Czechs thrashed Argentina 6-1 while Northern Ireland ensured a play-off against the Czechs by drawing 2-2 with West Germany. Manchester United's Harry Gregg was marvellous in goal, and Aston Villa's Peter McParland scored both Irish goals. In Group 2 France were fortunate to squeeze a 2-1 win over Scotland while Yugoslavia just did enough in forcing a 3-3 draw with Paraguay to go through to the next stage.

Hungary overwhelmed Mexico 4-0 while the Swedes and the Welsh played out a goalless draw, which meant that Group 3 would send Sweden through to the quarter-finals along with the winner of a play-off between Wales and Hungary, while in Group 4 yet another play-off was required after Brazil, at last playing Pele and Garrincha, beat the Soviet Union 2-0 and England drew with Austria.

So Scotland were out, but the other three British representatives were involved in play-offs. Amazingly, it was England who faltered, going down 1-0 to the USSR in Gothenburg. The Northern Irish faced the Czechs in Malmo, where they were soon one down through a goal from Zikan, but McParland equalised on the stroke of half-time and scored the winner in extra time. Wales joined them in the quarter-finals by beating Hungary 2-1, also after extra time.

The teams who won through in play-offs had to face their well-rested quarter-final opponents only forty-eight hours later, which was a cruel handicap. Nevertheless, Wales put up a marvellous performance against Brazil, and although the South American wonder team were clearly in a higher class, they were fortunate in that the only goal of the match came from a mis-kick from the seventeen-year-old Pele which screwed past Jack Kelsey into the Welsh net after deflecting off the boot of Williams. When his career was over, Pele would look back and say that it was the most important goal he ever scored.

The Irish were not only weary after their play-off, but were forced to undertake an eight-hour coach journey covering the two hundred and ten miles between Tylosand and Norrkoping on the day before their quarter-final with France. Also, they were depleted by injuries. Gregg had torn ligaments, but had to play in place of the even more severely injured Uprichard, and the injured Casey was also obliged to turn out. In the first half they held out well, but Wisnieski scored for France just before half-time and Fontaine, with two more goals, and Piantoni wrapped it up after the interval.

In Stockholm, it was apparent that Swedish supporters still lacked belief in their team, and a meagre crowd of less than 32,000 turned out for the quarter-final clash with the Soviet Union. The Swedes found the going tough at first, but the Soviets had been involved in a play-off only two days before (v England) and tired in the second half, when goals from Hamrin and Simonsson saw the home side through.

The Germans faced the Yugoslavs in the last quarter-final and once again had reason to be thankful to Helmut Rahn, who scored the only goal of the match after twelve minutes. The World Champions were through to the last four, although they had begun to acquire a reputation for some pretty ruthless tackling and were rather fortunate that one particular effort by Erhardt on Milutinovic near the end didn't result in a penalty.

The semi-final between Sweden and West Germany was the tournament's most dramatic struggle, and was preceded by some extraordinary behaviour by the Swedish authorities. They allowed the Swedish cheerleaders to go through their pre-match routine on the pitch, while confining the German cheerleaders to the running track in the Gothenburg stadium. The Germans were outraged by this appallingly inhospitable decision, and were further infuriated when it was discovered that there was an insufficient number of seats for the German supporters. Seats were provided under threat of withdrawal by the German team, and the match got under way.

The Swedes controlled the first twenty minutes without being able to score, and it was the Germans who opened the scoring with a spectacular twenty-five-yard volley from Schaefer in the twenty-fourth minute after a cross from Seeler. Sweden's equaliser soon afterwards was blemished by a dreadful error by the Hungarian referee Istvan Zsolt. Liedholm clearly controlled the ball with his hand before supplying Skoglund with the pass from which he scored.

Things started to roughen up after the interval when Hamrin kicked the German full-back Juskowiak. The German was silly enough to kick him back, for which he was sent off while Hamrin rolled about in apparently excruciating agony. As soon as Juskowiak had departed, Hamrin made an immediate recovery. Sixteen minutes from the end Parling, the Swedish left-half, joined Juskowiak in the dressing rooms after a murderous foul on the German captain Fritz Walter. Walter had to go off for treatment, and although he came back a couple of minutes later, the Germans were virtually down to nine men.

In the last nine minutes the Swedes finished the job with goals from thirty-eight-year-old Gunnar Gren and Hamrin, who finished a mesmerising dribble with a fine shot past Herkenrath. Once again the host country was through to the World Cup final.

The Stockholm semi-final between France and Brazil was too one-sided to be called a classic. Didi, Garrincha and Pele combined to lay on the first goal for Brazil after two minutes, scored by Vava, and although Fontaine equalised a few minutes later, Didi put the Brazilians back in front within two minutes and in the second half the Brazilians cut loose, with Pele getting a hat-trick. Piantoni scored a late second for France. At least the French had managed to score against the Brazilians, a feat which had eluded all their other opponents in this tournament, and they had the dubious consolation of trouncing the Germans 6-3 in the play-off for third place.

Before the final got under way, FIFA's World Cup Committee insisted that the match be played at Stockholm rather than Gothenburg, preferred by the Swedes for its fanatically chauvanistic atmosphere, and they also ruled out any suggestion that Swedish cheerleaders be allowed on the pitch.

On the day of the final, 29 June 1958, it poured with rain nearly all day, and this was thought not to favour the South Americans, whose artistry had been honed on the firm pitches of their homeland. It was also widely believed that should the Brazilians fall behind, their supposed weakness of character would be exposed and they would panic. Both of these theories proved to be wildly wrong.

Within four minutes the Brazilians were behind – for the first time in the tournament – to a goal from Liedholm. Far from showing signs of panic, they continued to play with their usual easy fluency and were level within six minutes. The amazing Garrincha tore down the right wing, swerving past Parling and Axbom with breath-taking ease, and sent in a vicious low cross which Vava hammered home past a helpless Svensson. After thirty-two minutes the crowd were treated to an almost exact replica of the first goal, and Brazil were 2-1 up.

Ten minutes into the second half Pele did something special, something almost arrogant in the way in which he displayed supreme skill allied to supreme confidence in his own ability. In the centre of the Swedish penalty area, with his back to goal, he caught the ball on his thigh, flicked it over his head, spun on the spot and crashed a perfectly-timed volley past Svensson. Swedish hopes died with that flash of brilliance.

Thirteen minutes from the end Zagalo jinked past two defenders before slotting home the fourth, and although Simonsson pulled one back soon afterwards, it was Pele again, this time with a thudding header, who scored the fifth goal.

The Brazilians were overcome with emotion. They had shown that skill could beat strength, that brains were better than brawn. They played perfect football. They hardly ever tackled anybody, preferring to 'steal' the ball with a combination of lightning reactions and astonishing anticipation. They played as a true team, subordinating their individual brilliance to the common good. Their control was magical. They seemed able to take the ball from any height or angle and, without a moment's delay, to bring it under control or pass it to any one of several team-mates who always seemed to be in space. Their behaviour was impeccable. They only lost self-control when congratulating their scorers with hugs, kisses, and even tears. There was no doubt about it – the World Cup had been won by the best team in the world.

Sweden 1958 – Results

Pool 1
West Germany (2)3, Argentina (1)1
Northern Ireland (1)1, Czechoslovakia (0)0
West Germany (1)2, Czechoslovakia (0)2
Argentina (1)3, Northern Ireland (1)1
West Germany (1)2, Northern Ireland (1)2
Czechoslovakia (3)6, Argentina (1)1

	P	W	D	L	F	A	Pts
West Germany	3	1	2	0	7	5	4
Czechoslovakia	3	1	1	1	8	4	3
Northern Ireland	3	1	1	1	4	5	3
Argentina	3	1	0	2	5	10	2

Play-off: Northern Ireland (1)2, Czechoslovakia (1)1 *(after extra time)*

Pool 2

France (2)7, Paraguay (2)3
Yugoslavia (1)1, Scotland (0)1
Yugoslavia (1)3, France (1)2
Paraguay (2)3, Scotland (1)2
France (2)2, Scotland (0)1
Yugoslavia (2)3, Paraguay (1)3

	P	W	D	L	F	A	Pts
France	3	2	0	1	11	7	4
Yugoslavia	3	1	2	0	7	6	4
Paraguay	3	1	1	1	9	12	3
Scotland	3	0	1	2	4	6	1

Pool 3

Sweden (1)3, Mexico (0)0
Hungary (1)1, Wales (1)1
Wales (1)1, Mexico (1)1
Sweden (1)2, Hungary (0)1
Sweden (0)0, Wales (0)0
Hungary (1)4, Mexico (0)0

	P	W	D	L	F	A	Pts
Sweden	3	2	1	0	5	1	5
Hungary	3	1	1	1	6	3	3
Wales	3	0	3	0	2	2	3
Mexico	3	0	1	2	1	8	1

Play-off: Wales (0)2, Hungary (1)1

Pool 4

England (0)2, USSR(1)2
Brazil (1)3, Austria (0)0
England (0)0, Brazil (0)0
USSR (1)2, Austria (0)0
Brazil (1)2, USSR (0)0
England (0)2, Austria (1)2

	P	W	D	L	F	A	Pts
Brazil	3	2	1	0	5	0	5
England	3	0	3	0	4	4	3
USSR	3	1	1	1	4	4	3
Austria	3	0	1	2	2	7	1

Play-off: USSR (0)1, England (0)0

Quarter-finals
Norrkopping
France (1)4 *(Wisnieski, Fontaine 2, Piantoni)*
Northern Ireland (0)0
France: Abbes; Kaebel, Lerond, Penverne, Jonquet, Marcel, Wisnieski, Fontaine, Kopa, Piantoni, Vincent.
Northern Ireland: Gregg; Keith, McMichael, Blanchflower, Cunningham, Cush, Bingham, Casey, Scott, McIlroy, McParland.

Malmo
West Germany (1)1 *(Rahn)*
Yugoslavia (0)0
West Germany: Herkenrath; Stollenwerk, Juskowiak, Eckel, Erhardt, Szymaniak, Rahn, Walter, Seeler, Schmidt, Schaefer.
Yugoslavia: Krivocuka; Sijakovic, Crnkovic, Krstic, Zebec, Boskov, Petakovic, Veselinovic, Milutinovic, Ognjanovic, Rajkov.

Stockholm
Sweden (0)2 *(Hamrin, Simonsson)*
USSR (0)0
Sweden: Svensson; Bergmark, Axbom, Boerjesson, Gustavsson, Parling, Hamrin, Gren, Simonsson, Liedholm, Skoglund.
USSR: Yashine; Kessarev, Kuznetsov, Voinov, Krijevski, Tsarev, Ivanov A., Ivanov V., Simonian, Salnikov, Ilyin.

Gothenburg
Brazil (0)1 *(Pele)*
Wales (0)0
Brazil: Gilmar; De Sordi, Santos N., Zito, Bellini, Orlando, Garrincha, Didi, Mazzola, Pele, Zagalo.
Wales: Kelsey; Williams, Hopkins, Sullivan, Charles M., Bowen, Medwin, Hewitt, Webster, Allchurch, Jones.

Semi-finals
Stockholm
Brazil (2)5 *(Vava, Didi, Pele 3)*
France (1)2 *(Fontaine, Piantoni)*
Brazil: Gilmar; De Sordi, Santos N., Zito, Bellini, Orlando,
Garrincha, Didi, Vava, Pele, Zagalo.
France: Abbes; Kaelbel, Lerond, Penverne, Jonquet,
Marcel, Wisnieski, Fontaine, Kopa, Piantoni, Vincent.

Gothenburg
Sweden (1)3 *(Skoglund, Gren, Hamrin)*
West Germany (1)1 *(Schaefer)*
Sweden: Svensson; Bergmark, Axbom, Boerjesson,
Gustavsson, Parling, Hamrin, Gren, Simonsson, Liedholm,
Skoglund.
West Germany: Herkenrath; Stollenwerk, Juskowiak, Eckel,
Erhardt, Szymaniak, Rahn, Walter, Seeler, Schaefer,
Cieslarczyk.

Third Place Play-off
Gothenburg
France (3)6 *(Fontaine 4, Kopa pen., Douis)*
West Germany (1)3 *(Cieslarczyk, Rahn, Schaefer)*
France: Abbes; Kaelbel, Lerond, Penverne, Lafont, Marcel,
Wisnieski, Douis, Kopa, Fontaine, Vincent.
West Germany: Kwiatowski; Stollenwerk, Erhardt,
Schnellinger, Wewers, Szymaniak, Rahn, Sturm, Kelbassa,
Schaefer, Cieslarczyk.

Final   Stockholm, 29 June 1958
Brazil (2)5 *(Vava 2, Pele 2, Zagalo)*
Sweden (1)2 *(Liedholm, Simonsson)*
Brazil: Gilmar; Santos D., Santos N., Zito, Bellini, Orlando,
Garrincha, Didi, Vava, Pele, Zagalo.
Sweden: Svensson; Bergmark, Axbom, Boerjesson,
Gustavsson, Parling, Hamrin, Gren, Simonsson, Liedholm,
Skoglund.

Chile 1962

Chile nearly lost her chance of staging the 1962 World Cup when the country was devastated by a series of earthquakes at the time the venue was being decided, but Carlos Dittborn, President of the Chilean Football Federation, pleaded with FIFA: 'We must have the World Cup, or we have nothing'. He got his wish, and the Chileans set about building a magnificent new stadium in Santiago.

In some senses, Chile was a strange choice. It was very much an under-developed country, but enormously hospitable and enthusiastic for all that. Sadly for the organisers, the tournament would turn out to be a largely disappointing one, marred by one particularly nasty match between Chile and Italy, and nobody except the Czechs was able to come anywhere near beating the reigning champions, Brazil.

The format for the tournament was exactly the same as in 1958, with sixteen finalists organised into four groups and two teams from each group going forward to the quarter-finals. Brazil, with a new manager named Aymore Moreira, brother of 1954's Zeze, were put into Group 3, based at Vina, along with Czechoslovakia, Mexico and Spain. The champions still had many of the same faces as in 1958 and Pele, still only twenty-one, was widely regarded as the best player in the world.

The Czech squad, based on the army team of Dukla Prague, were known to be a hard-working and well-disciplined side, and they were the only ones of whom the Brazilians professed to be scared. Perhaps their most outstanding player was the midfielder Josef Masopust. The Spanish also had a team full of talent, which included Puskas, now a Spanish citizen following his defection from Hungary after the 1956 uprising. There were doubts, however, which proved to be justified, about their effectiveness as a team. Finally there was Mexico, taken seriously by nobody, who would at least provide the tournament with one genuine shock.

In Rancagua, Group 4 consisted of England, Hungary, Bulgaria and Argentina. Walter Winterbottom was in charge of England for his fourth and last World Cup, assisted as coach by Burnley's Jimmy Adamson, just voted Footballer of the Year in England. The England squad was radically different from that of 1958, but Johnny Haynes was still there, as captain. The remarkable young Jimmy Greaves was there, and another East London lad had just won his place in the team – Bobby Moore. One of the full-backs was Ray Wilson, the other Jimmy Armfield. Ron Springett was first choice goalkeeper, Bobby Charlton was there, and so was Peter Swan, who was destined to undergo an experience in Vina del Mar which would make sure that future England parties travelled with a doctor, an omission which seems incredible with hindsight.

Hungary had regained some prowess since the lean times of 1958, and had beaten England in Budapest in 1960. Argentina had a new young manager, Juan Carlos Lorenzo, and the Bulgarians, another East European team built around an army side (CDNA Sofia), had qualified by beating France in a play-off.

Group 2, based in Santiago, comprised Italy, Chile, West Germany and Switzerland. Italy arrived in South America at a time when *catenaccio* had Italian football firmly in its negative grip. The former champions had qualified by beating Israel, against whom they were two down at one point, and now they faced hostility in a continent from where their clubs had poached many fine players. A report which appeared in an Italian newspaper accusing Chile of being a backward country didn't help.

The West Germans, with such as Uwe Seeler and Karl-Heinz Schnellinger, had qualified without difficulty by beating Greece and Northern Ireland, and were still managed by Sepp Herberger in what was to be his last World Cup. Switzerland had defeated the 1958 runners-up, Sweden, to qualify, but were not fancied, and very little was known about Chile, although they had recently beaten Hungary.

Group 1 was based thousands of miles to the north, in Arica, and consisted of Uruguay, the Soviet Union, Yugoslavia and Colombia. The first three were well-known football forces, but little Colombia had descended from their mountains after surprisingly beating Peru to qualify.

The host nation started brightly by beating Switzerland 3-1 in front of 65,000 ecstatic fans in Santiago. The following day the Italians and West Germans both decided to play Italian-style football, and the result was a dreary goalless draw. However, the Italians looked the more skilful side, and so it was surprising when they made six changes for the match against Chile. It would be their undoing.

Meanwhile Argentina started with a 1-0 win over Bulgaria

while England went down 2-1, unable to break down the solid defence of Hungary. Brazil beat Mexico, but only by 2-0, while the feared Czechs got the only goal of the game ten minutes before time to overcome Spain. In the remote outpost of Arica, Colombia took the lead against mighty Uruguay, and the former champions had their work cut out to fashion a 2-1 victory with very little time left. On the following day the Russians beat Yugoslavia 2-0, but it was a dour struggle and when Mujic broke Dubinski's leg, his Yugoslavian bosses sent him straight home.

The second round of matches got under way with one of the most infamous games in the history of the sport – The Battle of Santiago. As already mentioned, Italy were not exactly popular in Chile, but on the other hand their players allowed themselves to be far too easily provoked. From the start the Chileans were spitting in the faces of their opponents and before long the most dreadful brawl started. The English referee, Ken Aston, was unsighted when Sanchez delivered a left hook which broke Maschio's nose, and the linesman, who must have seen the incident, said nothing. Sanchez was therefore spared from punishment while Ferrini was sent off in only the seventh minute for a foul on Landa and David followed him soon afterwards for trying to kick Sanchez in the head. The Italians, with only nine men, held out until a quarter of an hour from the end, and then the Chileans managed to get two late goals through Ramirez and Toro.

Chile lost their last match 2-0 to West Germany, while Italy scored an inconsequential 3-0 victory over Switzerland, and so West Germany and Chile went through to the quarter-finals.

England got themselves together to beat Argentina 3-0 in Rancagua, with Bobby Charlton getting one of the goals, while the Hungarians thrashed Bulgaria 6-1 with the help of a hat-trick from the remarkable Florian Albert. Hungary went on to get the point they needed in a 0-0 draw with Argentina, and England did the same in a disappointing performance against Bulgaria. England and Hungary therefore went through, but England, as Group 4 runners-up, faced the more difficult quarter-final, against Brazil.

For their part, the champions had lost Pele with a torn thigh muscle in their 0-0 draw with Czechoslovakia. He would take no further part. Brazil's final game was against Spain, who had recorded a dismal 1-0 victory over Mexico but would prove to be difficult opponents for Brazil. Led by Puskas, but without di Stefano, the Spanish played with flair and commitment in an entertaining match and took the lead through Adelardo in the thirty-fourth minute. The Spanish manager, Herrera, had been the arch-exponent of *catenaccio* in a spell as manager of Internazionale in Milan, and now his Spanish players used this method to withstand the Brazilian onslaught for a further thirty-eight minutes before Amarildo headed the equaliser. Four minutes from the end Garrincha went on one of his dazzling runs, crossed, and there was Amarildo again to clinch the points.

It was in the final game in Group 3 that the Mexicans provided their big shock, beating Czechoslovakia 3-1 in one of the finest performances of their long and lacklustre World Cup history. Unfortunately for Mexico, the result made no difference to anybody, and Brazil went through with Czechoslovakia.

In far-off Arica the Russians, who had recently beaten Uruguay 5-0 in a Moscow friendly, found them to be a vastly different proposition in a South American World Cup, and just managed to scrape a 2-1 win against a side which had been reduced to ten men for an hour by an injury to Alvarez. This result was a great relief to the Russians, who had amazingly only managed to draw with Colombia. The Russians had been 3-0 up after ten minutes, but the match finished at 4-4. The sudden collapse was blamed in many quarters on that legendary goalkeeper Lev Yashine, and some newspapers predicted that this tournament would herald the end of his great career, but he was still there in England four years later.

Yugoslavia, meanwhile, beat Uruguay 3-1 and a weary Colombia 5-0 to go through to the quarter-finals with the Russians. There they would face, for the third consecutive World Cup, the West Germans.

In the quarter-finals, England were taken apart by Brazil, and in particular Garrincha. Poor Ray Wilson just couldn't cope with him, and even Maurice Norman, at six foot two, was outjumped by him (Garrincha was only five foot seven) as he headed Brazil's first goal from a corner. In the second half he added another as well as making a goal for Vava, while England's consolation goal was scored by Gerry Hitchens. Brazil were through and England went home to prepare for greater things ahead.

It was third time lucky for Yugoslavia, who at last beat the

Germans in a World Cup quarter-final. The Germans played defensively, while the Yugoslavs played four men up front, and for a long time it was anybody's game, but just when extra time seemed inevitable, Radakovic fired in a shot from just inside the penalty area and Yugoslavia were through.

In Arica, the host nation surprised everyone, not least the home crowd, by beating Russia 2-0, with Yashine once more in questionable form. One of the Chilean goals was scored from thirty-five yards, and a goalkeeper of Yashine's class should never have fallen for that.

Finally, in Rancagua, Hungary completely dominated their quarter-final against Czechoslovakia but succumbed to a goal scored early on in what was a rare breakaway by the Czechs. After that the woodwork and the brilliant goalkeeping of Schroiff kept the Magyars at bay.

The semi-final between Brazil and Chile was so one-sided as to be uninteresting. Garrincha was in devastating form again, scoring twice in the first half-hour, and although Chile gamely fought back with goals by Toro and a Sanchez penalty either side of Brazil's third goal by Vava, they never looked like getting on terms. Their fate was sealed by a second Vava goal before Garrincha, fed up with being kicked by Rojas, retaliated and was sent off. As he walked back to the dressing room, his head was cut open by a bottle thrown from the crowd, and not long afterwards the Chilean centre-forward Landa followed him.

In Vina del Mar a paltry 5,000 spectators turned out to see Czechoslovakia, against the odds, join Brazil in the final. Once again the Czech goalkeeper, Schroiff, was in superb form, and soon after the interval his side took the lead through Kadraba. Jerkovic equalised a few minutes later, but Schroiff would not be beaten again, and two goals from Scherer, the second a penalty, saw the Czechs through to the final, where they would once more face Brazil.

The host nation won third place in a play-off which the Yugoslavians clearly regarded as an irrelevance, and so the stage was set for a final in which the Brazilians were, of course, firm favourites.

Sadly for Czechoslovakia, Schroiff chose this, of all matches, to lose his form. Even so, the Czechs took the lead through Masopust after sixteen minutes. In every World Cup final since the war the eventual losers had scored first, a remarkable statistic which would be repeated at Wembley four years later. It didn't take Brazil long to equalise with a powerful far post drive from Amarildo which Schroiff wrongly thought would be coming in at the near post.

Amarildo was proving to be a marvellous replacement for the injured Pele, and it was Amarildo who provided a deadly cross in the sixty-ninth minute from which Zito headed Brazil into the lead. Thirteen minutes from the end Djalma Santos lobbed the ball high into the Czech penalty area. Schroiff, possibly blinded by the sun, dropped it, and Vava was on hand to tap it home. The World Cup stayed where it was.

Chile 1962 – Results

Group 1
Uruguay (0)2, Colombia(1)1
USSR (0)2, Yugoslavia (0)0
Yugoslavia (2)3, Uruguay (1)1
USSR (3)4, Colombia (1)4
USSR (1)2, Uruguay (0)1
Yugoslavia (2)5, Colombia (0)0

	P	W	D	L	F	A	Pts
USSR	3	2	1	0	8	5	5
Yugoslavia	3	2	0	1	8	3	4
Uruguay	3	1	0	2	4	6	2
Colombia	3	0	1	2	5	11	1

Group 2
Chile (1)3, Switzerland (1)1
West Germany (0)0, Italy (0)0
Chile (0)2, Italy (0)0
West Germany (1)2, Switzerland (0)1
West Germany (1)2, Chile (0)0
Italy (1)3, Switzerland (0)0

	P	W	D	L	F	A	Pts
West Germany	3	2	1	0	4	1	5
Chile	3	2	0	1	5	3	4
Italy	3	1	1	1	3	2	3
Switzerland	3	0	0	3	2	8	0

Group 3
Brazil (0)2, Mexico (0)0
Czechoslovakia (0)1, Spain (0)0
Brazil (0)0, Czechoslovakia (0)0
Spain (0)1, Mexico (0)0
Brazil (0)2, Spain (1)1
Mexico (2)3, Czechoslovakia (1)1

	P	W	D	L	F	A	Pts
Brazil	3	2	1	0	4	1	5
Czechoslovakia	3	1	1	1	2	3	3
Mexico	3	1	0	2	3	4	2
Spain	3	1	0	2	2	3	2

Group 4
Argentina (1)1, Bulgaria (0)0
Hungary (1)2, England (0)1
England (2)3, Argentina (0)1
Hungary (4)6, Bulgaria (0)1
Argentina (0)0, Hungary (0)0
England (0)0, Bulgaria (0)0

	P	W	D	L	F	A	Pts
Hungary	3	2	1	0	8	2	5
England	3	1	1	1	4	3	3
Argentina	3	1	1	1	2	3	3
Bulgaria	3	0	1	2	1	7	1

Quarter-finals
Santiago
Yugoslavia (0)1 *(Radakovic)*
West Germany (0)0
Yugoslavia: Soskic; Durkovic, Jusufi, Radakovic, Markovic, Popvic, Kovacevic, Sekularac, Jerkovic, Galic, Skoblar.
West Germany: Fahrian; Novak, Schnellinger, Schulz, Erhardt, Giesemann, Haller, Szymaniak, Seeler, Brulls, Schaefer.

Vina del Mar
Brazil (1)3 *(Garrincha 2, Vava)*
England (1)1 *(Hitchens)*
Brazil: Gilmar; Santos D., Mauro, Zozimo, Santos N., Zito, Didi, Garrincha, Vava, Amarildo, Zagalo.

England: Springett; Armfield, Wilson, Moore, Norman, Flowers, Douglas, Greaves, Hitchens, Haynes, Charlton.

Arica
Chile (2)2 *(Sanchez L., Rojas)*
USSR (1)1 *(Chislenko)*
Chile: Escutti; Eyzaguirre, Contreras, Sanchez R., Navarro, Toro, Rojas, Ramirez, Lands, Tobar, Sanchel L.
USSR: Yashine; Tchokelli, Ostrovski, Voronin, Maslenkin, Netto, Chislenko, Ivanov, Ponedelnik, Mamikin, Meshki.

Rancagua
Czechoslovakia (1)1 *(Scherer)*
Hungary (0)0
Czechoslovakia: Schroiff; Lala, Novak, Pluskal, Popluhar, Masopust, Pospichal, Scherer, Kvasniak, Kadraba, Jelinek.
Hungary: Grosios; Matrai, Sarosi, Solymosi, Meszoly, Sipos, Sandor, Rakosi, Albert, Tichy, Fenyvesi.

Semi-finals
Santiago
Brazil (2)4 *(Garrincha 2, Vava 2)*

Chile (1)2 *(Toro, Sanchez L. pen)*
Brazil: Gilmar; Santos D., Mauro, Zozimo, Santos N., Zito, Didi, Garrincha, Vava, Amarildo, Zagalo.
Chile: Escutti; Eyzaguirre, Contreras, Sanchez R., Rodriguez, Toro, Rojas, Ramirez, Lands, Tobar, Sanchez L.

Vina del Mar
Czechoslovakia (0)3 *(Kadraba, Scherer 2)*
Yugoslavia (0)1 *(Jerkovic)*
Czechoslovakia: Schroiff; Lala, Novak, Pluskal, Popluhar, Masopust, Pospichal, Scherer, Kvasniak, Kadraba, Jelinek.
Yugoslavia: Soskic; Durkovic, Jusufi, Radakovic, Markovic, Popovic, Sujakovic, Sekularac, Jerkovic, Galic, Skoblar.

Third Place Play-off
Santiago
Chile (0)1 *(Rojas)*
Yugoslavia (0)0
Chile: Godoy; Eyzaguirre, Cruz, Sanchez R., Rodriguez,

Toro, Rojas, Ramirez, Campos, Tobar, Sanchez L.
Yugoslavia: Soskic; Durkovic, Svinjarevic, Radakovic, Markovic, Popovic, Kovacevic, Sekularac, Jerkovic, Galic, Skoblar.

Final   Santiago, 17 June 1962
Brazil (1)3 *(Amarildo, Zito, Vava)*
Czechoslovakia (1)1 *(Masopust)*
Brazil: Gilmar; Santos D., Mauro, Zozimo, Santos N., Zito, Didi, Garrincha, Vava, Amarildo, Zagalo.
Czechoslovakia: Schroiff; Tichy, Novak, Pluskal, Popluhar, Masopust, Pospichal, Scherer, Kvasniak, Kadraba, Jelinek.

England 1966

When England returned from Chile in 1962, the FA decided that they would now appoint a full-time team manager. First choice was Jimmy Adamson, the former Burnley player who had been coaching assistant to Walter Winterbottom in Chile, but he turned the offer down. The FA turned to Alf Ramsey. His League career had started with Southampton, who had discovered him in the army, but it was with Arthur Rowe's famous push and run Tottenham side of the early fifties than he came to prominence and he soon settled down as a regular choice for club and country at full-back. He had been in the side which suffered that incredible defeat at the hands of the USA in 1950, and there again when England were overwhelmed by Hungary in 1953.

A quiet and thoughtful man, he became manager of lowly Ipswich Town when his playing days ended and took the obscure East Anglian side from the Third Division, which they joined only in 1937, to the First Division Championship. It was a startling feat, achieved with unremarkable players, but he knew that they were past their peak when the FA asked him to take over as England manager, and so he accepted. Characteristically, he insisted that he, and he alone, would pick the side, and so the FA Selection Committee disappeared for ever.

One of Ramsey's main strengths was that he was a player's man, rather than an establishment figure like his predecessor, and the players responded enthusiastically. He was loyal to them, and they to him, and although he exercised discipline, he had the knack of doing so in a manner which the players accepted readily. The atmosphere in the England camp was serene. When, in 1963, Ramsey predicted that England would win the next World Cup, most people just smiled at his confidence, some thought it dangerous to tempt fate, but Ramsey was right. Perhaps, even then, he knew it.

Having said that, England got off to an inauspicious start under Ramsey, losing 5-2 to France in Paris in a European Nations Cup fixture early in 1963. Ramsey immediately set about rebuilding the side and also did something which had never been done for England before – he appointed a team doctor. Peter Swan, given the wrong treatment, had almost died during the 1962 World Cup, and the FA were now ready to follow Ramsey's advice. The Arsenal team doctor, Alan

Bass, was chosen, and he proved a good choice, getting on marvellously with Ramsey and all the players.

By the summer of 1963, Ramsey's rebuilding was starting to take effect, and the England summer tour that year was a great success. After drawing 1-1 with Brazil at Wembley, they went off round Europe, beating Czechoslovakia 4-2, East Germany 2-1 and Switzerland 8-1. England under Ramsey were on their way.

By the summer of 1966, the composition of the England side was established, and centred round the brilliant Gordon Banks in goal, the excellent full-backs Ray Wilson and George Cohen, Bobby Moore and Nobby Stiles in front of them, and Bobby Charlton, Geoff Hurst and Martin Peters further forward. Then there was a small red-haired Blackpool inside-forward named Alan Ball, who would be a revelation. Others included Bobby Charlton's brother Jack, from Leeds United, Liverpool's Roger Hunt, and the brilliant goalscorer Jimmy Greaves, who was destined not to take part in England's moment of glory.

England was placed in Group 1, along with Uruguay, France and Mexico, and would play all their matches at Wembley. This has caused much controversy and discussion since the event, and it was unfortunate that the FA, in a booklet explaining the competition, more or less said that should England win their group, they would play their quarter-final at Wembley. No such decision had yet been made by the Organising Committee, and it was only after an acrimonious meeting that they eventually did so, no doubt thinking, as usual, of the gate receipts. This was certainly the case when it came to settling the venues for the semi-finals. The stadiums would be Wembley and Goodison, and whereas England v Portugal would guarantee a capacity crowd at Wembley, Russia v West Germany would probably only half-fill the stadium, whereas Goodison would be full whoever played there. It seemed like common sense, and was eventually accepted.

Group 2, consisting of Argentina, West Germany, Spain and Switzerland, was based in Birmingham and Sheffield. Argentina were looking formidable once more, and while the Swiss had perhaps been fortunate to qualify just ahead of Northern Ireland, who had been frustrated by a draw in Albania, the Germans were known to be dangerous. Uwe Seeler was still there – complete with an artificial Achilles tendon – along with Helmut Haller, Wolfgang Overath and a supposedly gifted young midfielder from Bayern Munich by the name of Franz Beckenbauer.

In the north-eastern Group 4 were the Italians, the Russians, Chile and North Korea, the latter, of course, standing no chance. Managed by Edmondo Fabbri, the Italians had an impressive recent record, despite their occasional lapses into *catenaccio,* and their progress through the first round seemed assured. The Russians still had Yashine, and notable among their outfield players was a fine young winger in Chislenko. Chile did not look particularly impressive, and as for North Korea . . . well! Most of the Afro-Asian qualifying block had withdrawn because they would be sending only one representative to England, and so the Koreans had only had to beat Australia to qualify. In the event they beat the Aussies 6-1 and 3-1. Sir Stanley Rous had been there, and came back with a warning that the Koreans had to be taken seriously. Nobody took Rous seriously.

Group 3, based in Liverpool and Manchester, contained Portugal, Hungary, Brazil and Bulgaria. The Brazilians were an ageing side, but they still had Pele, twenty-five years old and at the peak of his career. The Hungarians had qualified without losing a match, and although the Portuguese had struggled to qualify, they too had a genuine star in Eusebio – the nearest that Europe have ever been to producing a Pele.

As is sometimes the case in the World Cup, the opening game was a disappointment, England and Uruguay drawing 0-0 at Wembley. The Uruguayans defended solidly and Hunt and Greaves could find no way through. Brazil, on the other hand, started brightly, beating Bulgaria 2-0 at Everton, with Pele and Garrincha each scoring direct from free kicks. At Old Trafford Portugal beat Hungary 3-1 against the run of play, and in Sheffield the West Germans enjoyed a good practice match against Switzerland, trouncing them 5-0. Beckenbauer scored twice.

Spain went down 2-1 against Argentina at Villa Park in a slightly rough game, while the North Koreans surprised nobody by losing 3-0 against Russia at Ayresome Park, Middlesbrough. The Italians opened their programme with a laboured 2-0 win over Chile while, back in England's group, there was another dull draw between France and Mexico. In their next match, France went down 2-1 to Uruguay, and their chance was gone.

The second round of games produced what for many people was the finest game of the tournament, between Hungary and Brazil. Pele couldn't play because of injury, and his place was taken by Tostao, but it was the Hungarians who stole the show, once again thanks largely to the wonderful Florian Albert. Hungary took the lead after only three minutes through Bene, and although Tostao equalised minutes later, the Hungarians would not be denied. Farkas volleyed them back into the lead and, near the end, they sealed it with a surely taken penalty by Meszoli after Bene had been fouled. It was Brazil's first World Cup defeat since 1954.

Pele was brought back for the final match against Portugal, but in one of the most sadly memorable moments of the competition, with Portugal already two up and Pele only half fit anyway, a totally unnecessary double foul by Morais put Pele out for good. The ridiculous English referee, George McCabe, allowed Morais to stay on the field for some reason which only he understood, and Brazil, with only ten men, were finished. Portugal and Hungary duly went through to the quarter-finals.

England woke up against Mexico and opened their scoring account with a splendid long-range effort by Bobby Charlton. Hunt added another in the second half, and England followed up with another 2-0 victory against France to ensure their quarter-final place. Near the end of the game against France, Nobby Stiles committed a dreadful foul on Jacky Simon, and afterwards some FA officials tried to insist that Ramsey withdraw Stiles from the squad. Typically loyal, Ramsey said that if Stiles went, so would he. They both stayed. However, perhaps the most significant event of the game, in which both England goals were scored by Roger Hunt, was that Jimmy Greaves sustained an injury that would keep him out of the quarter-final against Argentina. He was never recalled.

The Argentinians had drawn 0-0 with West Germany and beaten the Swiss 2-0, while Germany beat Spain 2-1 in a hard game at Birmingham, where Seeler got the winner with minutes to spare. Meanwhile, Italy had lost narrowly against the USSR, but what did that matter? They only had to beat North Korea to go through.

The North Koreans had, to the delight of the friendly Middlesbrough crowd, drawn 1-1 with Chile. Indeed, they had nearly won. Perhaps the Italians didn't heed the warning.

In any event they were down to ten men after half an hour when Bulgarelli, obviously unfit, hurt his knee in a tackle and was unable to continue. Just before half-time the immortal Pak Doo Ik beat Albertosi with a fierce shot. There was no further score, and the Italians went home with their tails betwen their legs to face a barrage of abuse from the fans at the airport. Manager Fabbri was sacked. For their part, Russia beat Chile 2-1 at Sunderland to go through with maximum points.

The Wembley quarter-final between England and Argentina was astonishing. Hurst had been brought in to replace the injured Greaves, and would keep his place through to the final, where he would make his mark in football history. But all that seemed a long way off as the Argentinians set about committing one cynical foul after the other – an effective way of stifling England's attacking ambitions. The German referee, Kreitlein, had his book in his hand almost as much as his whistle, and it seemed that every time he made an entry, the tall Argentinian captain, Rattin, was looming over him to protest. Ten minutes before half-time, Kreitlein had had enough, and sent Rattin off. The trouble was, Rattin didn't want to go.

For an incredible ten minutes he held out, until Ken Aston, veteran of the Battle of Santiago and now in charge of World Cup referees on behalf of FIFA, walked on to the pitch to sort it out. Rattin left, still reluctant, and slowly made his way round the perimeter track, occasionally pausing to watch the match, sometimes to argue with the crowd.

The Argentinians held out with ten men until a quarter of an hour from the end when Hurst rose to head home a cross from his West Ham team-mate Martin Peters, and England were through. Such was the violent behaviour of the Argentinian players in the tunnel after the game that Ramsey was provoked into calling them 'animals'. That remark still rankles in Argentina today.

At Hillsborough, the West Germans overcame Uruguay 4-0, helped no doubt by the fact that two Uruguayans got their marching orders. Meanwhile Hungary, following their splendid performance against Brazil, fell apart against the Soviet Union, losing 2-1.

The quarter-final at Goodison, between Portugal and North Korea, was sensational. The Koreans were one up within a minute, scored by Pak Seung Jin. Twenty minutes later, they were two up, through Li Dong Woon this time. As if this wasn't incredible enough, they went even further ahead a few minutes later with a goal from Yang Sung Kook. Eusebio then came into his own to start Portugal's recovery. Simoes fed him the pass for his first goal after twenty-eight minutes and just before half-time he got his second from the penalty spot after Torres had been chopped down.

Fifteen minutes after the restart, Eusebio raced through to equalise, and soon after that he was hacked down himself in the penalty area and scored for Portugal to take the lead. Augusto got the fifth from a corner, and the wonderful Koreans were out, to disappear back into obscurity.

The semi-final between West Germany and Russia was a poor, ill-tempered affair. Sabo was soon out of it, having tried to foul Beckenbauer and only succeeded in nearly crippling himself in the process. Then, just before half-time, Chislenko was injured in a tackle from Schnellinger. The ball ran loose to Haller, who scored. The Russians sent the limping Chislenko back out for the second half. He was immediately beaten, easily, by Held, and kicked out in his frustration. The famous Sicilian referee, Concetto Lo Bello, sent him off at once, and so the Russians were down to nine men. Even so, the Germans only scored once more. It was, of course, enough.

The England v Portugal semi-final at Wembley was altogether a finer match, played in a marvellous spirit. It was here that Stiles silenced his critics once and for all by simply cutting Eusebio out of the game, as well as urging his mates on with all the infectious enthusiasm for which he was famous. Bobby Charlton played brilliantly, and scored the first goal after Pereira had only blocked a shot from Hunt. England held on until half-time, but had missed a number of chances, and the match was by no means over.

After the interval, Portugal started to press really hard, but could find no way through a splendid England defence, and so England started to regain command. Ten minutes from time, Charlton scored again, this time from a cross by Geoff Hurst, who was still preferred to the fit-again Jimmy Greaves. Eusebio scored from the penalty spot a couple of minutes later after Jack Charlton had punched the ball clear, but it made no difference. England were in the World Cup final.

Would Ramsey recall Greaves? Hurst was clearly playing too well to be dropped, but Roger Hunt could possibly make way. While Ramsey was pondering this matter, his German counterpart, Helmut Schoen, was worried about his goal-keeper. Tilkowski was slightly injured and in any case had proved less than adequate in dealing with high crosses. Schoen would have preferred the young Bayern goalkeeper, Sepp Maier, but he was too badly injured even to be considered.

So Tilkowski stayed where he was and Ramsey announced that the team which had won both quarter-final and semi-final would remain unchanged. It would also remain unchanged for the next three games after the World Cup, a six-match run which is still an England record. Portugal, meanwhile, beat Russia 2-1 in the third-place match with the help of yet another Eusebio penalty, and attention focussed on the final.

At that time, England had never lost to Germany, East, West or otherwise. Schoen knew the magnitude of the task that faced him and perhaps therefore made the mistake of detailing the marvellously gifted Beckenbauer to do nothing else but mark Bobby Charlton. Beckenbauer was still doing this four years later in Leon, until Ramsey took Charlton off with the match apparently won, but that's another story.

England were soon a goal adrift, scored by Haller after a mistake by Wilson, but within six minutes the scores were level. Bobby Moore took a free kick quickly, and with the German defence unprepared, Hurst ran in to nod the ball past the furious Tilkowski. Both sides had further chances in the half, but failed to take them, and the score remained 1-1 at the interval.

The second half started in pouring rain, and for a while the match seemed to be damped down. Tension seemed to be affecting both sides, and it wasn't until twelve minutes from the end that England took the lead. Ball took a corner, Hurst fired in a shot, Weber blocked it, and the ball spun through the air to be met by Martin Peters. His shot was accurate. 2-1.

With less than a minute left the crowd were beginning to celebrate, but then Held and Jack Charlton went up together for a header. It looked as if Held had backed into Charlton, but Dienst, the Swiss referee, had seen it differently, and the England wall formed to face the German free kick. Emmerich fired the kick into the goal area, where it seemed to ricochet from player to player until Weber, virtually on the goal-line, stabbed it home. Now there would be extra time for the first time since 1934.

Ten minutes into extra time came perhaps the most controversial incident ever seen in a World Cup final. Ball, still full of running after a hundred minutes, centred to Hurst, who crashed an unstoppable shot past Tilkowski. The ball hit the underside of the bar and bounced down, then out. Roger Hunt, who was closest and could easily have finished it off, turned in triumph. He was sure the ball had crossed the line. Referee Dienst was not, and went across to consult the Russian linesman, Bakhramov. The linesman was sure. The goal was given. England were delighted, the Germans furious.

Many years later a photograph, taken by a photographer at the other end of the pitch through a telescopic lens, was discovered which seemed to end the controversy. It shows the ball just as it had bounced up from the ground, and you can clearly see the white mark left by the damp goal-line marking on the orange ball. Clearly, it had not crossed the line.

However, it was Geoff Hurst again, seconds from the end, who wrapped it up for England. He broke free on the left, hurtled towards the goal and hit the ball as hard as he could, reckoning, he said afterwards, that if he missed, at least it would take so long to get the ball back from the back of the stand that England would be home and dry. He needn't have worried about time, for the ball went straight into the back of the net, not the stand, and the World Cup was England's. Hurst was the first man to score a hat-trick in a World Cup final, and the Cup had settled in the country where the game began.

England 1966 – Results

Group 1
England (0)0, Uruguay (0)0
France (0)1, Mexico (0)1
Uruguay (2)2, France (1)1
England (1)2, Mexico (0)0
Uruguay (0)0, Mexico (0)0
England (1)2, France (0)0

	P	W	D	L	F	A	Pts
England	3	2	1	0	4	0	5
Uruguay	3	1	2	0	2	1	4
Mexico	3	0	2	1	1	3	2
France	3	0	1	2	2	5	1

Group 2
West Germany (3)5, Switzerland (0)0
Argentina (0)2, Spain (0)1
Spain (0)2, Switzerland (1)1
Argentina (0)0, West Germany (0)0
Argentina (0)2, Switzerland (0)0
West Germany (1)2, Spain (1)1

	P	W	D	L	F	A	Pts
West Germany	3	2	1	0	7	1	5
Argentina	3	2	1	0	4	1	5
Spain	3	1	0	2	4	5	2
Switzerland	3	0	0	3	1	9	0

Group 3
Brazil (1)2, Bulgaria (0)0
Portugal (1)3, Hungary (0)1
Hungary (1)3, Brazil (1)1
Portugal (2)3, Bulgaria (0)0
Portugal (2)3, Brazil (0)1
Hungary (2)3, Bulgaria (1)1

	P	W	D	L	F	A	Pts
Portugal	3	3	0	0	9	2	6
Hungary	3	2	0	1	7	5	4
Brazil	3	1	0	2	4	6	2
Bulgaria	3	0	0	3	1	8	0

Group 4
USSR (2)3, North Korea (0)0
Italy (1)2, Chile (0)0
Chile (1)1, North Korea (0)1
USSR (0)1, Italy (0)0
North Korea (1)1, Italy (0)0
USSR (1)2, Chile (1)1

	P	W	D	L	F	A	Pts
USSR	3	3	0	0	6	1	6
North Korea	3	1	1	1	2	4	3
Italy	3	1	0	2	2	2	2
Chile	3	0	1	2	2	5	1

Quarter-finals
Wembley
England (0)1 *(Hurst)*
Argentina (0)0
England: Banks; Cohen, Wilson, Stiles, Charlton J., Moore, Ball, Hurst, Charlton R., Hunt, Peters.
Argentina: Roma; Ferreiro, Perfumo, Albrecht, Marzolini, Gonzalez, Rattin, Onega, Solari, Artime, Mas.

Sheffield (Hillsborough)
West Germany (1)4 *(Held, Beckenbauer, Seeler, Haller)*
Uruguay (0)0
West Germany: Tilkowski; Hottges, Weber, Shulz, Schellinger, Beckenbauer, Haller, Overath, Seeler, Held, Emmerich.
Uruguay: Mazurkiewicz; Troche, Ubinas, Goncalves, Manicera, Caetano, Salva, Rocha, Silva, Cortes, Perez.

Liverpool (Goodison)
Portugal (2)5 *(Eusebio 4, 2 pens, Jose Augusto)*
North Korea (3)3 *(Pak Seung Jin, Yang Sung Kook, Li Dong Woon)*
Portugal: Jose Pereira; Morais, Baptista, Vicente, Hilario, Graca, Coluna, Jose Augusto, Eusebio, Torres, Simoes.
North Korea: Li Chan Myung; Rim Yung Sum, Shin Yung Kyoo, Ha Jung Won, O Yoon Kyung, Pak Seung Jin, Jon Seung Hwi, Han Bong Jin, Pak Doo Ik, Li Dong Woon, Yang Sung Kook.

Sunderland
USSR (1)2 *(Chislenko, Porkujan)*
Hungary (0)1 *(Bene)*
USSR: Yashine; Ponomarev; Chesternijev, Voronin, Danilov, Sabo, Khusainov, Chislenko, Banichevski, Malafeev, Porkujan.
Hungary: Gelei; Matrai, Kaposzta, Meszoly, Sipos, Szepesi, Nagy, Albert, Rakosi, Bene, Farkas.

Semi-finals
Liverpool (Goodison)
West Germany (1)2 *(Haller, Beckenbauer)*
USSR (0)1 *(Porkujan)*
West Germany: Tilkowski; Hottges, Weber, Schulz, Schnellinger, Beckenbauer, Haller, Overath, Seeler, Held, Emmerich.
USSR: Yashine; Ponomarev, Chesternijev, Voronin, Danilov, Sabo, Khusainov, Chislenko, Banichevski, Malafeev, Porkujan.

Wembley
England (1)2 *(Charlton R. 2)*
Portugal (0)1 *(Eusebio pen.)*
England: Banks; Cohen, Wilson, Stiles, Charlton J., Moore, Ball, Hurst, Charlton R., Hunt, Peters.
Portugal: Jose Pereira; Festa, Baptista, Jose Carlos, Hilario, Graca, Coluna, Jose Augusto, Eusebio, Torres, Simoes.

Third Place Play-off
Wembley
Portugal (1)2 *(Eusebio pen., Torres)*
USSR (1)1 *(Malafeev)*
Portugal: Jose Pereira; Festa, Baptista, Jose Carlos, Hilario, Graca, Coluna, Jose Augusto, Eusebio, Torres, Simoes.
USSR: Yashine; Ponomarev, Khurtsilava, Korneev, Danilov, Voronin, Sichinava, Metreveli, Malafeev, Banichevski, Serebrianikov.

Final   Wembley, 30 July 1966
England (1)4 *(Hurst 3, Peters)*
West Germany (1)2 *(Haller, Weber)*
(after extra time, 90 mins 2-2)
England: Banks; Cohen, Wilson, Stiles, Charlton J., Moore, Ball, Hurst, Hunt, Charlton R., Peters.
West Germany: Tilkowski; Hottges, Schulz, Weber, Schnellinger, Haller, Beckenbauer, Overath, Seeler, Held, Emmerich.

Mexico 1970

Mexico had been awarded the 1970 World Cup finals as long ago as the FIFA Congress of 1964 in Tokyo, at the same time as it was decided that Mexico should host the 1968 Olympics. It was a poor choice, to say the least, because of the intense heat, which was exacerbated by the decision to start matches at noon in deference to European television, and the breathing difficulties which would be encountered in the rarified atmosphere 7,000 feet above sea level.

Although with the benefit of hindsight it still looks like a bad choice, favouring as it did the South American nations, the tournament was one of the most memorable of recent times, and once again the Brazilians would triumph. Their victory, based on their well-known virtues of dazzling attacking play combined with breath-taking skill, was all the sweeter in that they annihilated the Italians, who stood for all that was negative, in the final.

Acclimatisation was the name of the game, and most teams reckoned that they needed at least three, if not four, weeks at altitude in order to settle down. Important lessons had been learned in the 1968 Olympics. Unfortunately, with the tournament again going to Mexico for 1986, some lessons were not learned.

The Brazilians had cruised through their qualifying group against Colombia, Paraguay and Venezuela, although they had to face the disruption of a sudden change of manager in March 1970 when Zagalo, their left-winger from 1958 and 1962, replaced Saldanha. Saldanha's choice of players had been erratic throughout 1969, and he made the fatal error, in March 1970, of publicly announcing that he was thinking of dropping Pele. That was too much for the Brazilian Federation to stomach, and he was out.

Zagalo was fortunate in as much as Tostao was fit again after two eye operations in Texas, and he pulled the master stroke of introducing Rivelino. Brazil prepared to face their first round opponents – England, Rumania and Czechoslovakia. Part of their preparation consisted of a massive public relations exercise, designed to win the good will of their Mexican hosts. It was something which, perhaps, Sir Alf Ramsey (he had been knighted in 1967) could have learned from.

Ramsey had many fine qualities, but diplomacy was never

one of them, and his relations with the press – especially the foreign press – were not of the best. As a result, England were becoming the team that the locals loved to hate, and things were not helped by Bobby Moore's unforgiveable treatment in Colombia.

Staying at a hotel in Bogota, prior to a pre-World Cup friendly against Colombia, Moore and Bobby Charlton paid a visit to the hotel jewellery shop. Seeing nothing they wanted, they left and were sitting in the lobby when they were approached by hotel staff and Moore was accused of stealing a bracelet. A few days later, travelling back through Bogota en route to Mexico after a further friendly in Ecuador, Moore was arrested and charged. He was bailed for the World Cup, and the whole affair, which was clearly a fabrication, was forgotten two years later when those responsible for making the false accusations were charged with conspiracy. Moore behaved impeccably throughout, but it didn't help the image of the England squad at the time.

In addition to some members of the 1966 team, England had acquired the services of such as Francis Lee, Colin Bell, Alan Mullery, Terry Cooper and Keith Newton, and their chances of retaining the trophy looked promising, despite the awful conditions. Alf Ramsey said years later that the 1970 squad was probably the best he ever had, and few people would disagree with him.

West Germany were certainly among the contenders, with Beckenbauer at the peak of his prowess and a young, feared striker from Bayern Munich named Gerd Müller, while the Italians had a strong squad, at least on paper, though their style of play would not produce the ultimate dividend. Names such as Riva, Mazzola, and Rivera were rightly respected – except by the Brazilians.

The North Koreans were not there to haunt the Italians this time, but Morocco and Israel had qualified. From the 1966 finals, Yugoslavia and Spain had failed to make it, and England was the only British representative.

Once again, the opening game was a dull, goalless draw, this time between Mexico and Russia. England, on the other hand, fresh from a series of successful friendlies, made a bright start, beating Rumania with a Geoff Hurst goal. If England were bright, the Brazilians were dazzling, thrashing the Czechs 4-1 and displaying, in addition to Pele, the fearsome trio of Gerson, Rivelino and Jairzinho.

In Group D the Peruvians, whose homelands had suffered from terrible earthquakes shortly before the tournament, recovered from a two-goal deficit to beat Bulgaria 3-2, while the West Germans were staggered by falling behind to Morocco. This was the first World Cup in which substitutes were allowed, and the Germans brought on Grabowski with great effect – and not for the last time in this tournament. The Germans duly scored twice in the second half and could breath again, but only just.

Belgium easily overcame the pathetic El Salvador by 3-0 in Group A, while Group B got off to a deadly start. Uruguay made very heavy weather of defeating Israel 2-0, and lost their super midfielder Rocha in the process with an injury which would keep him out for the rest of the tournament. Meanwhile Italy managed a 1-0 victory against Sweden – the only goal they would score in the opening round, but still they would go through.

By far the most attractive match of these opening rounds was the meeting between England and Brazil. Rumania had beaten the Czechs the day before, and it was also on the day before that England's problems started. As the afternoon wore on a crowd started to gather outside their hotel, and by nightfall their intentions were obvious. All night long they kept up a cacophony of noise, particularly chanting and car-horns, and they succeeded in destroying the chances of the England players getting any peace.

As it turned out, England played superbly the next day, and were unfortunate not to at least get a draw. They were the only team in the competition to give Brazil any real problems, and had not Jeff Astle missed a golden opportunity to equalise Jairzinho's ferociously hit Brazilian goal, the draw would have been theirs. As it was, both teams would qualify for the quarter-finals. The match was also notable for a save by Gordon Banks from Pele which has gone down in history as one of the greatest ever seen. With the temperature approaching one hundred degrees, no English player lost less than ten pounds in weight.

In Group A, Russia and Mexico went through, the Russians having knocked the heart out of a talented Belgian side with a 4-1 win, followed by a 2-0 victory against El Salvador. Mexico trounced El Salvador 4-0 and finished with a 1-0 win against a half-hearted Belgium. Goal difference was at last being used instead of play-offs, and this saw through

Uruguay in Group B. They joined Italy in the quarter-finals.

Brazil finished their first round campaign with a 3-2 win over Rumania, while England, with several changes, just managed to beat Czechoslovakia 1-0 with a goal by Allan Clarke. In Group D, West Germany sailed through with maximum points and were joined in the last eight by Peru.

In the quarter-finals, the Italians at last started to play, and they brushed aside the host nation 4-1, with Riva getting two goals, although it was the arrival of Rivera in the second half which really settled matters. The wild rejoicings of the Mexican crowds in the capital had started to assume frightening proportions, but now that would happen no more.

In the vast Aztec stadium in Mexico City, Uruguay beat Russia 1-0 in the last moments of extra time with a controversial goal. Before Cubilla supplied the final cross, the ball seemed to have gone out of play, but when the cross was thumped in by Esparrago the goal stood. The disappointed Russians packed their bags.

In Guadalajara Brazil progressed through to the semi-finals by beating Peru 4-2, but the match was surprisingly open and entertaining, with the lowly Peruvians scorning defence in much the same way as the Brazilians. There was, however, no way that they could actually beat Brazil.

In Leon, England faced disaster. Drawn against West Germany in this quarter-final, they were brimming with confidence forty-eight hours before the kick-off. Then Gordon Banks drank a bottle of beer. Within hours he had gone down with the debilitating stomach disorder known to visitors to Mexico as Montezuma's Revenge. There was no way he could possibly play, and his place went to the first reserve 'keeper, Peter Bonetti. To be fair to Bonetti, he was rather thrown into things at the last minute, but having said that he made a couple of gross errors, which didn't help. As it was, there were other factors which were still waiting to ensure England's downfall, as we shall see in a moment.

The match was certainly an attractive fixture, not least because it was a replay of the 1966 final. Since then the Germans had scored their first win over England – a 1-0 result in a friendly in Hanover – and were undoubtedly a stronger team than they had been then. Indeed, the Germans were favourites to win this tie, but England started well, and took the lead after half an hour when Mullery exchanged passes with Lee, pushed the ball out to Newton and then raced through to slam Newton's centre past Maier. Five minutes after half-time Newton supplied another deadly cross, and this time Martin Peters was there to finish it off.

The substitutions which followed soon after the second England goal were to be crucial, and indeed devastating for England. Schoen replaced Libuda with Grabowski. The newcomer was fresh, whereas Terry Cooper was suffering, but it was not to be Cooper who would be taken off by Ramsey.

Soon afterwards Beckenbauer scored a vital goal, and then Ramsey made what most people regarded as his biggest mistake. He replaced Charlton with Colin Bell, thus allowing Beckenbauer, who had been mostly taken up with looking after Charlton, to come forward and do even more damage. Perhaps Ramsey thought that the match was safe, and that Charlton should be saved for the semi-finals. In any event, the match wasn't safe, and Charlton's departure, with his record-breaking 106th England cap in the bank, heralded the last time this magnificent player would ever be seen in an England shirt.

At the same time, Norman Hunter replaced Martin Peters, a move which has never been satisfactorily explained, but nevertheless England still looked far from finished at this point. Bell was chopped down in the German penalty area with the ball nowhere in sight, but the referee didn't see it that way, and soon afterwards a tired-looking Labone made a mess of a clearance and Schnellinger lobbed the ball back into the goalmouth. The slow English defence had not quite managed to put Seeler offside, and Seeler back-headed the ball over Bonetti's despairing hands to equalise.

So, as in 1966, extra time was needed to separate these two teams, and although the psychological advantage was now with Germany, it was England who netted first, Hurst slamming the ball past Maier after being put through by Lee. The referee, with a decision which has never been explained, disallowed the goal, and soon afterwards Muller finished England off with a murderous close-range volley. The English players were desperately disappointed, and it would be twelve long years before another England team qualified for the World Cup finals.

West Germany went through to a semi-final tie against Italy in Mexico City, while the two remaining South American teams, Brazil and Uruguay, faced up to each other in Guadalajara. To most people's surprise, Brazil fell behind to an early goal from Cubilla, although the Brazilian goalkeeper, Felix, was largely to blame for not covering the extremely narrow angle from which Cubilla fired the ball home.

Clodoaldo equalised just before half-time, which was a great relief to the Brazilians not only for the obvious reason that they were back in the game, but also because the goal meant that Uruguay had to abandon the defensive attitude they had adopted when in front and reinforced with some cynical fouling which had frustrated the Brazilian forward line.

So it was that Brazil took over in the second half, and although Uruguay became even more ruthlessly physical, Jairzinho put Brazil 2-1 up and Pele laid on a lovely chance for Rivelino, who duly completed the job.

In Mexico City, the crowd was thrilled by the other semi-final. West Germany were tired after their gruelling match against England, and Italy were soon one up through Boninsegna. It was the only goal of the first half, but after half-time the Italians made what was nearly a fatal mistake by withdrawing into their old habits of *catenaccio,* which allowed Beckenbauer and the rest of the German midfield more space to create. Even so, it looked as though the Italians would get away with it as the match went into the third minute of injury time. Then, in the very nick of time – Grabowski – playing a whole match for a change, crossed and Schnellinger drifted into the goalmouth to equalise.

In extra time Beckenbauer played with his arm strapped to his side, the result of a cynical foul perfectly timed just *outside* the penalty area. Even so, the Germans started extra time convincingly with a goal from Müller, and after that the goals came thick and fast. Italy restored their lead with goals by Burgnich and Riva, and in the second period of extra time Müller popped up again to equalise. That goal ensured Müller's place as the tournament's leading scorer, but it was Rivera, from a cross by Boninsegna, who wrapped it up six minutes from time for the Italians.

So the final would be contested by two teams who had each won the World Cup twice before, which gave the match the added spice that the winners would win the Jules Rimet trophy outright. The Brazilians were favourites, but the Italians had plenty of skill in their team, and, should they decide to attack they at least had the comfort of knowing that the Brazilians had a defence which was hardly outstanding.

Unfortunately the Italians stayed in their defensive shell and let the Brazilians come at them, and for this serious error of judgement they paid dearly. Everybody else was delighted, however, because we were treated to another marvellous exhibition of attacking football from the Brazilians, even if cynics would later describe the match as little *other* than an exhibition.

Pele, in his last major international match, was superb, and after eighteen minutes he rose majestically to a cross from Rivelino and headed the ball home with impressive power. Even so, seven minutes before half-time, the Italians were able to exploit the known weaknesses of the Brazilian defence to equalise through Boninsegna. At this point Italy could have continued to press, but, for some reason best known to them, they didn't, and although their defence held out until the sixty-sixth minute, the Brazilians, inevitably, broke them down – it was a drive from Gerson which did the damage – and thereafter it was all over bar the shouting.

Five minutes later, Pele pushed the ball through to Jairzinho, who steamed in with typical power to make it 3-1 and then, after fruitless substitutions by Italy, it was Pele again providing the final pass – this time for Carlos Alberto – and the Brazilians had their fourth and final goal.

Once again the Brazilians had proved that football was a game to be enjoyed, and now they had the trophy permanently. Sadly, in 1984 it was reported that the trophy had been stolen and melted down, but a replica has been made to replace it. Who will ever replace those Brazilians?

Mexico 1970 – Results

Group 1
Mexico (0)0, USSR (0)0
Belgium (1)3, El Salvador (0)0
USSR (1)4, Belgium (0)1
Mexico (1)4, El Salvador (0)0
USSR (0)2, El Salvador (0)0
Mexico (1)1, Belgium (0)0

	P	W	D	L	F	A	Pts
USSR	3	2	1	0	6	1	5
Mexico	3	2	1	0	5	0	5
Belgium	3	1	0	2	4	5	2
El Salvador	3	0	0	3	0	9	0

Group 2

Uruguay (1)2, Israel (0)0
Italy (1)1, Sweden (0)0
Uruguay (0)0, Italy (0)0
Sweden (0)1, Israel (0)1
Sweden (0)1, Uruguay (0)0
Italy (0)0, Israel (0)0

	P	W	D	L	F	A	Pts
Italy	3	1	2	0	1	0	4
Uruguay	3	1	1	1	2	1	3
Sweden	3	1	1	1	2	2	3
Israel	3	0	2	1	1	3	2

Group 3

England (0)1, Rumania (0)0
Brazil (1)4, Czechoslovakia (1)1
Rumania (0)2, Czechoslovakia (1)1
Brazil (0)1, England (0)0
Brazil (2)3, Rumania (1)2
England (0)1, Czechoslovakia (0)0

	P	W	D	L	F	A	Pts
Brazil	3	3	0	0	8	3	6
England	3	2	0	1	2	1	4
Rumania	3	1	0	2	4	5	2
Czechoslovakia	3	0	0	3	2	7	0

Group 4

Peru (0)3, Bulgaria (1)2
West Germany (0)2, Morocco (1)1
Peru (0)3, Morocco (0)0
West Germany (2)5, Bulgaria (1)2
West Germany (3)3, Peru (1)1
Morocco (1)1, Bulgaria (0)1

	P	W	D	L	F	A	Pts
West Germany............	3	3	0	0	10	4	6
Peru.........................	3	2	0	1	7	5	4
Bulgaria....................	3	0	1	2	5	9	1
Morocco	3	0	1	2	2	6	1

Quarter-finals
Leon
West Germany (0)3 *(Beckenbauer, Seeler, Muller)*
England (1)2 *(Mullery, Peters)*
(after extra time, 90 mins 2-2)
West Germany: Maier; Schnellinger, Vogts, Hottges
(Schulz), Beckenbauer, Overath, Seeler, Libuda
(Grabowski), Muller, Loehr.
England: Bonetti; Newton, Cooper, Mullery, Labone,
Moore, Lee, Ball, Hurst, Charlton (Bell), Peters (Hunter).

Guadalajara
Brazil (2)4 *(Rivelino, Tostao 2, Jairzinho)*
Peru (1)2 *(Gallardo, Cubillas)*
Brazil: Felix; Carlos Alberto, Brito, Piazza, Marco Antonio,
Clodoaldo, Gerson (Paulo Cesar), Jairzinho (Roberto),
Tostao, Pele, Rivelino.
Peru: Rubinos; Campos, Fernandez, Chumpitaz, Fuentes,
Mifflin, Challe, Baylon (Sotil), Perico Leon (Eladio Reyes),
Cubillas, Gallardo.

Toluca
Italy (1)4 *(Domenghini, Riva 2, Rivera)*
Mexico (1)1 *(Gonzalez)*
Italy: Albertosi; Burgnich, Cera, Rosato, Facchetti, Bertini,
Mazzola (Rivera), De Sisti, Domenghini (Gori), Boninsegna,
Riva.
Mexico: Calderon; Vantolra, Pena, Guzman, Perez,
Gonzalez (Borja), Pulido, Munguia (Diaz), Valdivia,
Fragoso, Padilla.

Mexico City
Uruguay (0)1 *(Esparrago)*
USSR (0)0
(after extra time)
Uruguay: Mazurkiewicz; Ubinas, Ancheta, Matosas, Mujica,
Maneiro, Cortes, Monero Castillo, Cubilla, Fontes (Gomez),
Morales (Esparrago).

USSR: Kavazashvili; Dzodzuashvili, Afonin, Khurtsilava (Logofet), Chesternijev, Muntijan, Asatiani (Kiselev), Kaplichni, Evriuzhkinzin, Bychevetz, Khmelnitzki.

Semi-finals
Mexico City
Italy (1)4 *(Boninsegna, Burgnich, Riva, Rivera)*
West Germany (0)3 *(Schnellinger, Muller 2)*
(after extra time, 90 mins 1-1)
Italy: Albertosi; Cera, Burgnich, Rosato (Poletti), Facchetti, Domenghini, Mazzola (Rivera), De Sisti, Boninsegna, Riva.
West Germany: Maier; Schnellinger, Vogts, Schulz, Beckenbauer, Patzke (Held), Seeler, Overath, Grabowski, Muller, Loehr (Libuda).

Guadalajara
Brazil (1)3 *(Clodoaldo, Jairzinho, Rivelino)*
Uruguay (1)1 *(Cubilla)*
Brazil: Felix; Carlos Alberto, Brito, Piazza, Everaldo, Clodoaldo, Gerson, Jairzinho, Tostao, Pele, Rivelino.
Uruguay: Mazurkiewicz; Ubinas, Ancheta, Matosas, Mujica, Montero, Castillo, Cortes, Fontes, Cubilla, Maneiro (Esparrago), Morales.

Third Place Play-off
Mexico City
West Germany (1)1 *(Overath)*
Uruguay (0)0
West Germany: Wolter; Schnellinger (Lorenz), Patzke, Fichtel, Weber, Vogts, Seeler, Overath, Libuda (Loehr), Muller, Held.
Uruguay: Mazurkiewicz; Ubinas, Ancheta, Matosas, Mujica, Montero, Castillo, Cortes, Fontes (Sandoval), Cubilla, Maneiro (Esparrago), Morales.

Final   Mexico City, 21 June 1970
Brazil (1)4 *(Pele, Gerson, Jairzinho, Carlos Alberto)*
Italy (1)1 *(Boninsegna)*
Brazil: Felix; Carlos Alberto, Brito, Piazza, Everaldo, Clodoaldo, Gerson, Jairzinho, Tostao, Pele, Rivelino.
Italy: Albertosi; Cera, Burgnich, Bertini (Juliano), Rosato, Facchetti, Domenghini, Mazzola, De Sisti, Boninsegna (Rivera), Riva.

West Germany 1974

Along with the new trophy which FIFA had commissioned came a new format for the 1974 World Cup. After the first round of group matches, there would be two more groups of four teams, with the winners from each of these second phase groups meeting in the final. This was not a very popular format in some circles, as it went too far away from the cup principle of sudden-death knock-out football, and within a decade FIFA would be changing its mind yet again.

But this was above all the World Cup of total football, and the two teams which won through to the final were the arch-exponents of that style. West Germany, who had first won the World Cup twenty years before, and were now the European Champions, having beaten the Soviet Union in the 1972 final, would face the Netherlands, led by the man considered to be the successor to Pele's title of the world's greatest player – Johann Cruyff.

The Brazilians were no longer the force they had been four years earlier. Pele had gone, along with Tostao, Gerson and Clodoaldo, the latter taken out by injury shortly before the finals, and although the champions were still managed by Zagalo, they seemed to have adopted the defensive style which they had so brilliantly eschewed in previous competitions.

England had failed to qualify. After managing only a draw with Wales in a mediocre performance at Wembley, they were forced to seek a win against Poland in that same stadium one night in October 1973 to ensure qualification. Hopes were raised when they trounced Austria 7-0 three weeks earlier in a friendly, but the hopes were false, and despite attacking for most of the night at Wembley, they could get only a 1-1 draw. England were out, and a few months later Sir Alf Ramsey lost his job.

Scotland, however, were in the finals for the first time since 1958, having overcome Czechoslovakia on an emotional night at Hampden Park in September 1973 to ensure qualification. Managed now by Willie Ormond, they left for the finals on a wave of fanatical Scottish optimism but were destined to be eliminated, albeit unbeaten, after the first round.

Criticism of the new format for the World Cup was not limited to the final tournament. The qualifying competition was based on geographical zones, which meant that some representatives from weak areas were guaranteed a place in the finals at the expense of better European or South American teams. It didn't matter that the sixteen finalists were quite clearly not the best sixteen teams in the world. In the event, none of the weaker finalists even gave us the thrill of a shock result, as had the North Koreans in England. Zaire, Haiti and Australia were simply wiped out.

Also, in order to make a space for the weaker sides, Russia was forced to play a two-legged qualifying play-off against Chile. The first match, in Moscow, was a 0-0 draw, and then the Russians suddenly had an attack of the political morals and refused to play the second game in a Santiago stadium where left-wing prisoners had been incarcerated and, in some cases, shot. Chile were through by default.

The finals began with the usual, boring goalless draw, this time between Brazil and Yugoslavia in Frankfurt. The next day the Germans made a slow start and just scraped a 1-0 win over Chile. Their East German neighbours, in the same group, were no more impressive in their 2-0 win over Australia. Another of the outsiders, Haiti, promised a shock result by taking the lead against Italy. Centre-forward Sanon became the first man to beat Dino Zoff in 1,147 minutes of international football, but the Italians pulled themselves together to take the game 3-1.

Sadly for the Haitians, their centre-half, Ernst Jean-Joseph, produced a positive result in a dope test the next day, and despite his protests that he had only taken pills for asthma, Haitian officials dragged him out of the centre where the team were staying, beat him up, and sent him home. The Haitians were subsequently trounced by Poland and Argentina.

The latter result was especially important for Argentina, who had drawn with Italy and lost 2-3 to Poland in their previous games. In the end the four goals they got against Haiti were enough to see them through on goal difference at the expense of the Italians. In the last game in the group, with Italy needing only a point against Poland to go through, Szarmach and Deyna scored the two goals which sealed Italy's fate.

West Germany followed their win against Chile with a 3-0 victory over Australia. The scoreline is misleading though, because the Australians played well and were unlucky not to get closer to a result. Then came the first-ever meeting on a football field between the two Germanies. Security was tight, but it wasn't security that the West Germans had to worry about, for in the second half Sparwasser scored for East Germany and the match was won. Ironically, it turned out to be a good result for West Germany, because it meant that they qualified in second place and therefore went into a second phase group where they avoided Holland and Brazil.

The Dutch sailed through the first round, beating Uruguay and Bulgaria convincingly and getting a draw against a surprisingly good Swedish side which eventually qualified in second place. The Uruguayans, with their proud history in this competition, were a disappointment, offering more cynicism than skill, and finished a miserable last in the group, with only one point from a draw with Bulgaria.

Scotland failed to make progress after scoring only two goals against Zaire in their first match. Lorimer and Jordan got the goals, but Yugoslavia put nine past the Africans, and Brazil three, so although the Scots went on to get brave draws against Brazil and Yugoslavia, playing particularly well against the South Americans, they were out.

Group A in the final phase comprised Holland, Brazil, East Germany and Argentina. Brazil started well, beating East Germany with a wicked free kick from Rivelino, while Cruyff scored two of the four goals by which Holland overran the Argentinians. In the second round of matches the Dutch didn't find it quite as easy, but still succeeded, by virtue of goals from Rensenbrink and Neeskens. At the same time Brazil faced Argentina – the first time these two nations had met in the World Cup – and the Brazilians ran out 2-1 winners, thus setting up a crucial match between Holland and Brazil. In effect, this was the semi-final.

It was a sorry affair, with the Brazilians fouling cynically from the start. The Dutch retaliated in like manner, and the game was saved as a spectacle only by two quite superb Dutch goals in the second half. For the first, Neeskens lobbed a centre from Cruyff over the advancing Leao in the Brazilian goal, and for the second it was Cruyff himself who volleyed Krol's centre to perfection. The Dutch were in the final for the first time.

In the other group, which contained West Germany, Poland, Sweden and Yugoslavia, the Germans had a more difficult passage to the final. They beat old rivals Yugoslavia with goals from Breitner and Müller, and overcame the

Swedes 4-2 in atrocious weather in Dusseldorf, but there were times in both matches when the Germans looked anything but fluent.

The Poles also won their first two games, and with even less conviction. Against Sweden they were lucky that their opponents missed some good scoring chances early on, and even missed a penalty in the second half, meaning that the solitary goal from Lato was enough to secure the points. Against Yugoslavia they ran it even closer, and had Karasi not given away a needless penalty by fouling Szarmach, things might have been different. Karasi himself made amends by equalising, but then Lato headed home from a Gadocha corner, and we were faced with what was in effect a second semi-final, this time between Poland and West Germany.

The Germans had much to thank Sepp Maier for in Frankfurt that day. He made splendid first half saves from Lato and Gadocha, while his Polish counterpart Tomaszewski – described by Brian Clough as a clown before England's disastrous 1-1 draw at Wembley months earlier – saved a Hoeness penalty in the second half. In the end a Hoeness shot was deflected to Gerd Müller, who snapped up the chance with his usual killer instinct.

So the Germans, with home advantage, faced Holland in the final. The Dutch had Cruyff, the Germans Beckenbauer and the deadly Müller. The Dutch had more flair, but the Germans were strong and solid. The Dutch had the weaker defence, perhaps, but the Germans had no one who looked able to turn a match with one flash of brilliance, like Cruyff. It was a fascinating prospect.

The final started in sensational fashion, with English referee Jack Taylor awarding a penalty to Holland almost before a German had touched the ball. The Dutch kicked off and arrogantly kept possession without making any real progress, much to the annoyance of the home supporters. Then Cruyff broke away, went past Vogts, who had been detailed to mark him, and was brought down by a desperate tackle by Hoeness. Neeskens scored easily from the spot, sending Maier the wrong way.

The Dutch, perhaps for historical reasons, seemed to want to humiliate the Germans after that, and played clever possession football without really threatening for quite a long period. It was a dangerous tactic and after half an hour they paid the penalty – literally. Holzenbein cut into the Dutch area, beat one man and was then chopped down by Jansen. Breitner converted the penalty, and Germany were back in the match.

Two minutes before half-time Gerd Muller scored his sixty-eighth and most important goal for West Germany, latching on to a cross from Bonhof and sliding the ball home from close range. There was no further scoring, although the Dutch nearly equalised with a powerful Neeskens volley in the second half, and West Germany had added the World Cup to the European Championship. The new trophy had found its first home, and while the Germans had deserved victory, the Dutch had certainly been attractive losers.

West Germany 1974 – Results

First Phase

Group 1
West Germany (0)1, Chile (0)0
East Germany (0)2, Australia (0)0
West Germany (2)3, Australia (0)0
East Germany (0)1, Chile (0)0
East Germany (1)1, West Germany (0)0
Chile (0)0, Australia (0)0

	P	W	D	L	F	A	Pts
East Germany	3	2	1	0	4	1	5
West Germany	3	2	0	1	4	1	4
Chile	3	0	2	1	1	2	1
Australia	3	0	1	2	0	5	1

Group 2
Brazil (0)0, Yugoslavia (0)0
Scotland (2)2, Zaire (0)0
Brazil (0)0, Scotland (0)0
Yugoslavia (6)9, Zaire (0)0
Scotland (0)1, Yugoslavia (0)1
Brazil (1)3, Zaire (0)0

	P	W	D	L	F	A	Pts
Yugoslavia	3	1	2	0	10	1	4
Brazil	3	1	2	0	3	0	4
Scotland	3	1	2	0	3	1	4
Zaire	3	0	0	3	0	14	0

Group 3

Holland (1)2, Uruguay (0)0
Sweden (0)0, Bulgaria (0)0
Holland (0)0, Sweden (0)0
Bulgaria (0)1, Uruguay (0)1
Holland (2)4, Bulgaria (0)1
Sweden (0)3, Uruguay (0)0

	P	W	D	L	F	A	Pts
Holland	3	2	1	0	6	1	5
Sweden	3	1	2	0	3	0	4
Bulgaria	3	0	2	1	2	5	2
Uruguay	3	0	1	2	1	6	1

Group 4

Italy (0)3, Haiti (0)0
Poland (2)3, Argentina (0)2
Italy (1)1, Argentina (1)1
Poland (5)7, Haiti (0)0
Argentina (2)4, Haiti (0)1
Poland (2)2, Italy (0)1

	P	W	D	L	F	A	Pts
Poland	3	3	0	0	12	3	6
Argentina	3	1	1	1	7	5	3
Italy	3	1	1	1	5	4	3
Haiti	3	0	0	3	2	14	0

Second Phase

Group A

Brazil (0)1, East Germany (0)0
Holland (2)4, Argentina (0)0
Holland (1)2, East Germany (0)0
Brazil (1)2, Argentina (1)1
Holland (0)2, Brazil (0)0
Argentina (1)1, East Germany (1)1

	P	W	D	L	F	A	Pts
Holland	3	3	0	0	8	0	6
Brazil	3	2	0	1	3	3	4
East Germany	3	0	1	2	1	4	1
Argentina	3	0	1	2	2	7	1

Group B
Poland (1)1, Sweden (0)0
West Germany (1)2, Yugoslavia (0)0
Poland (1)2, Yugoslavia (1)1
West Germany (0)4, Sweden (1)2
Sweden (0)2, Yugoslavia (0)1
West Germany (0)1, Poland (0)0

	P	W	D	L	F	A	Pts
West Germany	3	3	0	0	7	2	6
Poland	3	2	0	1	3	2	4
Sweden	3	1	0	2	4	6	2
Yugoslavia	3	0	0	3	2	6	0

Third Place Play-off
Munich
Poland (0)1 *(Lato)*
Brazil (0)0
Poland: Tomaszewski; Szymanowski, Gorgon, Zmuda,
Musial, Kasperczak (Cmikiewicz), Deyna, Masczyk, Lato,
Szarmach (Kapka), Gadocha.
Brazil: Leao; Ze Maria, Alfredo, Marinho M., Marinho F.,
Paulo Cesar Carpeggiani, Rivelino, Ademir da Guia
(Mirandinha), Valdomiro, Jairzinho, Dirceu.

Final   Munich, 7 July 1974
West Germany (2)2 *(Breitner pen., Müller)*
Holland (1)1 *(Neeskens pen.)*
West Germany: Maier; Beckenbauer, Vogts, Schwarzenbeck,
Breitner, Bonhof, Hoeness, Overath, Grabowski, Müller,,
Holzenbein.
Holland: Jongbloed; Suurbier, Rijsbergen (De Jong), Haan,
Krol, Jansen, Neeskens, Van Hanegem, Rep, Cruyff,
Rensenbrink (Van der Kerkhof R.).

Argentina 1978

There were even more misgivings about the venue for the 1978 World Cup than there had been about Mexico in 1970. Scourged by galloping inflation, run by a ruthless military dictatorship and battered by constant urban guerrilla warfare involving political assassinations by the lorry-load, Argentina hardly seemed suitable. Apart from anything else, there was considerable concern for the safety of the players. Even the head of the local organising committee, General Omar Actis, had been assassinated on his way to a press conference.

Throughout the 1960s, Argentinian club sides had acquired a justified reputation for violent play, and local supporters were well-known for the way in which they intimidated referees, but despite rumours that the tournament would be re-allocated to Holland, it was eventually decided that it would go ahead as planned. Sadly, it would go ahead without Johann Cruyff, who announced some time ahead that there was no way he would play in Argentina.

The host country were managed by the charismatic, chain-smoking figure of Cesar Luis Menotti, who had promised that no team led by him would kick its way to the World Cup. He had some difficulty in assembling a team, as many of the best local players had migrated to Europe after the 1974 tournament. Menotti announced that he wanted to recall at least three of them – Kempes, Piazza and Wolff. In the event, only Kempes came back. He had been enjoying great success as a goalscorer with Valencia in the Spanish League, and would prove to be a vital element in the Argentinian team. Piazza was released by Saint-Etienne, but returned to France suddenly when his wife and child were injured in a car crash, and Wolff was unable to return at all because Real Madrid refused to release him at the end of March, when Menotti wanted to start his preparations in earnest.

Holland turned up, without Cruyff, but they still had Rep, Rensenbrink and Neeskens, as well as a new manager, the Austrian Ernst Happel. West Germany had also lost some of her stars. Beckenbauer had been lured to New York Cosmos by an astronomical $2,500,000 offer, and Müller, Grabowski and Overath had all retired from international football.

As in 1974, Scotland were the only British representatives. England, after three years of disappointing management by

Don Revie, had been eliminated by Italy, while Wales had been put out by Scotland. Scotland's place in the finals had been assured by a fine win over Czechoslovakia – again – and it was the more remarkable this time as the Czechs were the reigning European Champions. The euphoria which followed Scottish qualification was fanned by the over-confident managership of Ally MacLeod, and although he had some fine players at his disposal, including Souness, Hartford, Macari and Rioch, he would sorely miss Danny McGrain, possibly the best full-back in the world at the time, who was out with injury. Later, after Scotland's humiliating departure from the competition, MacLeod would be anything but the hero he seemed to be beforehand.

Brazil had another new manager, Claudio Coutinho, but although his side qualified easily in a group with Colombia and Paraguay, his efforts at educating his players in the art of total football were doomed to failure. The natural brilliance of the Brazilians, still present in many members of the squad, could not blossom in an atmosphere where they were expected to chase back and challenge. It just wasn't their style.

The Italians, too, had a new manager in Enzo Bearzot. He was keen on eradicating the negativity which had afflicted Italian football for so long, but it would take time, and time would prove that in 1978 the Italians were not ready for the World Cup – not quite.

Security worries were highlighted again when, only weeks before the tournament was due to begin, a bomb was discovered in the Buenos Aires Press Centre. It exploded as it was being removed, killing a policeman.

Once again, with monotonous regularity, the opening game in the final tournament was a goalless draw – this time between West Germany and Poland. The following day the hosts opened their programme with a match against Hungary. The Argentine team was welcomed by what would become a hallmark of these championships – a snowstorm of paper. But it was the Hungarians who stormed into the lead, after twelve minutes. Three minutes later Argentina equalised through Kempes, and in the second half, by which time the game had degenerated into a rough-house, we started to notice a tricky little midfielder called Osvaldo Ardiles, and Argentina took command. Seven minutes from the end Bertoni scored the winner. The Hungarians, who had expressed fears about the impartiality of referees in matches involving Argentina, had two players – Torocsik and Nyilasi – sent off in the second half, although both dismissals were justified.

In the same group, Italy started with a 2-1 win against France. Little Paolo Rossi got the winner, and a twenty-one-year-old Frenchman called Michel Platini was impressive in the losing side. At this point, all was not well in the French camp, and the players had even painted out the Adidas stripes on their boots because they wanted more money, but in their next match, against Argentina, they improved immeasurably. Sadly, two dreadful decisions by the Swiss referee – a penalty awarded to Argentina and another denied to France – ensured that once again the French went down 2-1. They went on to beat Hungary 3-1 in their final match, but it was too late.

Italy had also beaten Hungary, and so by the time Argentina lined up against the Italians for the last match in the group, both sides had qualified and the only thing at stake was the venue for second phase matches. The winners would stay in Buenos Aires, the losers would be sent to Rosario. In the event, it was a single goal from Bettega which won the match for Italy. They would stay in the capital, but later they would wish they hadn't.

The Poles and West Germans qualified from Group 2, as expected, and in Group 3 it was the Austrians and Brazilians who went through at the expense of Spain and Sweden. Brazil managed only one win, against Austria, and two draws, while the Austrians ensured progress by beating Spain and Sweden.

In Group 4, Scotland's nightmare began. Accused by the local press of being a team of drunks, the Scots were quite clearly unprepared for their first game, against Peru. They gave Cubillas the freedom of midfield, which was disastrous, and they paid for it. Astonishingly, Souness was not picked until the final game with Holland, and this also proved to be an expensive mistake.

Even so, Scotland made a good start against Peru, and were a goal up after fourteen minutes when Joe Jordan scored, Quiroga having been unable to hold a fierce drive from Rioch. But gradually Cubillas took control of midfield, and just before half-time he fed Cueto with the pass which enabled him to equalise. A quarter of an hour into the second half Masson missed a penalty, and that was the beginning of the end for Scotland. Cubillas himself scored two lovely goals inside the last twenty minutes, and it was all over.

After the match Willie Johnstone was one of two players singled out for a dope test. He failed. He had taken two Fencamfamin tablets, which he strenuously claimed were intended to combat hay fever, but they were just pep pills and Johnstone was packed off home in disgrace. FIFA suspended him from international competition for a year, but the SFA were having none of that – they banned him for life. A demoralised Scotland could manage only a draw against little Iran in their next match – even the Scottish goal was an own goal – and their World Cup was as good as over.

Holland, meanwhile, were doing just enough to qualify. They beat Iran easily enough, and were then held to a goalless draw by Peru. This meant that the result of their last game, against Scotland, didn't matter, provided they didn't let in too many goals. At last Scotland played Souness, and what a difference he made. Scotland needed a victory by three clear goals to go through to the final phase, and indeed they got three goals, but the Dutch got two and Scotland were on their way home.

In the final groupings (the absurd formula of final phase leagues was persevered with in Argentina) the home country seemed to have the easier task in reaching the final, being grouped with Brazil, Poland and Peru, but in the end they only scraped home on goal difference. Like Brazil, they won two and drew one (against Brazil), but whereas the Brazilians had only managed a 3-0 win against Peru, the Argentinians knocked in six without reply and so made the final.

In the other group, containing Holland, Italy, West Germany and Austria, the Dutch started with a fine 5-1 win against Austria, which gave them not only two points but also a healthy goal difference to be going forward with. Meanwhile, Italy and Germany started with a goalless draw and from that moment the Dutch were favourites to reach the final.

In the second round of matches, Italy scored two points with a 1-0 win over Austria, while Holland lined up against West Germany in a repeat of the 1974 final. It proved to be one of the best games of the tournament. The Germans took the lead after three minutes when Abramczik headed home, but Holland equalised with a thirty-five yard screamer from Haan which left Maier rooted to the spot. Twenty minutes from the end Germany re-established a lead with a goal by

Dieter Müller, but Rene van der Kerkhof beat three defenders and Maier seven minutes from time to give the Dutch another valuable point.

The Dutch went on to beat Italy 2-1 in Buenos Aires, and so the final match in the group, in which Austria overcame the Germans 3-2, was academic. Holland were through to their second successive final.

It was always doubtful whether the Dutch could win without Cruyff. No European team had ever won the World Cup in South America, but the Dutch were in splendid form and Argentina's defence was not regarded too highly. Both teams were capable of rough play on occasions, and people were wondering whether referee Gonella could handle them. He made a poor impression even before a ball was kicked.

The home side arrived on the pitch five minutes late and then proceeded to complain bitterly about the fact that Rene van der Kerkhof was wearing a bandage on his arm. It was a ridiculous protest, all the more so because the Dutchman had worn the same bandage in several previous games, but the weak Gonella allowed the protest to succeed, and van der Kerkhof left the field and simply covered the bandage with another.

The Dutch, incensed by this incident, started fouling almost straight from the kick-off – not a clever tactic in a match controlled by a weak referee who was clearly intimidated by the crowd and tended to give the benefit of the doubt to the home side on every occasion.

Even so, the match was an interesting one, if not a classic. Kempes, given too much room, opened the scoring seven minutes before half-time when he latched on to a cross from Luque, rode a desperate tackle from Haan, and drove the ball past Jongbloed in the Dutch goal. Right on half-time Fillol, much-maligned but nevertheless effective in the Argentinian goal, made a crucial save from Rensenbrink, and Argentina went in with their one-goal lead.

Soon after the interval Fillol made another fine save, this time from Neeskens, but gradually the Dutch got back into the game. Rep was substituted by Nanninga, and soon afterwards a clearly less than fit Ardiles was swopped for Larrosa. The Dutch substitution seemed to have paid off when, seven minutes from the end, Rene van der Kerkhof centred and Nanninga rose to head home the equaliser. In the last minute

Holland lost the World Cup when Rensenbrink, with the Argentinian defence in tatters, hit the post. Extra time was needed.

The Argentinians looked exhausted – the Dutch had been in control for most of the second half – but somehow Menotti lifted his players, and fourteen minutes into the first period Kempes made it 2-1 for Argentina. In the second period, the Dutch became desperate in their search for an equaliser, but it was not to be. With only five minutes remaining Kempes and Bertoni exchanged passes as they bore down on the Dutch goal, and Bertoni applied the finishing touch. Buenos Aires went wild. Argentina had for so long had a poor reputation in the world of football, but they had won a thrilling final and deserved the honour, just as the Dutch deserved sympathy for losing two consecutive finals.

Argentina 1978 – Results

First Phase

Group 1
Argentina (1)2, Hungary (1)1
Italy (1)2, France (1)1
Argentina (1)2, France (0)1
Italy (2)3, Hungary (0)1
France (3)3, Hungary (1)1
Italy (1)1, Argentina (0)0

	P	W	D	L	F	A	Pts
Italy	3	3	0	0	6	2	6
Argentina	3	2	0	1	4	3	4
France	3	1	0	2	5	5	2
Hungary	3	0	0	3	3	8	0

Group 2
West Germany (0)0, Poland (0)0
Tunisia (0)3, Mexico (1)1
Poland (1)1, Tunisia (0)0
West Germany (4)6, Mexico (0)0
Poland (1)3, Mexico (0)1
West Germany (0)0, Tunisia (0)0

	P	W	D	L	F	A	Pts
Poland.......................	3	2	1	0	4	1	5
West Germany............	3	1	2	0	6	0	4
Tunisia	3	1	1	1	3	2	3
Mexico	3	0	0	3	2	12	0

Group 3
Austria (1)2, Spain (1)1
Sweden (1)1, Brazil (1)1
Austria (1)1, Sweden (0)0
Brazil (0)0, Spain (0)0
Spain (0)1, Sweden (0)0
Brazil (1)1, Austria (0)0

	P	W	D	L	F	A	Pts
Austria......................	3	2	0	1	3	2	4
Brazil........................	3	1	2	1	2	1	4
Spain	3	1	1	1	2	2	3
Sweden......................	3	0	1	2	1	3	1

Group 4
Peru (1)3, Scotland (1)1
Holland (1)3, Iran (0)0
Scotland (1)1, Iran (0)1
Holland (0)0. Peru (0)0
Peru (3)4, Iran (1)1
Scotland (1)3, Holland (1)2

	P	W	D	L	F	A	Pts
Peru..........................	3	2	1	0	7	2	5
Holland	3	1	1	1	5	3	3
Scotland	3	1	1	1	5	6	3
Iran	3	0	1	2	2	8	1

Second Phase

Group A
Italy (0)0, West Germany (0)0
Holland (3)5, Austria (0)1
Italy (1)1, Austria (0)0
Austria (0)3, West Germany (1)2
Holland (0)2, Italy (1)1
Holland (1)2, West Germany (1)2

	P	W	D	L	F	A	Pts
Holland	3	2	1	0	9	4	5
Italy	3	1	1	1	2	2	3
West Germany	3	0	2	1	4	5	2
Austria	3	1	0	2	4	8	2

Group B
Argentina (1)2, Poland (0)0
Brazil (2)3, Peru (0)0
Argentina (0)0, Brazil (0)0
Poland (0)1, Peru (0)0
Brazil (1)3, Poland (1)1
Argentina (2)6, Peru (0)0

	P	W	D	L	F	A	Pts
Argentina	3	2	1	0	8	0	5
Brazil	3	2	1	0	6	1	5
Poland	3	1	0	2	2	5	2
Peru	3	0	0	3	0	10	0

Third Place Play-off
Buenos Aires
Brazil (0)2 *(Nelinho, Dirceu)*
Italy (1)1 *(Causio)*
Brazil: Leao; Nelinho, Oscar, Amaral, Neto, Cerezo
(Rivelino), Batista, Dirceu, Gil (Reinaldo), Mendonca,
Roberto.
Italy: Zoff; Scirea, Gentile, Cuccureddu, Cabrini, Maldera,
Antognoni (Sala C.), Sala P., Causio, Rossi, Bettega.

Final
Buenos Aires, 25 June 1978
Argentina (1)3 *(Kempes 2, Bertoni)*
Holland (0)1 *(Nanninga)*
(after extra time, 90 mins 1-1)
Argentina: Fillol; Olguin, Galvan, Passarella, Tarantini,
Ardiles (Larrosa), Gallego, Kempes, Bertoni, Luque, Ortiz
(Houseman).
Holland: Jongbloed; Krol, Poortvliet, Brandts, Jansen
(Suurbier), Van der Kerkhof W., Neeskens, Haan, Rep
(Nanninga), Rensenbrink, Van der Kerkhof R.

Spain 1982

There were radical changes in the format for the 1982 World Cup finals in Spain. The number of finalists were increased to twenty-four, who would be divided into six groups of four. The top two teams from each group then went forward to form four further groups of three teams, again playing on a league basis. The four second phase group winners would then go into knock-out semi-finals, the losers playing off for third place.

The vast qualifying tournament, by now a two-year process, was a happier time for British teams leading up to the 1982 championships. England qualified at last, finishing second to Hungary in a group which also contained Rumania, Switzerland and Norway. Even a humiliating defeat at the hands of the Norwegian part-timers along the way did not stop the progress of Ron Greenwood's side, and they were joined in Spain by Northern Ireland and Scotland, who both qualified from one group, thus excluding Sweden, Portugal and Israel.

Italy, without doing anything spectacular, qualified from their group in second place to Yugoslavia, but the losing finalists of the last two World Cups, Holland, finished a dismal fourth in a group which sent Belgium and a much-improved France, soon to be European Champions, to Spain. The West Germans headed their group, taking Austria along with them to the finals, and Brazil, Peru and Chile joined Champions Argentina as the South American representatives.

The enlarged finals meant that more teams from the weaker zones would be present in the finals, and so it was that Honduras, El Salvador, Algeria, Cameroon, Kuwait and New Zealand would all be there. With the exception of El Salvador, these teams were all new-comers to the final tournament.

The draw for the finals, which took place in Madrid in January 1982 was a shambles. There were four ranks of seeding, and although this was more complicated than in previous tournaments, it should not have been beyond the ability of the Spanish authorities and their collaborators from FIFA to organise the event properly. It was a showpiece occasion, televised world-wide, and must have been a source of considerable embarrassment for the Spanish hosts as teams were put in the wrong groups, then taken out again, and one mistake was compounded by another amid an atmosphere of increasing confusion. Eventually it was sorted out, and some interesting combinations were revealed.

In Group 1, Poland and Italy were combined with Cameroon and Peru. The Poles and Italians were favourites to go through, and indeed they did, but the Italians made it after three draws and by the narrowest of margins. Cameroon also had three points, and an identical goal difference, but the Italians had scored two goals, Cameroon only one. Nobody gave the Italians a second thought at the time, but they surely came to life in the next phase.

Group 2 consisted of West Germany, Austria, Algeria and Chile, and here again the two fancied European sides made it to the second phase, but only after a disgraceful match between themselves. The Germans had started with a shock 2-1 defeat at the hands of Algeria, then pulled themselves together to trounce Chile 4-1. The Austrians, meanwhile, amassed four points at the expense of Algeria and Chile. In their last match, Algeria beat Chile 3-2, so as the Germans and the Austrians took the field for the last game in the group, Germany needed two points which would assure that they went through on goal difference, while Austria could afford to lose, but only narrowly, to go through on the same basis, thus shutting out the plucky Algerians. That was exactly what happened, the Germans winning 1-0. The whole affair stank of a fix, but nothing could be proved.

Group 3 brought together Belgium, Argentina, Hungary and El Salvador. Belgium headed the group in unspectacular fashion thanks to narrow victories against Argentina and El Salvador, while Argentina recovered from their opening defeat by Belgium to beat Hungary and El Salvador and join Belgium in the second phase. Hungary's opening 10-1 win against El Salvador, which gave them such a fine start, was of no avail.

England made a great start in Group 4, with captain Bryan Robson scoring against France after only twenty-seven seconds – the fastest goal ever recorded in a World Cup final tournament match, and further goals from Mariner and Robson ensured a 3-1 victory. The English went on to beat the Czechs 2-0 and Kuwait, less impressively, 1-0. The fine French team recovered from their opening set-back to beat Kuwait and draw with Czechoslovakia, thus joining England in phase two.

Northern Ireland were the surprise of Group 5, for after registering draws against Yugoslavia and Honduras, a Gerry Armstrong goal beat Spain in front of an incredulous home crowd. Luckily for Spain, their three points from their other two games, against Honduras and Yugoslavia, saw them through in second place.

Finally, in Group 6, Brazil and Russia went through as expected. Scotland made a promising start, beating New Zealand 5-2, but they were drubbed 4-1 by a Brazilian side which once again looked ominously dangerous, and could manage only a 2-2 draw with the Soviet Union. Once again, they were out after the first round of matches, but this time they were not disgraced.

In the second phase, Group A consisted of Poland, Russia and Belgium. The Belgians lost both matches, and the final 0-0 draw between Poland and Russia meant that Poland reached the semi-finals by virtue of the goal difference they had built up in their opening 3-0 win over Belgium. In the light of what was happening in the Polish trade union movement at the time, it must have been a sweet result.

In Group B England threw away their chance of a place in semi-finals by playing two goalless draws against opponents Spain and West Germany. Kevin Keegan and Trevor Brooking, both so vital for England, had been plagued with injury, and although Keegan came on as a substitute in the final match with Spain, he missed an open goal and with it went England's last hope. West Germany, by virtue of a 2-1 win over Spain, went through.

Group C was the one in which the Italians started to make things happen. They faced Brazil and Argentina, with both South American teams in form, and after their first round performances, were not the fancied side, but they played spectacular football in beating Argentina 2-1 in the opening game. Even so, after Brazil had recorded a 3-1 victory against Argentina in the group's second game, Italy were faced with having to beat Brazil to go through, and so they did, with another fine performance and a 3-2 scoreline.

It was France, one of the most improved sides in Europe, which headed Group D. They started by beating Austria 1-0, and although Northern Ireland gave themselves a chance by drawing 2-2 with Austria in the next match, they had no answer to the French in the final game, and went down 4-1.

111

In the Barcelona semi-final, Italy continued their impressive progress by beating Poland 2-0 to reach their fourth World Cup final, but France were desperately unlucky in Seville, where they held the Germans to a 3-3 draw after extra time, only to lose 5-4 in the penalty competition. Dispirited, they went on to lose the third place play-off 3-2 to Poland in Alicante.

On the day of the final, 11 July in Madrid, the Italians had their tails up after their recent, impressive performances, especially those against the South Americans. They were favourites now, and not only with the bookmakers. The Germans had made no friends in their semi-final with France, especially when goalkeeper Schumacher had nearly killed the French substitute Battiston in a collision on the edge of the penalty area.

The first half was somewhat disappointing, and remained goalless, but things changed after half-time when Rossi, Tardelli and Altobelli scored three marvellous goals, to which the Germans had only the one reply, from Breitner. The artists of Italy had beaten the efficient mechanism of the Germans – also appearing in their fourth final – and the World Championship went back to Italy for the third time, and the first since 1938.

Spain 1982 – Results

First Phase

Group 1
Italy (0)0, Poland (0)0
Peru (0)0, Cameroon (0)0
Italy (1)1, Peru (0)1
Poland (0)0, Cameroon (0)0
Poland (0)5, Peru (0)1
Italy (0)1, Cameroon (0)1

	P	W	D	L	F	A	Pts
Poland	3	1	2	0	5	1	4
Italy	3	0	3	0	2	2	3
Cameroon	3	0	3	0	1	1	3
Peru	3	0	2	1	2	6	2

Group 2

Algeria (0)2, West Germany (0)1
Austria (1)1, Chile (0)0
West Germany (1)4, Chile (0)1
Austria (0)2, Algeria (0)0
Algeria (3)3, Chile (0)2
West Germany (1)1, Austria (0)0

	P	W	D	L	F	A	Pts
West Germany............	3	2	0	1	6	3	4
Austria.....................	3	2	0	1	3	1	4
Algeria.....................	3	2	0	1	5	5	4
Chile........................	3	0	0	3	3	8	0

Group 3

Belgium (0)1, Argentina (0)0
Hungary (3)10, El Salvador (0)1
Argentina (2)4, Hungary (0)1
Belgium (1)1, El Salvador (0)0
Belgium (0)1, Hungary (1)1
Argentina (1)2, El Salvador (0)0

	P	W	D	L	F	A	Pts
Belgium.....................	3	2	1	0	3	1	5
Argentina	3	2	0	1	6	2	4
Hungary	3	1	1	1	12	6	3
El Salvador...............	3	0	0	3	1	13	0

Group 4

England (1)3, France (1)1
Czechoslovakia (1)1, Kuwait (0)1
England (0)2, Czechoslovakia (0)0
France (2)4, Kuwait (0)1
France (0)1, Czechoslovakia (0)1
England (1)1, Kuwait (0)0

	P	W	D	L	F	A	Pts
England.....................	3	3	0	0	6	1	6
France.......................	3	1	1	1	6	5	3
Czechoslovakia	3	0	2	1	2	4	2
Kuwait	3	0	1	2	2	6	1

Group 5

Honduras (1)1, Spain (0)1
Northern Ireland (0)0, Yugoslavia (0)0
Spain (1)2, Yugoslavia (1)1
Honduras (0)1, Northern Ireland (1)1
Yugoslavia (0)1, Honduras (0)0
Northern Ireland (0)1, Spain (0)0

	P	W	D	L	F	A	Pts
Northern Ireland	3	1	2	0	2	1	4
Spain	3	1	1	1	3	3	3
Yugoslavia	3	1	1	1	2	2	3
Honduras	3	0	2	1	2	3	2

Group 6

Brazil (0)2, USSR (1)1
Scotland (3)5, New Zealand (0)2
Brazil (1)4, Scotland (1)1
USSR (1)3, New Zealand (0)0
Scotland (1)2, USSR (0)2
Brazil (2)4. New Zealand (0)0

	P	W	D	L	F	A	Pts
Brazil	3	3	0	0	10	2	6
USSR	3	1	1	1	6	4	3
Scotland	3	1	1	1	8	8	3
New Zealand	3	0	0	3	2	12	0

Second Phase

Group A

Poland (2)3, Belgium (0)0
USSR (0)1, Belgium (0)0
USSR (0)0, Poland (0)0

	P	W	D	L	F	A	Pts
Poland	2	1	1	0	3	0	3
USSR	2	1	1	0	1	0	3
Belgium	2	0	0	2	0	4	0

Group B
West Germany (0)0, England (0)0
West Germany (0)2, Spain (0)1
England (0)0, Spain (0)0

	P	W	D	L	F	A	Pts
West Germany......	2	1	1	0	2	1	3
England..........	2	0	2	0	0	0	2
Spain	2	0	1	1	1	2	1

Group C
Italy (0)2, Argentina (0)1
Brazil (1)3, Argentina (0)1
Italy (2)3, Brazil (1)2

	P	W	D	L	F	A	Pts
Italy.......	2	2	0	0	5	3	4
Brazil......	2	1	0	1	5	4	2
Argentina ..	2	0	0	2	2	5	0

Group D
France (1)1, Austria (0)0
Northern Ireland (1)2, Austria (0)2
France (1)4, Northern Ireland (0)1

	P	W	D	L	F	A	Pts
France...........	2	2	0	0	5	1	4
Austria..........	2	0	1	1	2	3	1
Northern Ireland...	2	0	1	1	3	6	1

Semi-finals
Barcelona
Italy (1)2 *(Rossi 2)*
Poland (0)0
Italy: Zoff; Bergomi, Collovati, Scirea, Cabrini,Oriali,
Antognoni (Marini), Tardelli, Conti, Rossi, Graziani
(Altobelli).
Poland: Mlynarczyk; Dziuba, Zmuda, Janas, Majewski,
Kupcewicz, Buncol, Matysik, Lato, Ciolek (Palasz),Smolarek
(Kusto).

Seville
West Germany (1)3 *(Littbarski, Rummenigge, Fischer)*
France (1)3 *(Platini pen., Tresor, Giresse)*
(after extra time, West Germany won 5-4 on penalties)
West Germany: Schumacher; Kaltz, Forster K-H., Stielike,
Forster B., Briegel (Rummenigge), Dremmler, Breitner,
Littbarski, Fischer, Magath (Hrubesch).
France: Ettori; Amoros, Janvion, Tresor, Bossis, Genghini
(Battiston) (Lopez), Tigana, Platini, Giresse, Rocheteau,
Six.

Third Place Play-off
Alicante
Poland (2)3 *(Szarmach, Majewski, Kupcewicz)*
France (1)2 *(Girard, Couriol)*
Poland: Mlynarczyk; Dziuba, Zmuda, Janas, Majewski,
Kupcewicz, Buncol, Matysik (Wojcicki), Lato, Boniek,
Szarmach.
France: Castenada; Amoros, Mahut, Tresor, Janvion
(Lopez), Girard, Larios, Tigana (Six), Couriol, Soler,
Bellone.

Final   Madrid, 11 July 1982
Italy (0)3 *(Rossi, Tardelli, Altobelli)*
West Germany (0)1 *(Breitner)*
Italy: Zoff; Bergomi, Cabrini, Collovati, Scirea, Gentile,
Oriali, Tardelli, Conti, Graziani (Altobelli) (Causio), Rossi.
West Germany: Schumacher; Kaltz, Forster K-H., Stielike,
Forster B., Breitner, Dremmler (Hrubesch), Littbarski,
Briegel, Fischer, Rummenigge (Muller).

CHAPTER TWO

WORLD CUP 1986
THE QUALIFYING
COMPETITION

Introduction

The member nations of FIFA are divided into six confederations: UEFA (Europe), CONMEBOL (South America), CONCACAF (North/Central America and the Caribbean), AFRICA, ASIA and OCEANIA/ISRAEL.

European teams were divided into seven groups, the winner of each group qualifying for the finals. The runners-up in Groups 2,3,4 and 6 also qualified, while the runners-up of Groups 1 and 5 played off for a place in the finals. The runners-up in Group 7 played off against the winners of the Oceania/Israel zone for a place in the finals.

The African zone was decided entirely on a knock-out cup basis, with the last two teams left in the competition qualifying for the finals.

The first round of the Concacaf zone was played on a cup system, with nine teams going through to the second round, where they were divided into three groups of three. The winners of these three mini-leagues went forward to the third round, which was again based on a league system, with the top team qualifying for the finals.

The first round of the Conmebol zone was played on a League basis, with the ten entrants divided into two groups of three and one group of four. The winners of each group qualified and the runners-up from the two groups of three joined the second and third-placed teams from the group of four in a two-legged knock-out competition, with the winner qualifying for the finals.

There were twenty-four entrants in the Asian zone qualifying tournament. The first round was played on a league basis, with the teams divided into eight sub-groups. The winners of each sub-group went forward to a knock-out competition to decide which two countries would qualify for the finals.

There were only four entrants in the Oceania/Israel zone, and a league competition decided which team should play off against the runners-up of the European Group 7 for a place in the finals.

UEFA

GROUP 1
(Albania, Belgium, Greece, Poland)

Brussels, 17 October 1984, attendance 11,000
Belgium (0)3 *(Claesen, Scifo, Voordeckers)*
Albania (0)1 *(Omuri)*
Belgium: Munaron; Grun, Devriese, Renquin, De Wolf, Leo Van der Elst (de Grijse), Vandereycken, Vercauteren, Scifo, Czerniatynski (Voordeckers), Claesen.
Albania: Musta; Zmijani, Targaj (Eksarko), Omuri, Demollari, Hodja, Josa, Muca, Ballgjini, Minga, Kola (Lame).
Zabrze, 17 October 1984, attendance 15,000

Poland (0)3 *(Smolarek, Dziekanowski 2)*
Greece (1)1 *(Mitropoulos)*
Poland: Kazimierski; Kubicki, Wdowczyk, Zmuda, Wojcicki, Palasz (Matysik), Boniek, Wijas, Buncol (Karas), Smolarek, Dziekanowski.
Greece: Sarganis; Xanthopoulos, Karulias, Mitsibonas, Micjos (Dintsikos), Vamvakulos (Ardizolu), Hadzopoulos, Semertsidis, Anastopoulos, Mitropoulos, Kofidis.

Mielec, 31 October 1984, attendance 25,000
Poland (1)2 *(Smolarek, Palasz)*
Albania (0)2 *(Omuri, Josa)*
Poland: Kazimierski; Kubicki, Zmuda, Wojcicki (Dziuba), Wdowczyk, Buda (Komorwicki), Boniek, Matysik, Palasz, Dziekanowski, Smolarek.
Albania: Musta; Rragami, Targaj, Hodja, Omuri, Muca, Ballgjini (Lame) (Eksarko), Demollari, Josa, Kola, Minga.

Athens, 19 December 1984, attendance 15,000

Greece (0)0
Belgium (0)0
Greece: Sarganis; Xanthopoulos T., Karulias; Kyrastas, Manolos, Alavandes, Saravakos, Vamvakulas (Kostkos), Anastopoulos, Mitropoulos, Papaioannou.
Belgium: Munaron; Grun, Jaspers, Franky Van der Elst, Renquin, De Groote, Ceulemans, Scifo, Vercauteren, Czerniatynski (Voordeckers), Claesen.

Tirana, 22 December 1984, attendance 20,000
Albania (0)2 *(Josa, Minga)*
Belgium (0)0
Albania: Musta; Rragami, Targaj, Hodja, Zmijani, Ocelli, Muca, Demollari, Minga, Kola, Josa.
Belgium: Pfaff; Grun, Jaspers, Renquin, De Groote, Franky Van der Elst, Scifo (Clijsters), Vercauteren, Ceulemans, Claesen, Czerniatynski (Voordeckers).

Athens, 27 February 1985, attendance 20,000
Greece (2)2 *(Saravakos, Antoniou)*
Albania (0)0
Greece: Sarganis; Alavandas, Karulias, Kyrastas, Manolas, Michos, Saravakos (Batsinilas), Antoniou, Anastopoulos, Kofidis, Papaioannou (Semertsidis).
Albania: Musta; Zmijani, Ocelli, Targaj, Demollari, Hodja (Ahmetiz), Josa, Muca, Ballgjini (Zagami), Minga, Kola.

Brussels, 27 March 1985, attendance 41,500
Belgium (0)2 *(Vercauteren, Scifo)*
Greece (0)0
Belgium: Pfaff; Grun, De Wolf, Plessers, Renquin, Vercauteren, Vandereycken, Scifo, Vandenbergh, Voordeckers, Ceulemans.
Greece: Sarganis; Alavantas, Karulias, Kyrastas, Manolas, Michos, Saravakos (Dimopoulos), Antoniou (Kofidis), Anastopoulos, Mitropoulos, Papaioannou.

Brussels, 1 May 1985, attendance 48,310
Belgium (1)2 *(Vandenbergh, Vercauteren)*
Poland (0)0
Belgium: Munaron; Grun, Franky Van der Elst, Plessers, Renquin, Vercauteren (Mommens), Vandereycken, Scifo (Clijsters), Vandenbergh, Voordeckers, Ceulemans.
Poland: Mlynarczyk; Pawlak, Zmuda, Ostrowski, Wojcicki, Matysik, Buncol, Jalocha (Komornicki), Boniek,

Dziekanowski (Palasz), Smolarek.

Athens, 19 May 1985, attendance 52,500
Greece (0)1 *(Anastopoulos)*
Poland (1)4 *(Smolarek, Ostrowski, Boniek, Dziekanowski)*
Greece: Sarganis; Alavantas, Kyrastas, Mitsibonas (Saravakos), Karulias (Skartados), Antoniou, Michos, Dimopoulos, Papaioannou, Anastopoulos, Mitropoulos.
Poland: Mlynarczyk; Pawlak, Wojcicki, Przybys, Ostowski, Tarasziewicz (Dziekanowski), Matysik, Buncol, Urban, Boniek, Smolarek.

Tirana, 30 May 1985, attendance 20,000
Albania (0)0
Poland (1)1 *(Boniek)*
Albania: Musta; Zmijani, Omuri, Targaj, Hadja, Jera, Josa, Demollari (Marko), Muca (Mile), Minga, Kola.
Poland: Mlynarczyk; Pawlak, Przybys, Ostrowski, Wojcicki, Matysik, Buncol, Urban (Tarasiewicz), Boniek, Dziekanowski, Smolarek.

Chorzow, 11 September 1985, attendance 70,000
Poland (0)0
Belgium (0)0
Poland: Mlynarczyk; Pawlak, Wojcicki, Przybys, Ostrowski, Matysik, Komornicki, Urban, Boniek (Buncol), Smolarek (Palasz), Dziekanowski.
Belgium: Pfaff; Gerets, Grun (De Grijse), Plessers, Renquin, Franky Van der Elst, Ceulemans, Scifo, Vandereycken, Vandenbergh (Clijsters), Voordeckers.

Tirana, 30 October 1985, attendance 17,000
Albania (1)1 *(Omuri)*
Greece (0)1 *(Skartados)*
Albania: Musta; Zmijani, Hodja, Targaj, Bino, Josa, Demollari, Muca, Omuri, Minga, Abazi (Kola).
Greece: Sarganis; Alavantas, Michos, Manolas, Mavriosis, Skartados, Papaioannou P. (Antoniou), Papaioannou A. (Semertsidis), Kofidis, Mitropoulos, Anastopoulos.

Final Table	P	W	D	L	F	A	Pts	GD
Poland	6	3	2	1	10	6	8	+4
Belgium	6	3	2	1	7	3	8	+4
Albania	6	1	2	3	6	9	4	−3
Greece	6	1	2	3	5	10	4	−5

POLAND QUALIFY, BELGIUM PLAY OFF

GROUP 2
(Czechoslovakia, Malta, Portugal, Sweden, West Germany)

Norrkoping, 23 May 1984, attendance 18,819
Sweden (2)4 *(Sunesson 2, Corneliusson, Erlandsson)*
Malta (0)0
Sweden: Ravelli T.: Erlandsson, Hysen, Dahlqvist, Fredriksson, Eriksson, Prytz (Ramberg), Stromberg, Holmgren (Holmqvist), Sunesson, Corneliusson.
Malta: Midsuf; Buttigieg, Aquilana, Holland, Borg, Alex Azzopardi, Alf Azzopardi (Teuma), Farrugia L., Vella, Degiorgio, Muscat (Gatt).

Stockholm, 12 September 1984, attendance 30,136
Sweden (0)0
Portugal (0)1 *(Gomes)*
Sweden: Ljung; Erlandsson, Hysen, Dahlqvist, Fredriksson, Eriksson, Bergman (Borg), Tord Holmgren, Tommy Holmgren, Sandberg, Holmqvist.
Portugal: Bento; Joao Pinto, Lima Pereira, Eurico, Inacio, Frasco, Jaime Pacheco, Carlos Manuel, Sousa, Gomes (Futre), Diamantino (Vermelinho).

Oporto, 14 October 1984, attendance 32,500
Portugal (1)2 *(Diamantino, Carlos Manuel)*
Czechoslovakia (1)1 *(Jarolim)*
Portugal: Bento; Joao Pinto, Lima Pereira, Eurico, Inacio, Carlos Manuel (Virgilio), Frasco, Jaime Pacecho, Jaime Magalhaes, Gomes, Diamantino (Futre).
Czechoslovakia: Miklosko; Jacubec, Prokes, Fiala, Rada, Berger, Janecka, Jarolim, Ondra (Levy), Zelensky, Knoflicek (Micinec).

Cologne, 17 October 1984, attendance 60,000
West Germany (0)2 *(Rahn, Rummenigge K-H.)*
Sweden (0)0
West Germany: Schumacher; Herget, Forster K-H., Jakobs, Matthaus, Brehme, Falkenmeyer (Allofs K.), Magath (Rahn), Briegel, Voller, Rummenigge K-H.
Sweden: Ravelli T.; Erlandsson (Borg), Hysen, Dahlqvist, Fredriksson, Eriksson, Stromberg, Tord Holmgren, Tommy Holmgren, Corneliusson (Holmqvist), Gren.

Prague, 31 October 1984, attendance 4000
Czechoslovakia (2)4 *(Janecka 2, Jarolim, Berger)*
Malta (0)0

121

Czechoslovakia: Miklosko; Straka, Ondra, Fiala, Levy (Jakubec), Berger, Jarolim, Zajaros, Visek, Griga (Micinec), Janecka.
Malta: Mifsud; Aquilina, Scicluna, Holland, Alex Azzopardi (Buttigieg), Ed Farrugia, Vella, Alf Azzopardi, Degiorgio, Gatt, Muscat (Mizzi).

Lisbon, 14 November 1984, attendance 45,000
Portugal (1)1 *(Jordao)*
Sweden (3)3 *(Prytz 2, 1 pen, Nilsson T.)*
Portugal: Bento; Joao Pinto, Lima Pereira, Eurico, Inacio (Sousa), Jaime Magalhaes, Carlos Manuel, Frasco (Futre), Diamantino, Gomes, Jordao.
Sweden: Ravelli T.; Erlandsson, Hysen, Dahlqvist, Fredriksson, Prytz, Stromberg, Larsson (Tord Holmgren), Nilsson T., Gren, Tommy Holmgren (Eriksson).

Valletta, 16 December 1984, attendance 25,000
Malta (1)2 *(Busuttil, Xuereb R.)*
West Germany (1)3 *(Forster K-H., Allofs K.)*
Malta: Mifsud; Aquilina, Xuereb G., Holland (Alf Azzopardi), Scicluna, Busuttil, Woods, Vella, Xuereb R., Muscat (Gatt), Degiorgio.
West Germany: Schumacher; Forster K-H., Herget, Jakobs (Thon), Matthaus, Rahn, Brehme, Briegel, Rummenigge K-H., Voller, Allofs K.

Valletta, 11 February 1985, attendance 15,000
Malta (0)1 *(Farrugia L.)*
Portugal (2)3 *(Carlos Manuel, Gomes 2)*
Malta: Mifsud; Buttigieg, Aquilina (Em Farrugia), Woods, Alex Azzopardi, Scicluna (Muscat), Busuttil, Vella, Degiorgio, Farrugia L., Xuereb R.
Portugal: Bento; Joao Pinto, Lima Pereira, Eurico, Inacio, Andre, Jaime Magalhaes, Frasco (Virgilio), Carlos Manuel, Futre (Diamantino), Gomes.

Lisbon, 24 February 1985, attendance 60,000
Portugal (0)1 *(Diamantino)*
West Germany (2)2 *(Littbarski, Voller)*
Portugal: Bento; Joao Pinto, Lima Pereira (Sousa), Eurico, Inacio, Jaime Magalhaes, Andre (Daimantino), Carlos Manuel, Jaime Pacheco, Gomes, Futre.
West Germany: Schumacher; Berthold, Herget, Frontzeck, Jakobs, Matthaus, Falkenmeyer, Magath, Brigel, Voller, Littbarski.

Saarbrucken, 27 March 1985, attendance 37,600
West Germany (5)6 *(Rahn 2, Magath, Littbarski, Rummenigge K-H. 2)*
Malta (0)0
West Germany: Schumacher; Berthold, Forster K-H., Hergot, Frontzeck, Rahn (Thon), Magath, Briegel (Brehme), Littbarski, Voller, Rummenigge K-H.
Malta: Bonello; Alex Azzopardi, Holland, Buttigieg, Em Farrugia (Aquilina), Busuttil, Vella, Woods, Farrugia L., Mizzi (Xuereb R.), Degiorgio.

Valletta, 21 April 1985, attendance 12,000
Malta (0)0
Czechoslovakia (0)0
Malta: Bonello; Mifsud, Aquilina, Buttigieg, Xuereb G., Alex Azzopardi, Holland, Theuma, Alf Azzopardi, Woods, Busuttil (Xuereb R.).
Czechoslovakia: Borovicka; Hasek, Fiala, Prokes, Kukucka, Chaloupka (Micinec), Berger, Sloup, Janecka, Griga, Knoflicek (Zelensky).

Prague, 1 May 1985, attendance 35,000
Czechoslovakia (0)1 *(Griga)*
West Germany (4)5 *(Berthold, Littbarski, Matthaus, Herget, Allofs K.)*
Czechoslovakia: Borovicka; Fiala, Hasek, Prokes, Kukucka, Berger, Chaloupka (Zelensky), Sloup (Chovanec), Vizek, Griga, Janecka.
West Germany: Schumacher; Jakobs, Berthold, Forster K-H., Brehme, Herget, Matthaus (Thon), Magath, Rahn (Allofs K.), Littbarski, Voller.

Stockholm, 5 June 1985, attendance 33,891
Sweden (0)2 *(Prytz, pen, Larsson)*
Czechoslovakia (0)0
Sweden: Ravelli T.; Dahlqvist, Ravelli A., Hysen, Fredriksson, Erlandsson, Prytz, Stromberg, Svensson, Nilsson T., Truedsson (Larsson).
Czechoslovakia: Miklosko; Bazant, Fiala, Straka, Pelc (Brezina), Berger, Chovanec, Kubic, Kula, Vizek, Hruska.

Malmo, 25 September 1985, attendance 39,157
Sweden (0)2 *(Corneliusson, Mats Magnusson)*
West Germany (2)2 *(Voller, Herget)*
Sweden: Ravelli T.; Erlandsson, Hysen, Dahlqvist, Fredriksson, Prytz, Stromberg, Jan Svensson (Holmqvist), Ravelli

123

A. (Magnusson), Nilsson T., Corneliusson.
West Germany: Schumacher; Augenthaler, Brehme, Forster T., Jakobs, Herget, Berthold, Briegel, Littbarski, Voller, Rummenigge.

Prague, 25 September 1985, attendance 9000
Czechoslovakia (1)1 *(Hruska)*
Portugal (0)0
Czechoslovakia: Mikiosko; Hasek, Straka, Chovanec, Ondra, Chaloupka (Micinec), Berger, Kula, Vizek, Griga (Lauda), Hruska.
Portugal: Bento; Joao Pinto, Frederico, Venancio, Inacio, Jose Luis, Carlos Manuel, Andre, Sousa (Ribeiro), Gomes, Futre (Xavier).

Lisbon, 12 October 1985, attendance 5000
Portugal (1)3 *(Gomes 2, Rafael)*
Malta (0)2 *(Frederico og, Degiorgio)*
Portugal: Bento; Joao Pinto, Frederico, Venancio, Alvaro, Jaime Pacheco, Litos, Carlos Manuel, Palhares (Jaime), Gomes, Jordao (Jose Rafael).
Malta: Bonello; Buttigieg, Aquilina, Woods, Holland, Alex Azzopardi, Vella (Degiorgio), Busuttil, Scerri, Gregory (Xuereb R.), Farrugia L.

Prague, 16 October 1985, attendance 11,500
Czechoslovakia (1)2 *(Vizek 2)*
Sweden (1)1 *(Corneliusson)*
Czechoslovakia: Miklosko; Levy, Chovanec, Straka, Ondra, Hasek, Berger, Kula, Vizek, Lauda (Luhovy), Micinec (Novak).
Sweden: Ravelli T.; Erlandsson, Hysen, Dahlqvist, Fredriksson, Prytz, Ravelli A. (Holmqvist), Stromberg, Svensson (Magnusson), Nilsson T., Corneliusson.

Stuttgart, 16 October 1985, attendance 60,000
West Germany (0)0
Portugal (0)1 *(Carlos Manuel)*
West Germany: Schumacher; Berthold, Forster K., Jakobs (Grundel), Brehme, Allgower, Herget, Briegel, Meier, Littbarksi (Allofs T.), Rummenigge K-H.
Portugal: Bento; Joao Pinto, Venancio, Frederico, Inacio, Carlos Manuel (Litos), Jaime Pacheco, Veloso, Jose Antonio, Gomes (Jose Rafael), Mario Jorge.

Munich, 17 November 1985, attendance 15,000

West Germany (1)2 *(Brehme, Rummenigge K-H)*
Czechoslovakia (0)2 *(Novak, Lauda)*
West Germany: Schumacher; Brehme, Briegel (Frontzek), Forster K, Augenthaler, Rolff, Littbarski (Rahn), Allgower, Kogl, Thon, Rummenigge K-H.
Czechoslovakia: Miglosko; Hasek, Straka, Kula, Ondra, Berger, Vizek, Chovanec, Lauda (Luhovy), Novak, Levy.

Valletta, 17 November 1985, attendance 10,000
Malta (0)1 *(Farrugia)*
Sweden (1)2 *(Prytz, Stromberg)*
Malta: Bonello; Aquilina (Camilleri), Scicluna, Woods, Holland, Buttigieg, Busuttil, Vella, Gregory (Xuereb), Farrugia, De Giorgio.
Sweden: Wernersson; Ravelli A., Larsson P., Dahlqvist, Fredriksson, Eriksson, Prytz (Tord Holmgren), Stromberg, Sanders (Larsson L.), Holmqvist, Tommy Holmgren.

Final Table	P	W	D	L	F	A	Pts	GD
West Germany	8	5	2	1	22	9	12	+13
Portugal	8	5	0	3	12	10	10	+2
Sweden	8	4	1	3	14	9	9	+5
Czechoslovakia	8	3	2	3	11	12	8	−1
Malta	8	0	1	7	6	25	1	−19

WEST GERMANY AND PORTUGAL QUALIFY

GROUP 3
(England, Finland, Northern Ireland, Rumania, Turkey)

Pori, 27 May 1984, attendance 8115
Finland (0)1 *(Valvee)*
Northern Ireland (0)0
Finland: Huttonen; Tekonen, Kymalainen, Ikalainen (Europaeus), Petaja, Turunen, Houtsonen, Ukkonen, Rantanen (Kousa), Rautiainen, Valvee.
Northern Ireland: Jennings; Nicholl J., McClelland, McElhinney, Donaghy, O'Neill M., McIlroy (Worthington), Armstrong (Cochrane), Hamilton, Whiteside, Stewart.

Belfast, 12 September 1984, attendance 18,000
Northern Ireland (1)3 *(Iorgulescu og, Whiteside, O'Neill M.)*
Rumania (1)2 *(Hagi, Geolgau)*
Northern Ireland: Jennings; Nicholl J., McClelland, McElhinney, Donaghy, Armstrong, O'Neill M., McCreery, Stewart, Hamilton, Whiteside.

Rumania: Lung; Rednic, Stefanescu, Iorgulescu, Ungureanu, Ticleanu (Movila). Andone, Klein, Irimescu (Geolgau), Augustin, Hagi.

Wembley, 17 October 1984, attendance 47,234
England (2)5 *(Hateley 2, Woodcock, Robson, Sansom)*
Finland (0)0
England: Shilton; Duxbury (Stevens), Sansom, Williams, Wright, Butcher, Robson (Chamberlain), Wilkins, Hateley, Woodcock, Barnes.
Finland: Huttunen; Pekonen, Kymalainen, Lahtinen, Petaja, Haaskivi (Turunen), Houtsonen, Ukkonen, Ikalainen, Rautiainen, Valvee (Hjelm).

Antalya, 31 October 1984, attendance 10,000
Turkey (0)1 *(Tufekci)*
Finland (1)2 *(Hjelm, Lipponen)*
Turkey: Arif; Muharrem, Abdulkerim, Riza (Mujdat), Rasit, Cem, Aykut (Ridvan), Ismail, Tufekci, Erdal, Hasan.
Finland: Huttunen; Lahtinen, Kymalainen, Ikalainen, Pekonen, Turunen, Virtanen, Houtsonen, Ukkonen, Lipponen, Hjelm (Valvee).

Belfast, 14 November 1984, attendance 25,000
Northern Ireland (1)2 *(O'Neill J., Armstrong)*
Finland (1)1 *(Lipponen)*
Northern Ireland: Jennings; Nicholl J., O'Neill J., McClelland, Donaghy, O'Neill M., McIlroy, Armstrong, Quinn, Whiteside, Stewart.
Finland: Huttonen; Pekonen, Kymalainen, Lahtinen, Ikalainen, Turunen, Europaeus, Ukkonen, Houtsonen, Hjelm, Lipponen.

Istanbul, 14 November 1984, attendance 40,000
Turkey (0)0
England (3)8 *(Robson 3, Woodcock 2, Barnes 2, Anderson)*
Turkey: Yasar; Ismail, Yusuf, Kemal, Cem, Rasit, Mujdat, Ridvan, Ahmet, Tufekci (Tuncay), Erdal.
England: Shilton; Anderson, Sansom, Williams (Stevens), Wright, Butcher, Robson, Wilkins, Withe, Woodcock (Francis), Barnes.

Belfast, 27 February 1985, attendance 28,000
Northern Ireland (0)0
England (0)1 *(Hateley)*

Northern Ireland: Jennings; Nicholl J., McClelland, O'Neill J., Donaghy, McIlroy, Ramsey, Armstrong, Stewart, Quinn, Whiteside.
England: Shilton; Anderson, Martin, Butcher, Sansom, Steven, Wilkins, Stevens, Woodcock (Francis), Hateley, Barnes.

Craiova, 3 April 1985, attendance 35,000
Rumania (3)3 *(Hagi, Camataru 2)*
Turkey (0)0
Rumania: Lung; Negrila, Iorgulescu, Stefanescu, Ungureanu, Rednic, Irimescu, Mateut (Lacatus), Hagi, Coras (Balaci), Camataru.
Turkey: Arif; Semih, Abdulkerim, Kemal, Mujdat, Senol (Hasan), Huseyin, Yusuf, Metin, Selcuk (Iskender), Ridvan.

Belfast, 1 May 1985, attendance 18,000
Northern Ireland (1)2 *(Whiteside 2)*
Turkey (0)0
Northern Ireland: Jennings; Nicholl J., McClelland, O'Neill J., Donaghy, McIlroy, Ramsey, Brotherston, Whiteside, Quinn, Stewart.
Turkey: Erhan; Rasit, Abdulkerim, Semih, Hasan, Yusuf, Ismail, Metin, Tufekci, Mujdat, Hasan.

Bucharest, 1 May 1985, attendance 70,000
Rumania (0)0
England (0)0
Rumania: Lung; Negrila, Iorgulescu (Iovan), Stefanescu, Ungureanu, Rednic, Hagi, Coras (Lacatus), Boloni, Klein, Camataru.
England: Shilton; Anderson, Butcher, Wright, Sansom, Wilkins, Robson, Steven, Barnes (Waddle), Mariner (Lineker), Francis.

Helsinki, 22 May 1985, attendance 30,000
Finland (1)1 *(Rantanen)*
England (0)1 *(Hateley)*
Finland: Huttunen; Lahtinen (Petaja), Ikalainen, Kymalainen, Nieminen, Houtsonen, Rautiainen, Turunen, Ukkonen (Hjelm), Rantanen, Lipponen.
England: Shilton; Anderson, Fenwick, Butcher, Sansom, Steven (Waddle), Wilkins, Robson, Francis, Hateley, Barnes.

Helsinki, 6 June 1985, attendance 22,000

Finland (1)1 *(Lipponen)*
Rumania (1)1 *(Hagi)*
Finland: Huttunen; Lahtinen, Kymalainen, Ikalainen, Nieminen, Turunen, Houtsonen, Ukkonen, Lipponen, Rautiainen, Rantanen.
Rumania: Lung; Negrila, Stefanescu, Ungureanu, Rednic, Iorgulescu, Coras, Klein, Camataru, Boloni, Hagi.

Timisoara, 28 August 1985, attendance 45,000
Rumania (1)2 *(Hagi, Mateut)*
Finland (0)0
Rumania: Moraru; Rednic, Stefanescu, Ungureanu, Mateut, Iorgulescu (Iovan), Coras (Gabor), Klein, Camataru, Boloni, Hagi.
Finland: Huttunen; Houtsonen, Nieminen, Europaeus, Ikalainen, Rautiainen, Ukkonen (Petaja), Hjelm, Lipponen, Rantanen, Turunen.

Izmir, 11 September 1985, attendance 42,500
Turkey (0)0
Northern Ireland (0)0
Turkey: Yasar; Ismail, Rasit, Sedat, Erdogan, Ilyas (Bahattin), Mujdat, Hasan, Metin, Senol, Erdal (Tanju).
Northern Ireland: Jennings; Nicholl J., McClelland, O'Neill, Donaghy, Ramsey, Quinn, McIlroy (McCreery), Penney, Armstrong, Worthington.

Wembley, 11 September 1985, attendance 59,500
England (1)1 *(Hoddle)*
Rumania (0)1 *(Camataru)*
England: Shilton; Stevens, Wright, Fenwick, Sansom, Hoddle, Robson, Reid, Hateley, Lineker (Woodcock), Waddle (Barnes).
Rumania: Lung; Negrila, Stefanescu, Ungureanu, Rednic, Iovan, Coras (Gabor), Klein (Mateut), Camataru, Boloni, Hagi.

Tampere, 25 September 1985, attendance 3500
Finland (1)1 *(Rantanen)*
Turkey (0)0
Finland: Huttunen; Lahtinen, Kymalainen, Rantanen, Nieminen (Petaja), Turunen, Houtsonen, Ukkonen (Lipponen), Ikalainen, Rautiainen, Hjelm.
Turkey: Yasar; Ismail, Sedat, Rasit, Erdogan, Yusuf, Mujdat, Arif (Tufekci), Selcuk, Hasan, Senol Corlu.

Bucharest, 16 October 1985, attendance 45,000
Rumania (0)0
Northern Ireland (1)1 *(Quinn)*
Rumania: Lung; Negrila (Geolgau), Iovan, Ungureanu, Mateut, Iorgulescu, Rednic, Klein, Coras (Piturca), Boloni, Hagi.
Northern Ireland: Jennings; Nicholl J., Donaghy, O'Neill J., McDonald, McCreery, Penney (Armstrong), McIlroy, Quinn, Whiteside, Stewart (Worthington).

Wembley, 16 October 1985, attendance 52,500
England (4)5 *(Waddle, Lineker 3, Robson)*
Turkey (0)0
England: Shilton; Stevens, Wright, Fenwick, Sansom, Hoddle, Wilkins, Robson (Steven), Lineker, Hateley (Woodcock), Waddle.
Turkey: Yasar; Ismail, Yusuf, Rasit, Sedat, Abdulkerim, Huseyin, Mujdat, Senol (Hasan Sengun), Hasan, Vezir, Selcuk.

Wembley, 13 November 1985, attendance 70,500
England (0)0
Northern Ireland (0)0
England: Shilton; Stevens, Sansom, Hoddle, Wright, Fenwick, Bracewell, Wilkins, Dixon, Lineker, Waddle.
Northern Ireland: Jennings; Nicholl J., Donaghy, O'Neill, McDonald, McCreery, Penney (Armstrong), McIlroy, Quinn, Whiteside, Stewart (Worthington).

Izmir, 13 November 1985, attendance 35,000
Turkey (0)1 *(Metin)*
Rumania (2)3 *(Iorgulescu, Coras, Boloni)*
Turkey: Ocan; Mujdat, Ismail I., Yusuf, Erdogan, Riza, Metin, Unal, Senol (Ismail II), Tanju, Selcuk.
Rumania: Lung; Iovan, Iorgulescu, Stefanescu, Barbulescu, Rednic, Boloni, Klein, Hagi, Coras (Geolgau), Piturca (Camataru).

Final Table	P	W	D	L	F	A	Pts	GD
England	8	4	4	0	21	2	12	+19
Northern Ireland	8	4	2	2	8	5	10	+3
Rumania	8	3	3	2	12	7	9	+5
Finland	8	3	2	3	7	12	8	−5
Turkey	8	0	1	7	2	24	1	−22

ENGLAND AND NORTHERN IRELAND QUALIFY

GROUP 4
(Bulgaria, East Germany, France, Luxembourg, Yugoslavia)

Belgrade, 29 September 1984, attendance 11,000
Yugoslavia (0)0
Bulgaria (0)0
Yugoslavia: Stojic; Zoran Vujovic (Gracan), Baljic, Gudelj, Hadzibegic, Radanovic, Sestic, Sliskovic, Vokrri (Pancev), Bazdarevic, Zlatko Vujovic.
Bulgaria: Mikhailov; Petrov, Arabov, Markov, Dimitrov, Zdravkov, Yanchev (Tanev), Sadakov, Velitchkov, Gospodinov, Mladenov.

Luxembourg, 13 October 1984, attendance 9000
Luxembourg (0)0
France (4)4 *(Battiston, Platini, Stopyra 2)*
Luxembourg: Van Rijswick; Michaud, Scheuer, Petry, Meunier, Schonkert, Hellers, Weis, Dresch, Langers, Reiter.
France: Bats; Bibard, Battiston, Bossis, Amoros, Fernandez, Tusseau, Giresse, Platini (Ferreri), Stopyra, Brisson (Anziani).

Leipzig, 20 October 1984, attendance 63,000
East Germany (1)2 *(Glowatzky, Ernst)*
Yugoslavia (1)3 *(Bazdarevic, Vokrri, Sestic)*
East Germany: Muller; Kreer, Dorner, Stahmann, Zotsche, Rohde, Ernst (Streich), Troppa, Steinbach, Minge, Glowatzky.
Yugoslavia: Stojic; Radovic, Hadzibegic, Radanovic, Baljic, Gudelj, Zajec, Bazdarevic, Sestic (Josk), Vokrri (Deveric), Zlatko Vujovic.

Esch-sur-Alzette, 17 November 1984, attendance 2000
Luxembourg (0)0
East Germany (0)5 *(Ernst 3, Minge 2)*
Luxembourg: Van Rijswick; Girres, Schonkert, Weis, Scheuer, Meunier, Hellers, Petry, Malget (Dresch), Langers (Bossi), Reiter.
East Germany: Muller; Kreer, Stahmann (Stubner), Dorner, Doschner, Thom, Troppa, Ernst, Steinbach, Minge, Glowatzky (Liebers).

Paris, 21 November 1984, attendance 45,000
France (0)1 *(Platini)*
Bulgaria (0)0
France: Bats; Bibard, Senac, Bossis, Amoros, Fernandez,

Tigana, Platini, Genghini, Stopyra (Toure) (Tusseau), Bellone.
Bulgaria: Mikhailov; Nikolov, Arabov, Dimitrov, Markov, Zdravkov, Sadakov, Gochev (Gospodinov), Sirakov, Iskrenov, Mladenov (Spassov).

Sofia, 5 December 1984, attendance 15,000
Bulgaria (2)4 *(Sirakov, Velitchkov, Mladenov, Dimitrov)*
Luxembourg (0)0
Bulgaria: Mikhailov; Nikolov, Arabov, Markov (Getov), Dimitrov, Zdravkov, Gochev (Mladenov), Sirakov, Velitchkov, Spassov, Pashev.
Luxembourg: Van Rijswick; Schonkert, Scheuer, Weis, Petry, Meunier, Girres, Hellers, Reiter (Bossi), Dresch, Malget (Hoscheid).

Paris, 8 December 1984, attendance 43,174
France (1)2 *(Stopyra, Anziani)*
East Germany (0)0
France: Bats; Bibard, Senac, Bossis, Amoros, Giresse, Tigana, Fernandez, Platini, Stopyra (Anziani), Bellone.
East Germany: Muller; Trautmann, Stahmann, Dorner, Doschner, Liebers, Troppa, Stubner, Steinbach (Richter), Minge (Glowatzky), Thom.

Zenica, 27 March 1985, attendance 28,500
Yugoslavia (1)1 *(Gudelj)*
Luxembourg (0)0
Yugoslavia: Stojic; Zoran Vujovic, Hadzibegic, Baljic, Radanovic, Gudelj, Sliskovic, Bazdarevic, Zlatko Vujovic, Durovski, Pasic (Sestic).
Luxembourg: Van Rijswick; Schonkert, Wagner, Rohmann, Bossi, Barboni, Hellers, Weis (Malget), Dresch, Langers, Reiter.

Sarajevo, 3 April 1985, attendance 53,500
Yugoslavia (0)0
France (0)0
Yugoslavia: Stojic; Capljic, Baljic, Gudelj, Hadzibegic, Radanovic, Sestic (Sliskovic), Zajec, Halilhodzic, Bazdarevic, Zlatko Vujovic (Durovski M.).
France: Bats; Ayache, Amoros, Specht, Battiston, Fernandez (Tusseau), Tigana, Giresse, Stopyra (Toure), Platini, Bellone.

Sofia, 6 April 1985, attendance 50,000
Bulgaria (0)1 *(Mladenov)*

East Germany (0)0
Bulgaria: Mikhailov; Iliev, Arabov, Petrov, Dimitrov, Zdrav-kov, Gochev (Getov), Sadakov, Mladenov, Sirakov (Velitch-kov), Iskrenov.
East Germany: Muller; Kreer, Dorner, Stahmann, Doschner, Stubner, Krause, Backs (Schulz), Minge (Weidemann), Ernst, Thom.

Luxembourg, 1 May 1985, attendance 7000
Luxembourg (0)0
Yugoslavia (0)1 *(Vokrri)*
Luxembourg: Van Rijswick, Schonkert, Wagner, Bossi, Roh-mann, Barboni, Hellers, Dresch, Reiter, Weis (Girres), Langers.
Yugoslavia: Stojic; Milius, Baljic, Hadzibegic, Zejec, Rad-anovic (Durovski M.), Zlatko Vujovic (Pancev), Gudelj, Vok-rri, Bazdarevic, Mlinaric.

Sofia, 2 May 1985, attendance 60,000
Bulgaria (1)2 *(Dimitrov, Sirakov)*
France (0)0
Bulgaria: Mikhailov; Nikolov, Arabov, Petrov, Dimitrov, Zdravkov, Getov (Pashev), Sirakov, Velitchkov (Jeliaskov), Sadakov, Mladenov.
France: Bats; Ayache, Amoros, Specht, Bossis, Fernandez (Tusseau), Toure, Tigana, Stopyra, Platini, Bellone.

Babelsberg, 18 May 1985, attendance 9000
East Germany (3)3 *(Minge 2, Ernst, pen)*
Luxembourg (0)1 *(Langers)*
East Germany: Muller; Kreer, Dorner, Rohde (Doschner), Zotsche, Pilz, Ernst, Liebers, Kirsten, Minge, Thom.
Luxembourg: Van Rijswick; Schonkert (Meunier), Rohmann, Bossi, Wagner, Weis, Barboni, Dresch, Hellers, Reiter (Mal-get), Langers.
Sofia, 1 June 1985, attendance 60,000
Bulgaria (1)2 *(Getov 2)*
Yugoslavia (1)1 *(Durovski)*
Bulgaria: Mikhailov; Nikolov, Arabov, Petrov, Dimitrov, Zdravkov, Getov, Sirakov (Jeliaskov), Velitchkov (Kos-tadinov), Sadakov, Mladenov.
Yugoslavia: Stojic; Caplijc, Radanovic, Hadzibegic, Zajec, Gudelj, Bahtic (Mrkela) Mlinaric, Vokrri, Bajdarevic, Durovski.

Leipzig, 11 September 1985, attendance 69,000
East Germany (0)2 *(Ernst, Kreer)*
France (0)0
East Germany: Muller; Kreer, Rohde, Sanger, Zotzsche, Stubner, Liebers, Minge, Thom, Kirsten, Ernst.
France: Bats; Bibard, Ayache, Le Roux, Bossis, Fernandez, Poullain (Bellone), Giresse, Platini, Rocheteau, Toure.
Luxembourg, 25 September 1985, attendance 2500
Luxembourg (0)1 *(Langers, pen)*
Bulgaria (3)3 *(Petrov, Kostadinov, Dimitrov G.)*
Luxembourg: Van Rijswick; Schonkert, Dresch, Scheuer, Meunier, Jeitz, Weis (Girres), Hellers, Barboni (Malget), Retier, Langers.
Bulgaria: Valov; Zdravkov, Arabov, Petrov P., Dimitrov G., Sadkov, Getov (Kolev), Gochev, Kostadinov, Gospodinov, Iskrenov (Pashev).

Belgrade, 28 September 1985, attendance 45,000
Yugoslavia (0)1 *(Skoro)*
East Germany (0)2 *(Thom 2)*
Yugoslavia: Ljukovcan; Elsner, Gracan, Radanovic, Kapetanovic, Gudelj (Capljic), Skoro, Bazdarevic, Nikolic (Durovski), Bursac, Zlatko, Vujovic.
East Germany: Muller; Rohde, Kreer, Sanger, Zotzsche, Pilz, Minge, Liebers, Thom, Kirsten (Heun), Ernst.

Paris, 30 October 1985, attendance 20,000
France (4)6 *(Rocheteau 3, Toure, Giresse, Fernandez, pen)*
Luxembourg (0)0
France: Bats; Ayache, Battiston, Bossis (Le Roux), Amoros, Tigana, Fernandez, Giresse, Platini, Rocheteau (Bellone), Toure.
Luxembourg: Van Rijswick; Meunier, Bossi, Dresch, Schonkert, Weis, Jeitz (Wagner), Hellers, Hoscheid (Scholten), Langers, Girres.

Paris, 16 November 1985, attendance 50,000
France (1)2 *(Platini 2)*
Yugoslavia (0)0
France: Bats; Ayache, Amoros, Le Roux, Battiston, Fernandez, Tigana, Giresse, Rocheteau (Stopyra), Platini, Toure.
Yugoslavia: Stojic; Miljus, Kapetanovic, Gudelj, Veremezovic, Radanovic, Stojkovic (Soro), Sliskovic, Bursac, Bazdarevic, Zlatko Vujovic.

Karl-Marz-Stadt, 16 November 1985, attendance 35,000
East Germany (2)2 *(Zotzsche, pen, Liebers)*
Bulgaria (1)1 *(Gochev)*
East Germany: Muller; Kreer, Rohde, Sanger, Zotzsche, Stubner, Liebers, Pilz, Kirsten (Heun), Ernst (Glowatzki), Minge.
Bulgaria: Valov; Dimitrov E., Dimitrov G., Koev, Petrov, Zdravkov (Kolev Kh.), Zeliaskov, Gochev, Gospodinov, Kostadinov, Iskrenov (Getov).

Final Table	P	W	D	L	F	A	Pts	GD
France	8	5	1	2	15	4	11	+11
Bulgaria	8	5	1	2	13	5	11	+8
East Germany	8	5	0	3	16	9	10	+7
Yugoslavia	8	3	2	3	7	8	8	−1
Luxembourg	8	0	0	8	2	27	0	−25

GROUP 5
(Austria, Cyprus, Hungary, Netherlands)

Nicosia, 2 May 1984, attendance 10,000
Cyprus (0)1 *(Kristoforou)*
Austria (1)2 *(Gisinger, Prohaska)*
Cyprus: Konstantinou; Miamiliotis, Kezos, Pantziaras N., Erotokritou. Kouis (Tsingis), Dimitrou, Giakoudakis, Kounnas, Fotis (Kristoforou), Theophanos.
Austria: Koncilia; Krauss, Lainer, Obermayer, Pezzey, Gisinger, Prohaska, Weber, Hormann, Schachner, Niederbacher (Willfurth).

Budapest, 26 September 1984, attendance 20,000
Hungary (0)3 *(Nagy A., Esterhazy, Kardos)*
Austria (1)1 *(Schachner)*
Hungary: Andrusch; Csuhay (Sallai), Roth, Garaba, Varga, Kardos, Nagy A., Detari, Kiprich, Nyilasi, Esterhazy.
Austria: Koncilia; Dihanich, Pezzey, Messlender, Pregesbauer, Prohaska, Weber, Gasselich (Hormann), Gisinger (Drabits), Schachner, Polster.

Rotterdam, 17 October 1984, attendance 55,000
Netherlands (1)1 *(Kieft)*
Hungary (1)2 *(Detari, Esterhazy)*
Netherlands: Van Breukelen; Rijkaard, Spelbos, Silooy, Wijnstekers, Valke (Koeman E.), Gullit, Van der Kerkhof, Van Basten (Houtman), Kieft, Van der Gijp.
Hungary: Andrusch; Sallai, Roth, Varga, Kardos, Garaba

(Csongradi), Kiprich (Bodonyi), Nyilasi, Nagy A., Detari, Esterhazy.

Vienna, 14 November 1984, attendance 15,000
Austria (1)1 *(Valke og)*
Netherlands (0)0
Austria: Koncilia; Pezzey, Weber, Messlender (Lainer), Prohaska, Jara, Hormann, Brauneder, Schachner, Polster, Steinkogler.
Netherlands: Van Breukelen; Spelbos, Ophof, Boeve (Van der Gijp), Brandts, Van Tiggelen, Lokhoff (Been), Van der Kerkhof, Valke, Van Basten, Gullit.

Nicosia, 17 November 1984, attendance 8000
Cyprus (1)1 *(Fotis)*
Hungary (0)2 *(Roth, Nyilasi)*
Cyprus: Konstantinou A.; Pantzarias K., Pantzarias N. (Konstantinou K.), Klitos, Miamiliotis, Marangos, Savides (Damianou), Yiangudakis, Mavris, Fotis, Sikous.
Hungary: Andrusch; Sallai, Roth, Garaba, Varga, Csongradi (Dajka), Nagy A., Detari, Kiprich (Bodonyi), Nyilasi, Esterhazy.

Nicosia, 23 December 1984, attendance 3000
Cyprus (0)0
Netherlands (0)1 *(Houtman)*
Cyprus: Konstantinou A.; Kouis, Pantzarias N., Erotokritou, Miamiliotis, Yiangudakis, Mavris, Marangos, Tsikos, Savides, Fotis.
Netherlands: Van Breukelen; Boeve, Spelbos, Brandts, Wijnstekers, Valke, Van der Kerkhof, Gullit, Houtman, Van Basten, Van der Gijp.

Amsterdam, 27 February 1985, attendance 25,000
Netherlands (3)7 *(Koeman E., Kieft 2, Schoenaker 2, Pantziaras K. og, Van Basten)*
Cyprus (1)1 *(Marangos)*
Netherlands: Van Breukelen; Wijnstekers, Brandts, Van der Kerkhof, Boeve, Schoenaker, Koeman E., Gullit (Van der Gijp), Kieft, Van Basten, Tahamata.
Cyprus: Konstantinou A.; Pantziaras K., Miamiliotis, Erotokritou, Pantziaras N., Konstantinou K., Maragos, Kouis (Damianou), Savides (Nicholau), Tsikos, Fotis.

Budapest, 3 April 1985, attendance 10,000
Hungary (0)2 *(Nyilasi, Szokolai)*

Cyprus (0)0
Hungary: Disztl P.; Sallai, Roth, Garaba, Varga, Kardos, Detari, Nagy A., Bodonyi (Szokolai), Nyilasi, Esterhazy (Kiprich).
Cyprus: Konstantinou A.; Klitos, Karseras (Nikolau), Pantziaras N., Miamiliotis, Konstantinou K., Marangos, Tsingis, Yiangudakis, Savides (Mavridis), Fotis.

Vienna, 17 April 1985, attendance 20,000
Austria (0)0
Hungary (2)3 *(Kiprich 2, Detari)*
Austria: Koncilia; Lainer, Hormann, Degeorgi (Turmer), Pezzey, Weber, Schachner, Prohaska, Krankl, Oberacher (Polster), Jara.
Hungary: Disztl P.; Sallai, Roth, Peter, Kardos, Garaba, Kiprich, Nyilasi, Nagy A., Detari, Esterhazy.

Rotterdam, 1 May 1985, attendance 52,000
Netherlands (0)1 *(Kieft)*
Austria (0)1 *(Schachner)*
Netherlands: Van Breukelen; Rijkaard, Van de Korput, Brandts, Wijnstekers, Schoenaker, Van der Kerkhof, Koeman E., Van der Gijp (De Wit), Kieft, Tahamata.
Austria: Koncilia; Lainer, Pezzey, Turmer, Brauneder, Hormann (Hrstic), Prohaska, Willfurth, Kienast, Schachner, Polster.

Vienna, 7 May 1985, attendance 15,000
Austria (2)4 *(Hrstic, Polster, Schachner, Willfurth)*
Cyprus (0)0
Austria: Koncilia; Lainer, Pezzey, Turmer, Brauneder, Hormann, Prohaska, Hrstic, Willfurth, Schachner, Polster (Pacult).
Cyprus: Konstantinou A.; Konstantinou K., Pantzarias N. (Pantzarias K.), Erotokritou, Paktikis, Marangos, Yiangudakis, Nikolau, Tsingis (Kristofi), Savides, Fotis.

Budapest, 14 May 1985, attendance 83,000
Hungary (0)0
Netherlands (0)1 *(De Wit)*
Hungary: Disztl P.; Sallai, Kardos, Roth, Garaba, Peter, Nagy A. (Varga), Nyilasi, Detari, Kiprich, Esterhazy (Meszaros).
Netherlands: Van Breukelen; Wijnstekers, Van de Korput, Van Tiggelen, Lokhoff (De Wit), Rijkaard, Schoenaker, Van der Kerkhof (Koeman R.), Kieft, Tahamata, Van Basten.

Final Table

	P	W	D	L	F	A	Pts	GD
Hungary	6	5	0	1	12	4	10	+8
Netherlands	6	3	1	2	11	5	7	+6
Austria	6	3	1	2	9	8	7	+1
Cyprus	6	0	0	6	3	18	0	−15

HUNGARY QUALIFY, NETHERLANDS PLAY OFF

GROUP 6
(Denmark, Eire, Norway, Switzerland, USSR)

Dublin, 12 September 1984, attendance 28,000
Eire (0)1 *(Walsh)*
USSR (0)0
Eire: McDonagh; Devine, O'Leary, Lawrenson, Hughton, Whelan, Grealish, Brady, Robinson, Walsh (O'Keefe), Galvin.
USSR: Dasayev; Sulakvelidze, Chivadze, Demianenko, Baltacha, Oganesian (Gotsmanov), Litovchenko, Bessonov (Zigmantovich), Aleinikov, Rodionov, Blokhin.

Oslo, 12 September 1984, attendance 14,431
Norway (0)0
Switzerland (1)1 *(Egli, pen)*
Norway: Thorstvedt; Hareide, Soler, Kojedal, Grondalen, Herlovsen, Ahlsen, Davidsen, Giske (Albertsen), Dokken, Brandhaug (Seland).
Switzerland: Engel; In-Albon, Wehrli, Egli, Schallibaum, Koller, Geiger, Hermann, Brigger, Barberis, Sutter.

Copenhagen, 26 September 1984, attendance 45,000
Denmark (1)1 *(Elkjaer)*
Norway (0)0
Denmark: Qvist; Busk, Olsen M., Nielsen, Christofte, Bertelsen, Molby, Berggren (Brylle), Olsen J. (Lauridsen), Laudrup, Elkjaer.
Norway: Thorstvedt; Fjaelberg, Kojedal, Hareide, Grondalen, Soler, Ahlsen, Davidsen, Vaadal (Moen), Jacobsen P. (Mathiesen), Laudrup, Elkjaer.

Oslo, 10 October 1984, attendance 13,789
Norway (0)1 *(Thoresen, pen)*
USSR (0)1 *(Litovchenko)*
Norway: Thorstvedt; Fjaelberg, Kojedal, Hareide, Mordt, Soler, Ahlsen, Davidsen (Johansen E.), Thoresen, Okland, Jacobsen P.

USSR: Dasayev; Sulakvelidze, Bubnov, Baltacha, Pozdnyakov, Litovchenko, Gotsmanov, Oganesian (Zigmantovich), Aleinikov, Protasov (Kondratiev), Rodionov.

Berne, 17 October 1984, attendance 37,000
Switzerland (1)1 *(Barberis)*
Denmark (0)0
Switzerland: Engel; Schallibaum, In-Albon, Egli, Wehrli, Hermann, Bregy, Barberis (Ponte), Brigger (Sutter), Geiger, Zwicker.
Denmark: Qvist; Busk, Olsen M., Nielsen, Molby (Brylle), Bertelsen, Olsen J., Berggren (Sivebaek), Laudrup, Elkjaer, Christofte.

Oslo, 17 October 1984, attendance 12,468
Norway (1)1 *(Jacobsen P.)*
Eire (0)0
Norway: Thorstvedt; Fjaelberg (Davidsen), Kojedal, Hareide, Mordt, Soler, Ahlsen, Herlovsen, Okland, Jacobsen P.(Henriksen), Thoresen.
Eire: McDonagh; Devine, Hughton, Lawrenson, O'Leary, Brady, Whelan (O'Callaghan), Grealish, Galvin, Stapleton, Robinson (Walsh).

Copenhagen, 14 November 1984, attendance 43,500
Denmark (1)3 *(Elkjaer 2, Lerby)*
Eire (0)0
Denmark: Qvist; Siveback, Olsen M., Nielsen, Busk, Arnesen, Berggren, Bertelsen (Molby), Lerby, Laudrup, Elkjaer (Brylle).
Eire: McDonagh; Lawrenson, McCarthy, O'Leary, Beglin, Sheedy, Brady, Grealish, Galvin (O'Callaghan), Stapleton, Walsh.

Berne, 17 April 1985, attendance 50,000
Switzerland (1)2 *(Bregy, pen, Egli)*
USSR (1)2 *(Gavrilov, Demianenko)*
Switzerland: Engel; Ludi, In-Albon, Egli, Wehrli, Hermann, Barberis (Schallibaum), Geiger, Brigger, Bregy, Cina.
USSR: Dasayev; Vishnevsky, Demianenko, Baltacha, Litovchenko (Zigmantovich), Larionov, Gotsmanov, Aleinikov, Gavrilov, Protasov, Kondratiev.

Dublin, 1 May 1985, attendance 16,000
Eire (0)0
Norway (0)0
Eire: Bonner; Langan (McGrath), Lawrenson, O'Leary, Beglin, Waddock, Daly, Brady (Whelan), Galvin, Stapleton, Robinson.
Norway: Thorstvedt; Fjaelberg, Kojedal, Hareide, Henriksen, Herlovsen (Erlandsen), Ahlsen, Soler, Okland, Thorsen, Moen (Jacobsen P.).

Moscow, 2 May 1985, attendance 19,000
USSR (4)4 *(Protasov 2, Kondratiev 2)*
Switzerland (0)0
USSR: Dasayev; Larionov, Vishnevsky, Demianenko, Sulakvelidze, Aleinikov, Gotsmanov, Litovchenko (Belanov), Kondratiev (Cherenkov), Gavrilov, Protasov.
Switzerland: Engel; Wehrli, In-Albon, Ludi, Egli, Schallibaum, Barberis (Matthey), Brigger, Geiger, Bregy (Braschler), Hermann.

Dublin, 2 June 1985, attendance 20,000
Eire (2)3 *(Sheedy, Stapleton, Grealish)*
Switzerland (0)0
Eire: McDonagh; Langan, O'Leary, McCarthy, Beglin, Daly (Whelan), Grealish (McGrath), Brady, Sheedy, Robinson, Stapleton.
Switzerland: Engel (Burgener); Wehrli, In-Albon, Ludi, Geiger, Hermann, Decastel, Egli, Matthey, Barberis (Bregy), Braschler.

Copenhagen, 5 June 1985, attendance 45,700
Denmark (2)4 *(Elkjaer 2, Laudrup 2)*
USSR (1)2 *(Protasov, Gotsmanov)*
Denmark: Qvist; Olsen M., Nielsen, Busk, Berggren, Bertelsen, Olsen J. (Frimann), Lerby, Arnesen (Andersen), Elkjaer, Laudrup.
USSR: Dasayev; Baltacha, Podznyakov, Sulakvelidze, Demianenko, Litovchenko (Zigmantovich), Aleinikov, Gavrilov, Gotsmanov, Protasov, Belanov (Kondratiev).

Berne, 11 September 1985, attendance 24,000
Switzerland (0)0
Eire (0)0

Switzerland: Engel; Schallibaum (Brigger), In-Albon, Egli, Geiger, Hermann, Perret, Koller, Luthi, Bregy, Matthey.
Eire: McDonagh; Hughton, Beglin, McCarthy, O'Leary, Brady, Daly (McGrath), Lawrenson, Cascarino, Stapleton, Sheedy (O'Callaghan).

Moscow, 25 September 1985, attendance 100,000
USSR (0)1 *(Protasov)*
Denmark (0)0
USSR: Dasayev; Morozov, Chivadze, Demianenko, Bubnov, Larionov (Savarov), Gotsmanov, Cherenkov, Aleinikov, Protasov, Blokhin (Kondratiev).
Denmark: Rasmussen; Siveback, Busk, Olsen M., Nielsen (Molby), Lerby, Bertelsen, Arnesen, Berggren, Elkjaer (Frimann), Laudrup.

Copenhagen, 9 October 1985, attendance 45,600
Denmark (0)0
Switzerland (0)0
Denmark: Rasmussen; Busk, Olsen M., Nielsen, Berggren, Bertelsen, Simonsen, Arnesen, Lerby, Laudrup, Elkjaer.
Switzerland: Engel; Egli, Geiger, In-Albon, Ludi, Schallibaum, Bregy, Hermann, Koller, Matthey, Sutter.

Oslo, 16 October 1985, attendance 19,420
Norway (1)1 *(Sundby)*
Denmark (0)5 *(Laudrup, Lerby, pen, Elkjaer, Berggren 2)*
Norway: Thorstvedt; Fjaelberg (Kojedal), Ahlsen, Hareide (Jacobsen P.), Henriksen, Davidsen, Herlovsen, Sundby, Andersen, Okland, Thoresen.
Denmark: Rasmussen; Siveback, Busk, Olsen M., Nielsen, Lerby, Bertelsen (Molby), Arnesen (Frimann), Berggren, Elkjaer, Laudrup.

Moscow, 16 October 1985, attendance 100,000
USSR (0)2 *(Cherenkov, Protasov)*
Eire (0)0
USSR: Dasayev; Morozov, Chivadze, Demianenko, Bubnov, Zavarov (Bessonov), Gotsmanov, Cherenkov, Aleinikov, Protasov, Blohkin (Kondratiev).
Eire: McDonagh; Hughton, Beglin (O'Callaghan), McCarthy, O'Leary, Brady, Waddock, Lawrenson, Cascarino, Stapleton, Grealish (Whelan).

Moscow, 30 October 1985, attendance 40,000
USSR (0)1 *(Kondratiev)*

Norway (0)0
USSR: Dasayev; Morozov, Chivadze, Demianenko, Bubnov, Zavarov, Gotsmanov, Cherenkov, Aleinikov (Bessonov), Protasov (Gavrilov), Kondratiev.
Norway: Thorstvedt; Henriksen, Kojedal, Hareide, Mordt, Davidsen, Herlovsen, Sundby, Andersen (Brandhaug), Okland, Thoresen.

Lucerne, 13 November 1985, attendance 4500
Switzerland (0)1 *(Matthey)*
Norway (1)1 *(Sundby)*
Switzerland: Engle; Schallibaum, Ludi, Egli, In-Albon, Hermann, Geiger, Matthey, Brigger, Bregy (Koller), Sulser (Cina).
Norway: Thorstvedt; Henriksen, Kojedal, Hareide, Mordt, Davidsen, Herlovsen, Ahlsen (Brandhaug), Sundby, Oekland (Andersen), Thoresen.

Dublin, 13 November 1985, attendance 12,000
Eire (1)1 *(Stapleton)*
Denmark (2)4 *(Elkjaer 2, Laudrup, Siveback)*
Eire: McDonagh; Lawrenson, Beglin, Moran, O'Leary, Brady, McGrath, Grealish (Byrne P.), Cascarino, Stapleton, Sheedy (Robinson).
Denmark: Rasmussen; Siveback, Busk, Olsen M.(Arnesen), Nielsen, Lerby (Bertelsen), Molby, Olsen J., Berggren, Elkjaer, Laudrup.

Final Table	P	W	D	L	F	A	Pts	GD
Denmark	8	5	1	2	17	6	11	+11
USSR	8	4	2	2	13	8	10	+5
Switzerland	8	2	4	2	5	10	8	−5
Eire	8	2	2	4	5	10	6	−5
Norway	8	1	3	4	4	10	5	−6

DENMARK AND USSR QUALIFY

GROUP 7
(Iceland, Scotland, Spain, Wales)

Reykjavik, 12 September 1984, attendance 14,500
Iceland (0)1 *(Bergs)*
Wales (0)0
Iceland: Sigurdsson; Thrainsson, Sveinsson, Bergs, Sigi Jonsson, Sigurvinsson, Edvaldsson, Thorbjornsson, Gudlaugsson, Petursson, Gratarsson.

Wales: Southall; Slatter, Hopkins, Ratcliffe, Jones, Davies G. (Charles), Jackett, Thomas, Davies A., James, Hughes.

Seville, 17 October 1984, attendance 42,500
Spain (1)3 *(Rincon, Carrasco, Butragueno)*
Wales (0)0
Spain: Arconada; Goicoechea, Maceda, Camacho, Senor, Victor, Francisco (Roberto), Gordillo, Carrasco, Butragueno, Rincon (Julio Alberto).
Wales: Southall; Slatter, Charles, Ratcliffe, Jackett, Phillips, James, Nicholas, Thomas (Vaughan), Hughes, Curtis.

Hampden Park, 17 October 1984, attendance 52,829
Scotland (2)3 *(McStay 2, Nicholas)*
Iceland (0)0
Scotland: Leighton; Nicol, Albiston, Souness, McLeish, Miller, Dalglish (Nicholas), McStay, Johnston, Bett, Cooper.
Iceland: Sigurdsson; Thrainsson, Edvaldsson, Bergs, Margeirsson, Sigi Jonsson, Gudlaugsson, Gudjohnsen, Petursson, Sigurvinsson, Sveinsson.

Hampden Park, 14 November 1984, attendance 74,299
Scotland (2)3 *(Johnston 2, Dalglish)*
Spain (0)1 *(Goicoechea)*
Scotland: Leighton; Nicol, Albiston, Souness, McLeish, Miller, Dalglish, McStay, Johnston, Bett, Cooper.
Spain: Arconada; Urquiaga, Camacho, Maceda, Goicoechea, Gordillo, Senor, Victor, Santillana, Urtubi (Carrasco), Rincon (Butragueno).

Cardiff, 14 November 1984, attendance 10,506
Wales (1)2 *(Thomas, Hughes)*
Iceland (0)1 *(Petursson)*
Wales: Southall; Slatter, Charles (Hopkins), Ratcliffe, Jackett, Phillips, James, Davies G., Thomas, Hughes, Rush.
Iceland: Sigurdsson; Thrainsson, Sigi Jonsson, Bergs, Gretarsson (Eidsson), Saevar Jonsson, Gudjohnsen, Petursson, Margeirsson (Gislasson), Thorbjornsson, Sveinsson.

Seville, 27 February 1985, attendance 70,000
Spain (0)1 *(Clos)*
Scotland (0)0
Spain: Arconada; Gerardo, Goicoechea, Maceda, Camacho, Senor, Roberto, Gallego (Julio Alberto), Gordillo, Clos, Butragueno.
Scotland: Leighton; Gough, Miller, McLeish, Albiston,

McStay (Strachan), Bett, Souness, Cooper, Archibald (Nicholas), Johnston.

Hampden Park, 27 March 1985, attendance 62,424
Scotland (0)0
Wales (1)1 *(Rush)*
Scotland: Leighton; Nicol, Albiston (Hansen), McLeish, Miller, McStay (Nicholas), Dalglish, Souness, Cooper, Bett, Johnston.
Wales: Southall; Slatter, Jackett, Ratcliffe, Jones, Phillips, James, Nicholas, Rush, Thomas, Hughes.

Wrexham, 30 April 1985, attendance 23,494
Wales (1)3 *(Rush 2, Hughes)*
Spain (0)0
Wales: Southall; Slatter, Van den Hauwe, Ratcliffe, Jackett, James, Nicholas, Phillips, Thomas, Hughes, Rush.
Spain: Arconada; Gerardo, Liceranzu, Maceda, Goicoechea, Julio Alberto, Victor, Gallego (Caldere), Gordillo, Rojo, Rincon (Clos).

Reykjavik, 28 May 1985, attendance 16,000
Iceland (0)0
Scotland (0)1 *(Bett)*
Iceland: Gudmundsson; Thrainsson, Sigi Jonsson (Torfasson), Bergs, Petursson, Saevar Jonsson, Gudlaugsson, Edvaldsson, Thordarsson (Gretarsson), Thorbjornsson, Sveinsson.
Scotland: Leighton; Gough, Malpas, Aitken, McLeish, Miller, Strachan, Souness, Gray (Archibald), Bett, Sharp.

Reykjavik, 12 June 1985, attendance 10,400
Iceland (1)1 *(Thordarsson)*
Spain (0)2 *(Sarabia, Alonso)*
Iceland: Sigurdsson; Thrainsson, Bergs, Sigi Jonsson, Gudlaugsson, Torfasson, Edvaldsson, Margeirsson, Porbjorsson, Gretarsson, Pordarsson (Sveinsson) (Gislasson).
Spain: Zubizarreta; Gerardo, Goicoechea, Maceda, Camacho, Victor, Quique, Gallego (Caldere), Rincon (Sarabia), Santillana, Marcos.

Cardiff, 10 September 1985, attendance 39,500
Wales (1)1 *(Hughes)*
Scotland (0)1 *(Cooper, pen)*
Wales: Southall; Jones J., Van den Hauwe, Ratcliffe, Jackett, James R. (Lovell), Phillips, Nicholas, Thomas (Blackmore), Rush, Hughes.

Scotland: Leighton (Rough); Gough, Malpas, Aitken, McLeish, Miller, Nicol, Strachan (Cooper), Sharp, Bett, Speedie.

Seville, 25 September 1985, attendance 55,000
Spain (1)2 *(Rincon, Gordillo)*
Iceland (1)1 *(Thorbjornsson)*
Spain: Zubizarreta; Gerardo, Camacho, Maceda, Goicoechea, Gordillo (Julio Alberto), Rincon (Marcos), Victor, Butragueno, Gallego, Rojo.
Iceland: Sigurdsson; Thrainsson, Edvaldsson, Sav Jonsson, Thorbjornsson (Gislasson), Gudlaugsson, Sigi Jonsson, Gudjohnsson, Thordarsson, Sigurvinsson, Petursson, (Gretarsson).

Final Table	P	W	D	L	F	A	Pts	GD
Spain	6	4	0	2	9	8	8	+1
Scotland	6	3	1	2	8	4	7	+4
Wales	6	3	1	2	7	6	7	+1
Iceland	6	1	0	5	4	10	2	−6

SPAIN QUALIFY, SCOTLAND PLAY OFF

EUROPEAN PLAY-OFF
First Leg in Brussels, October 16 1985, attendance 36,500
Belgium (1)1 *(Vercauteren)*
Netherlands (0)0
Belgium: Pfaff; Gerets, Grun (Czerniatynski), Franky Van der Elst, Renquin, Leo Van der Elst, Ceulemans, Vandereycken, Vercauteren, Vandenbergh, Claesen.
Netherlands: Van Breukelen; Wijnstekers, Spelbos, Van de Korput, Van Tiggelen, Gullit (Ophof), Rijkaard, Van der Kerkhof W., Van Basten, Kieft, De Wit (Tahamata).

Second Leg in Rotterdam, 20 November 1985, attendance 55,000
Netherlands (0)2 *(Houtman, De Wit)*
Belgium (0)1 *(Grun)*
Netherlands: Van Breukelen; Wijnstekers, Spelbos, Van de Korput (Van Loen), Van Tiggelen, Gullit, Rojkaard, Valke, Tahamata (Silooy), Houtman, De Wit.
Belgium: Pfaff; Gerets, Broos, Franky Van der Elst (Veyt), De Wolf, Vercauteren, Vandereycken, Leo Van der Elst (Grun), Clijsters, Demet, Ceulemans.

BELGIUM QUALIFY

CONMEBOL

GROUP 1
(Argentina, Colombia, Peru, Venezuela)

Bogota, 26 May 1985, attendance 53,000
Colombia (1)1 *(Prince)*
Peru (0)0
Colombia: Zape; Prince, Luna, Molina, Porras, Sarmiento, Morales (Herrera), Ortiz, Barrios (Quinones), Iguaran, Lugo.
Peru: Acasuzo; Diaz, Rojas, Requena (Castullo), Olaechea, Cueto, Chirinos, Velasquez, Barbadillo, Navarro, Oblitas (Uribe).

San Cristobal, 26 May 1985, attendance 30,000
Venezuela (1)2 *(Torres, Marquez)*
Argentina (2)3 *(Maradona 2, Passarella)*
Venezuela: Baena; Acosta, Torres, Simonelli, Campos, Sanchez, Cedeno (Maldonado), Mendez (Marquez), Febles, Anor, Carrero.
Argentina: Fillol; Passarella, Clausen, Trossero, Garre, Russo, Ponce, Burruchaga, Gareca (Marcico), Maradona, Pasculli (Valdano).

Bogota, 2 June 1985, attendance 53,000
Colombia (0)1 *(Prince)*
Argentina (1)3 *(Pasculli 2, Burruchaga)*
Colombia: Zape (Gomez); Molina, Gil, Prince, Lopez, Morales, Sarmiento, Quinones (Herrera), Cordoba, Ortiz, Iguaran.
Argentina: Fillol; Passarella, Clausen, Trossero, Garre, Giusti, Russo, Maradona, Trobbiani (Barbas), Burruchaga, Pasculli.

San Cristobal, 2 June 1985, attendance 20,000
Venezuela (0)0
Peru (0)1 *(Uribe)*
Venezuela: Baena; Becerra, Torres, Acosta, Campos, Carrero (Cedeno), Sanchez, Maldonado (Febles), Marquez, Anor, Mendez.
Peru: Acasuzo; Olaechea, Rojas, Chirinos, Gastulo, Cueto, Velasquez, Uribe, Barbadillo, Navarro, Oblitas.

Buenos Aires, 9 June 1985, attendance 55,000
Argentina (1)3 *(Russo, Clausen, Maradona)*
Venezuela (0)0

Argentina: Fillol; Passarella, Clausen, Trossero, Garre, Giusti, Russo, Maradona, Valdano, Pasculli, Burruchaga.
Venezuela: Baena; Torres, Acosta, Bicerra, Campos, Sanchez, Ellie (Mendez) (Nada), Cedeno, Carrero, Anor, Febles.

Lima, 9 June 1985, attendance 40,000
Peru (0)0
Colombia (0)0
Peru: Acasuzo; Olaechea, Rojas, Chirinos, Gastulo, Cueto, Diaz, Uribe, Barbadillo (Malasquez), Navarro, Hirano (Larosa).
Colombia: Gomez; Molina, Gil, Prince, Lopez, Morales, Sarmiento, Quinones, Cordoba (Borras), Ortiz, Iguaran (Lugo).

Buenos Aires, 16 June 1985, attendance 35,000
Argentina (1)1 *(Valdano)*
Colombia (0)0
Argentina: Fillol; Clausen, Passarella, Trossero, Garre, Giusti, Russo (Barbas), Burruchaga, Pasculli, Maradona, Valdano.
Colombia: Gomez; Luna, Soto, Prince, Porras, Sarmiento (Quinones), Morales, Lugo (Ricuarte), Cordoba, Ortiz, Iguaran.

Lima, 16 June 1985, attendance 10,000
Peru (2)4 *(Barbadillo, Navarro, Hirano, Cueto)*
Venezuela (1)1 *(Mendez)*
Peru: Acasuzo; Rojas, Diaz, Olaechea, Gastulo, Velasquez, Cueto, Malasquez (Hirano), Barbadillo, Navarro (La Rosa), Oblitas.
Venezuela: Baena; Torres, Acosta, Simonetti, Sanchez, Campos, Landaeta, Mendez (Carrero), Marquez (Maldonado), Anor, Febles.

Lima, 23 June 1985, attendance 43,000
Peru (1)1 *(Oblitas)*
Argentina (0)0
Peru: Acasuzo; Olaechea, Rojas, Velasquez, Gastulo, Cueto, Diaz, Reyna (Chirinos), Barbadillo (Uribe), Navarro, Oblitas.
Argentina: Fillol; Passarella, Clausen (Ruggieri), Trossero, Garre, Giusti, Russo (Pasculli), Barbas, Maradona, Valdano, Burruchaga.

San Cristobal, 23 June 1985, attendance 25,000
Venezuela (1)2 *(Cedeno, Anor)*
Colombia (1)2 *(Ortiz, Herrera)*

Venezuela: Baena; Landaeta (Maldonado), Acosta, Simonelli, Sanchez, Campos, Deceno (Carrero), Torres, Mendez, Anor, Marquez.
Colombia: Gomez; Porras, Luna, Prince, Soto, Morales, Sarmiento, Quinones (Herrera), Barrios, Ortiz, Lugo (Reyes).

Buenos Aires, 30 June 1985, attendance 75,000
Argentina (1)2 *(Pasculli, Gareca)*
Peru (2)2 *(Velasquez, Barbadillo)*
Argentina: Fillol; Passarella, Camino (Gareca), Trossero, Garre, Giusti, Barbas (Trobbiani), Maradona, Valdano, Pasculli, Burruchaga.
Peru: Acasuzo; Olaechea, Rojas, Velasquez, Gastulo, Cueto, Diaz, Reyna (Chirino), Barbadillo, Navarro (Uribe), Oblitas.

Bogota, 30 June 1985, attendance 10,000
Colombia (2)2 *(Cordoba, Herrera)*
Venezuela (0)0
Colombia: Navarro; Escobar, Reyes, Luna, Porras, Sarmiento, Herrera (Barrios), Ricuarte (Caudrado), Cordoba, Ortiz, Lugo.
Venezuela: Nicolai; Torres, Acosta, Gonzalez, Betancour, Carrera (Ellie), Sanchez, Maldonado, Cedeno (Mendez), Marquez, Febles.

Final Table	P	W	D	L	F	A	Pts	GD
Argentina	6	4	1	1	12	6	9	+6
Peru	6	3	2	1	8	4	8	£4
Colombia	6	2	2	2	6	6	6	0
Venezuela	6	0	1	5	5	15	1	−10

ARGENTINA QUALIFY, PERU AND COLOMBIA PLAY OFF

GROUP 2
(Chile, Ecuador, Uruguay)

Quito, 3 March 1985, attendance 56,000
Ecuador (1)1 *(Maldonado, pen)*
Chile (1)1 *(Letelier)*
Ecuador: Rodriguez; Perlaza, Quinonez H., Armas, Maldonado, Hurtado, Villafuerte (Cuvi), De Negri, Baldeon, Benitez, Moreno (Quinonez L.)
Chile: Rojas; Garrido, Soto, Hormazabel, Gomez, Hisis, Mardones (Herrera), Aravena, Yanez, Neira, Letelier.

Montevideo, 10 March 1985, attendance 70,000
Uruguay (1)2 *(Aguilera, Ramos)*
Ecuador (0)1 *(Cuvi)*
Uruguay: Rodriguez; Montelongo, Gutierrez, Acevedo, Martinez, Barrios (Ramos), Bossio, Francescoli, Aguilera, Nadal, Da Silva (Cabrera).
Ecuador: Rodriguez; Perlaza, Klinger, Armas, Maldonado, Hurtado, De Negri, Villafuerte, Baldeon (Benitez), Quinonez L. (Vazquez), Cuvi.

Santiago, 17 March 1985, attendance 70,000
Chile (4)6 *(Puebla, Caszely 2, Hisis, Aravena 2)*
Ecuador (2)2 *(Baldeon 2)*
Chile: Rojas; Garrido, Gomez, Soto, Hormazabel, Hisis, Neira, Aravena, Rubio (Herrera), Caszely (Mardones), Puebla.
Ecuador: Rodriguez; Perlaza, Klinger, Armas, Maldonado, De Negri, Hurtado, Villafuerte, Baldeon (Benitez), Quinonez L. (Vazquez), Cuvi.

Santiago, 24 March 1985, attendance 80,000
Chile (1)2 *(Rubio, Aravena)*
Uruguay (0)0
Chile: Rojas; Garrido, Gomez, Soto, Hormazabel, Neira, Hisis, Aravena, Rubio, Caszely, Puebla.
Uruguay: Rodriguez; Montelongo, Acevedo, Gutierrez, Diogo, Barrios (Nadal), Bossio, Santin, Francescoli, Aguilera, Cabrera.

Quito, 31 March 1985, attendance 30,000
Ecuador (0)0
Uruguay (2)2 *(Saralegui, Francescoli)*
Ecuador: Rodriguez; Capurro, Armas, Klinger, Maldonado, Villafuerte, Hurtado, De Negri, Baldeon, Quinonez L., Cuvi.
Uruguay: Rodriguez; Diogo, Gutierrez, Pereira, Batista, Saralegui, Bossio, Santin, Francescoli, Ramos, Nadal (Da Silva).

Montevideo, 7 April 1985, attendance 80,000
Uruguay (1)2 *(Batista, Ramos)*
Chile (1)1 *(Aravena)*
Uruguay: Rodriguez; Montelongo, Gutierrez, Pereira, Batista, Saralegui, Bossio, Santin, Ramos (Cabrera), Francescoli, Nadal (Da Silva).
Chile: Rojas; Valenzuela, Tabilo, Soto, Gomez (Letelier), Hormazabel, Neira, Hisis, Aravena, Rubio, Caszely.

Final Table

	P	W	D	L	F	A	Pts	GD
Uruguay	4	3	0	1	6	4	6	+2
Chile	4	2	1	1	10	5	5	+5
Ecuador	4	0	1	3	4	11	1	−7

URUGUAY QUALIFY, CHILE PLAY OFF

GROUP 3
(Bolivia, Brazil, Paraguay)

Santa Cruz, 26 May 1985, attendance 20,000
Bolivia (1)1 *(Rojas)*
Paraguay (0)1 *(Nunez)*
Bolivia: Galarza; Coimbra, Herrera, Vaca, Saldias, Melgar, Castill, Romero (Borja), Paniagua R., Sanchez, Rojas (Paniagua D.).
Paraguay: Almeida; Delgado, Caceres, Zavala, Torales, Chilavert (Guasch), Benitez, Nunez, Villabla, Ferreira, Mendoza (Mora).

Santa Cruz, 2 June 1985, attendance 25,000
Bolivia (0)0
Brazil (0)2 *(Casagrande, Noro, og)*
Bolivia: Galarza; Coimbra, Herrera, Vaca (Noro), Perez, Castillo, Sanchez, Melgar, Romero, Panigua R., Rojas.
Brazil: Carlos; Leandro, Oscar, Edinho, Junior, Cerezo, Socrates, Zico, Renato, Casagrande (Careca), Eder.

Asuncion, 9 June 1985, attendance 60,000
Paraguay (2)3 *(Mendoza, Jacquet, Romero)*
Bolivia (0)0
Paraguay: Almeida; Zavala, Caceres (Torales), Delgado, Jacquet, Romero, Benitez, Funes, Villabla E., Ferreira, Mendoza (Villabla J.)
Bolivia: Galarza; Avila, Coimbra, Noro, Perez, Melgar, Casperdes (Sanchez), Castillo, Paniagua, Romero, Rojas (Borja).

Asuncion, 16 June 1985, attendance 55,000
Paraguay (0)0
Brazil (1)2 *(Zico, Casagrande)*
Paraguay: Almeida; Zavala, Caceres, Delgado, Jacquet, Romero, Benitez (Villabla E.), Nunes, Villabla J., Ferreira, Mendoza.
Brazil: Carlos; Leandro, Oscar, Edinho, Junior, Socrates, Zico, Toninho, Casagrande, Renato (Alemao), Eder.

Rio de Janeiro, 23 June 1985, attendance 150,000
Brazil (1)1 *(Socrates)*
Paraguay (1)1 *(Romero)*
Brazil: Carlos; Edinho, Leando, Oscar, Junior, Cerezo, Socrates, Zico, Renato, Casagrande, Eder (Alemao).
Paraguay: Almeida; Zabala, Caceres, Delgado, Jacquet (Torales), Benitez, Sandoval, Romero, Ferreira, Nunez, Mendoza.

Sao Paulo, 30 June 1985, attendance 90,709
Brazil (1)1 *(Careca)*
Bolivia (0)1 *(Sanchez)*
Brazil: Carlos; Edinho, Edson, Oscar, Junior, Cerezo, Socrates, Zico, Renato, Careca, Eder.
Bolivia: Galarza; Spinosa, Avila, Saldias, Coimbra, Castillo, Melgar, Paniagua R. (Paniagua D.), Romero, Sanchez, Rojas (Borja).

Final Table	P	W	D	L	F	A	Pts	GD
Brazil	4	2	2	0	6	2	6	+4
Paraguay	4	1	2	1	5	4	4	+1
Bolivia	4	0	2	2	2	7	2	−5

BRAZIL QUALIFY, PARAGUAY PLAY OFF

CONMEBOL PLAY-OFF MATCHES

Asuncion, 27 October 1985, attendance 60,000
Paraguay (2)3 *(Hicks, Romero pen, Cabanas)*
Colombia (0)0
Paraguay: Fernandez; Torales, Delgado, Zavala, Schettina (Caceres), Romero, Nunes, Canete, Ferreira, Hicks, Cabanas (Guasch).
Colombia: Navarro Montoya; Polo, Prince (Ampudia), Escobar, Hoyos, Murillo, Morales, Hernandez (Valderrama), Gomes, Ortiz, Castano.

Santiago, 27 October 1985, attendance 40,000
Chile (3)4 *(Aravena 2, 1 pen, Rubio, Hisis)*
Peru (1)2 *(Navarro 2)*
Chile: Rojas; Garrido (Espinoza), Soto, Gomez, Hormazabal, Hisis, Neira (Leppe), Aravena, Yanez, Rubio, Puebla.
Peru: Acasuzo (Quiroga); Rojas, Diaz, Requena, Gastulo, Olaechea, Velasquez, Cueto (La Rosa), Uribe, Navarro, Barbadillo.

Cali, 3 November 1985, attendance 10,000
Colombia (0)2 *(Angulo, Ortiz)*
Paraguay (0)1 *(Ferreira)*
Colombia: Navarro Montoya; Luna, Prince, Alvaro Escobar, Ambuila, Murillo, Alex Escobar, Valderrama, De Avila (Lugo), Ortiz, Castano (Angulo).
Paraguay: Fernandez; Torales, Delgado, Zabala, Schettina, Romero, Nunes, Canete, Ferreira, Hicks (Mendoza), Cabanas (Guasch).

Lima, 3 November 1985, attendance 45,000
Peru (0)0
Chile (0)1 *(Aravena)*
Peru: Quiroga; Rojas, Requena, Duarte, Gastulo, Velasquez, Cueto (Malasquez), Uribe, Barbadillo, Navarro, Oblitas (Hirano).
Chile: Rojas; Garrido, Soto, Gomez, Hormazabal, Hisis, Leppe, Aravena, Puebla, Yanez (Espinoza), Rubio.

Play-Off Final
First Leg in Asuncion, 10 November 1985, attendance 35,000
Paraguay (1)3 *(Cabanas 2, Delgado)*
Chile (0)0
Paraguay: Fernandez; Torales, Delgado (Caceres), Zabala, Schettina, Romero, Chilavert, Canete, Ferreira, Hicks (Samaniego), Cabanas.
Chile: Rojas; Garrido, Soto, Gomez, Hormazabal, Leppe, Hisis, Aravena, Rubio, Letelier, Puebla.

Second Leg in Santiago, 17 November 1985, attendance 70,000
Chile (1)2 *(Rubio, Munoz)*
Paraguay (2)2 *(Schettina, Romero)*
Chile: Rojas; Espinoza, Herrera (Letelier), Soto, Hormazabal, Hisis, Neira, Aravena, Yanez, Rubio (Munoz), Puebla.
Paraguay: Fernandez; Torales, Zabala, Schettina, Delgado, Cabral, Chilavert, Romero (Guasch), Canete, Ferreira, Cabanas.

PARAGUAY QUALIFY

CONCACAF

First Round *(Cup System)*

Group 1
29.7.84	San Salvador	El Salvador (4)5, Puerto Rico (0)0
5.8.84	San Juan	Puerto Rico (0)0, San Salvador (2)3
	Canada v Jamaica	*– Jamaica expelled 14.3.84*
29.9.84	Curacao	Neth. Antilles (0)0, USA (0)0
6.10.84	St Louis	USA (0)4, Neth. Antilles (0)0

El Salvador, Canada, USA qualified for Second Round

Group 2
	Barbados v Costa Rica	*– Barbados withdrew 7.3.84*
15.6.84	Colon	Panama (0)0, Honduras (2)3
24.6.84	Tegucigalpa	Honduras (0)1, Panama (0)0
	Guatemala	*– walkover*

Costa Rica, Honduras, Guatemala qualified for Second Round

Group 3
	Trinidad/Tobago v Grenada	*– Grenada withdrew 24.2.84*
4.8.84	Port-au-Prince	Antigua (0)0, Haiti (2)4
7.8.84	Port-au-Prince	Haiti (1)1, Antigua (1)2
15.8.84	Paramaribo	Surinam (1)1, Guyana (0)0
29.8.84	Georgetown	Guyana (1)1, Surinam (0)1

Trinidad/Tobago, Haiti, Surinam qualified for Second Round

Second Round *(League System)*

Group 1
(El Salvador, Honduras, Surinam)
24.2.85	San Salvador	Surinam (0)0, El Salvador (1)3
27.2.85	San Salvador	El Salvador (0)3, Surinam (0)0
3.3.85	Tegucigalpa	Surinam (1)1, Honduras (1)1
6.3.85	Tegucigalpa	Honduras (1)2, Surinam (0)1
10.3.85	San Salvador	El Salvador (0)1, Honduras (1)2
14.3.85	Tegucigalpa	Honduras (0)0, El Salvador (0)0

Final Table	P	W	D	L	F	A	Pts	GD
Honduras	4	2	2	0	5	3	6	+2
El Salvador	4	2	1	1	7	2	5	+5
Surinam	4	0	1	3	2	9	1	−7

Honduras qualified for Third Round

Group 2

13.4.85	Vancouver	Canada (2)2, Haiti (0)0
20.4.85	Vancouver	Canada (2)2, Guatemala (0)1
26.4.85	Port-au-Prince	Haiti (0)0, Guatemala (0)1
5.5.85	Guatemala	Guatemala (1)1, Canada (1)1
8.5.85	Port-au-Prince	Haiti (0)0, Canada (1)2
15.5.85	Guatemala	Guatemala (0)4, Haiti (0)0

Final Table	P	W	D	L	F	A	Pts	GD
Canada	4	3	1	0	7	2	7	+5
Guatemala	4	2	1	1	7	3	5	+4
Haiti	4	0	0	4	0	9	0	−9

(Canada qualified for Third Round)

Group 3

(USA, Costa Rica, Trinidad & Tobago)

24.4.85	San Jose	Trinidad/Tobago (0)0, Costa Rica (1)3
28.4.85	San Jose	Costa Rica (1)1, Trinidad/Tobago (0)1
15.5.85	St Louis	Trinidad/Tobago (1)1, USA (1)2
19.5.85	Los Angeles	USA (1)1, Trinidad/Tobago (0)0
26.5.85	San Jose	Costa Rica (1)1, USA (1)1
31.5.85	Los Angeles	USA (0)0, Costa Rica (1)1

Final Table	P	W	D	L	F	A	Pts	GD
Costa Rica	4	2	2	0	6	2	6	+4
USA	4	2	1	1	4	3	5	+1
Trinidad/Tobago	4	0	1	3	2	7	1	−5

(Costa Rica qualified for Third Round)

Third Round *(League System)*

11.8.85	San Jose	Costa Rica (1)2, Honduras (2)2
17.8.85	Toronto	Canada (0)1, Costa Rica (1)1
25.8.85	Tegucigalpa	Honduras (0)0, Canada (0)1
1.9.85	San Jose	Costa Rica (0)0, Canada (0)0
8.9.85	Tegucigalpa	Honduras (1)3, Costa Rica (1)1
14.9.85	St John's	Canada (1)2, Honduras (0)1

Final Table	P	W	D	L	F	A	Pts	GD
Canada	4	2	2	0	4	2	6	+2
Honduras	4	1	1	2	6	6	3	0
Costa Rica	4	0	3	1	4	6	3	−2

CANADA AND MEXICO (AS HOSTS) QUALIFY

ASIA

First Round *(League System)*

Group 1
Sub-Group 1A *(Saudi Arabia, United Arab Emirates – Oman withdrew)*
12.4.85 Riyadh   Saudi Arabia (0)0, UAE (0)0
19.4.85 Dubai   UAE (1)1, Saudi Arabia (0)0
(UAE qualified for Second Round)

Sub-Group 1B *(Iraq, Qatar, Jordan – Lebanon withdrew)*
15.3.85 Amman   Jordan (0)1, Qatar (0)0
29.3.85 Amman   Jordan (0)2, Iraq (1)3
5.4.85 Doha   Qatar (1)3, Iraq (0)0
12.4.85 Doha   Qatar (0)2, Jordan (0)0
19.4.85 Kuwait   Iraq (0)2, Jordan (0)0
5.5.85 Calcutta   Iraq (1)2, Qatar (1)1

Final Table	P	W	D	L	F	A	Pts	GD
Iraq	4	3	0	1	7	6	6	+1
Qatar	4	2	0	2	6	3	4	+3
Jordan	4	1	0	3	3	7	2	−4

(Iraq qualified for Second Round)

Group 2
Sub-Group 2A *(Kuwait, Yemen AR, Syria)*
22.3.85 Damascus   Syria (1)1, Kuwait (0)0
29.3.85 Sana'a   Yemen AR (0)0, Syria (0)1
5.4.85 Kuwait   Kuwait (1)5, Yemen AR (0)0
12.4.85 Kuwait   Kuwait (0)0, Syria (0)0
19.4.85 Damascus   Syria (2)3, Yemen AR (0)0
26.4.85 Sana'a   Yemen AR (0)1, Kuwait (2)3

Final Table	P	W	D	L	F	A	Pts	GD
Syria	4	3	1	0	5	0	7	+5
Kuwait	4	2	1	1	8	2	5	+6
Yemen AR	4	0	0	4	1	12	0	−11

(Syria qualified for Second Round)

Sub-Group 2B *(Bahrain, Yemen PDR – Iran excluded)*
29.3.85 Aden   Yemen PDR (0)1, Bahrain (2)4
12.4.85 Bahrain   Bahrain (0)3, Yemen PDR (1)3
(Bahrain qualified for Second Round)

Group 3
Sub-Group 3A *(Malaysia, Nepal, South Korea)*
2.3.85   Kathmandu   Nepal (0)0, South Korea (1)2
10.3.85 Kuala Lumpur   Malaysia (0)1, South Korea (0)0
16.3.85 Kathmandu   Nepal (0)0, Malaysia (0)0
31.3.85 Kuala Lumpur   Malaysia (5)5, Nepal (0)0
6.4.85   Seoul   South Korea (3)4, Nepal (0)0
19.5.85 Seoul   South Korea (2)2, Malaysia (0)0

Final Table	P	W	D	L	F	A	Pts	GD
South Korea	4	3	0	1	8	1	6	+7
Malaysia	4	2	1	1	6	2	5	+4
Nepal	4	0	1	3	0	11	1	−11

(South Korea qualified for Second Round)

Sub-Group 3B *(Thailand, India, Bangladesh, Indonesia)*
15.3.85 Jakarta   Indonesia (0)1, Thailand (0)0
18.3.85 Jakarta   Indonesia (0)2, Bangladesh (0)0
21.3.85 Jakarta   Indonesia (1)2, India (1)1
23.3.85 Bangkok   Thailand (1)3, Bangladesh (0)0
26.3.85 Bangkok   Thailand (0)0, India (0)0
29.3.85 Bangkok   Thailand (0)0, Indonesia (1)1
30.3.85 Dhaka   Bangladesh (1)1, India (1)2
2.4.85   Dhaka   Bangladesh (0)2, Indonesia (1)1
5.4.85   Dhaka   Bangladesh (0)1, Thailand (0)0
6.4.85   Calcutta   India (0)1, Indonesia (1)1
9.4.85   Calcutta   India (0)1, Thailand (0)1
12.4.85 Calcutta   India (1)2, Bangladesh (1)1

Final Table	P	W	D	L	F	A	Pts	GD
Indonesia	6	4	1	1	8	4	9	+4
India	6	2	3	1	7	6	7	+1
Thailand	6	1	2	3	4	4	4	0
Bangladesh	6	2	0	4	5	10	4	−5

(Indonesia qualified for Second Round)

Group 4
Sub-Group 4B *(China PR, Hong Kong, Macao, Brunei)*
17.2.85 Macao   Macao (0)2, Brunei (0)0
17.2.85 Hong Kong   Hong Kong (0)0, China PR (0)0
20.2.85 Macao   Macao (0)0, China PR (1)4
23.2.85 Hong Kong   Hong Kong (3)8, Brunei (0)0
26.2.85 Macao   China PR (4)8, Brunei (0)0
1.3.85   Hong Kong   Brunei (0)0, China PR (2)4
6.4.85   Band.S.B.   Brunei (1)1, Hong Kong (3)5

155

13.4.85	Band.S.B.	Brunei (0)1, Macao (0)2
28.4.85	Macao	Macao (0)0, Hong Kong (0)2
4.5.85	Hong Kong	Hong Kong (0)2, Macao (0)0
12.5.85	Beijing	China PR (3)6, Macao (0)0
19.5.85	Beijing	China PR (1)1, Hong Kong (1)2

Final Table	P	W	D	L	F	A	Pts	GD
Hong Kong	6	5	1	0	19	2	11	+17
China PR	6	4	1	1	23	2	9	+21
Macao	6	2	0	4	4	15	4	−11
Brunei	6	0	0	6	2	29	0	−27

(Hong Kong qualified for Second Round)

Sub-Group 4B *(Japan, North Korea, Singapore)*

19.1.85	Singapore	Singapore (1)1, North Korea (0)1
23.2.85	Singapore	Singapore (1)1, Japan (1)3
21.3.85	Tokyo	Japan (1)1, North Korea (0)0
30.4.85	Pyongyang	North Korea (0)0, Japan (0)0
18.5.85	Tokyo	Japan (0)5, Singapore (0)0
25.5.85	Pyongyang	North Korea (2)2, Singapore (0)0

Final Table	P	W	D	L	F	A	Pts	GD
Japan	4	3	1	0	9	1	7	+8
North Korea	4	1	2	1	3	2	4	+1
Singapore	4	0	1	3	2	11	1	−9

(Japan qualified for Second Round)

Second Round *(Cup System)*

20.9.85	Dubai	UAE(1)2, Iraq (1)3
27.9.85	Taif	Iraq (0)1, UAE (1)2
6.9.85	Bahrain	Bahrain (1)1, Syria (0)1
20.9.85	Damascus	Syria (1)1, Bahrain (0)0
21.7.85	Seoul	South Korea (0)2, Indonesia (0)0
30.7.85	Jakarta	Indonesia (0)1, South Korea (3)4
11.8.85	Kobe	Japan (2)3, Hong Kong (0)0
22.9.85	Hong Kong	Hong Kong (0)1, Japan (1)2

(Iraq, Japan, South Korea and Syria qualified for Third Round)

Third Round *(Cup System)*

15.11.85	Damascus	Syria (0)0, Iraq (0)0
29.11.85	Taif	Iraq (1)3, Syria (0)1
26.10.85	Tokyo	Japan (1)1, South Korea (2)2
3.11.85	Seoul	South Korea (0)1, Japan (0)0

IRAQ AND SOUTH KOREA QUALIFY

AFRICA

First Round *(Cup System)*

28.8.84	Cairo	Egypt (1)1, Zimbabwe (0)0
30.9.84	Harare	Zimbabwe (1)1, Egypt (1)1
13.10.84	Nairobi	Kenya (1)2, Ethiopia (1)1
28.10.84	Addis Ababa	Ethiopia (2)3, Kenya (0)3
15.7.84	Curecipe	Mauritius (0)0, Malawi (1)1
28.7.84	Lilongwe	Malawi (1)4, Mauritius (0)0
29.7.84	Ndola	Zambia (1)3, Uganda (0)0
25.8.84	Kampala	Uganda (0)1, Zambia (0)0
		Madagascar v Lesotho – *Lesotho refused to play and were excluded*
13.10.84	Mwanza	Tanzania (1)1, Sudan (0)1
27.10.84	Khartoum	Sudan (0)0, Tanzania (0)0
30.6.84	Freetown	Sierra Leone (0)0, Morocco (0)1
15.7.84	Rabat	Morocco (1)4, Sierra Leone (0)0
		Libya v Niger – *Niger withdrew 8.10.84*
28.10.84	Cotonou	Benin (0)0, Tunisia (0)2
13.11.84	Tunis	Tunisia (2)4, Benin (0)0
		Togo v Guinea – *Togo withdrew 13.4.84*
21.10.84	Abidjan	Ivory Coast (0)4, Gambia (0)0
4.11.84	Banjul	Gambia (1)3, Ivory Coast (1)2
20.10.84	Lagos	Nigeria (2)3, Liberia (0)0
4.11.84	Monrovia	Liberia (0)0, Nigeria (1)1
1.7.84	Luanda	Angola (0)1, Senegal (0)0
15.7.84	Dakar	Senegal (1)1, Angola (0)0
		Angola won 4-3 on penalties

Second Round *(Cup System)*

(Algeria, Cameroon, Ghana qualified by walkover)

7.4.85	Lusaka	Zambia (4)4, Cameroon (0)1
21.4.85	Yaounde	Cameroon (1)1, Zambia (1)1
7.4.85	Rabat	Morocco (1)2, Malawi (0)0
21.4.85	Lilongwe	Malawi (0)0, Morocco (0)0
31.3.85	Luanda	Angola (0)0, Algeria (0)0
19.4.85	Algiers	Algeria (2)3, Angola (0)2
6.4.85	Nairobi	Kenya (0)0, Nigeria (2)3
20.4.85	Lagos	Nigeria (2)3, Kenya (1)1
5.4.85	Cairo	Egypt (0)1, Madagascar (0)0
21.4.85	Antananarivo	Madagascar (0)1, Egypt (0)0
		Egypt won 4-2 on penalties

10.2.85	Conakry	Guinea (1)1, Tunisia (0)0
24.2.85	Tunis	Tunisia (1)2, Guinea (0)0
22.2.85	Khartoum	Sudan (0)0, Libya (0)0
8.3.85	Tripoli	Libya (0)4, Sudan (0)0
7.4.85	Abidjan	Ivory Coast (0)0, Ghana (0)0
21.4.85	Accra	Ghana (0)2, Ivory Coast (0)0

Third Round *(Cup System)*

13.7.85	Algiers	Algeria (1)2, Zambia (0)0
28.7.85	Lusaka	Zambia (0)0, Algeria (0)1
14.7.85	Accra	Ghana (0)0, Libya (0)0
26.7.85	Benghazi	Libya (1)2, Ghana (0)0
6.7.85	Lagos	Nigeria (0)1, Tunisia (0)0
20.7.85	Tunis	Tunisia (2)2, Nigeria (0)0
12.7.85	Cairo	Egypt (0)0, Morocco (0)0
28.7.85	Casablanca	Morocco (1)2, Egypt (0)0

Fourth Round *Cup System)*

6.10.85	Tunis	Tunisia (1)1, Algeria (2)4
18.10.85	Algiers	Algeria (2)3, Tunisia (0)0
6.10.85	Rabat	Morocco (1)3, Libya (0)0
18.10.85	Benghazi	Libya (1)1, Morocco (0)0

ALGERIA AND MOROCCO QUALIFY

OCEANIA/ISRAEL

First Round *(League System)*

3.9.85	Tel Aviv	Israel (3)6, Chinese Taipei (0)0
8.9.85	Tel Aviv	Chinese Taipei (0)0, Israel (2)5
21.9.85	Auckland	New Zealand (0)0, Australia (0)0
5.10.85	Auckland	New Zealand (3)5, Chinese Taipei (1)1
8.10.85	Tel Aviv	Israel (0)1, Australia (0)2
12.10.85	Christchurch	Chinese Taipei (0)0, New Zealand (2)5
20.10.85	Melbourne	Australia (1)1, Israel (0)1
23.10.85	Adelaide	Australia (2)7, Chinese Taipei (0)0
26.10.85	Auckland	New Zealand (2)3, Israel (1)1
27.10.85	Sydney	Chinese Taipei (0)0, Australia (1)8
3.11.85	Sydney	Australia (1)2, New Zealand (0)0
10.11.85	Tel Aviv	Israel (0)3, New Zealand (0)0

Final Table

	P	W	D	L	F	A	Pts	GD
Australia	6	4	2	0	20	2	10	+18
Israel	6	3	1	2	17	6	7	+11
New Zealand	6	3	1	2	13	7	7	+6
Chinese Taipei	6	0	0	6	1	36	0	−35

Second Round *(Home and away play-off against the Runner-up of UEFA Group 7)*

Glasgow, 20 November 1985, attendance 60,000
Scotland (0)2 *(Cooper, McAvennie)*
Australia (0)0
Scotland: Leighton; Nicol, Malpas, Souness, McLeish, Miller, Dalglish (Sharp), Strachan, McAvennie, Aitken, Cooper.
Australia: Greedy; Davidson, Jennings, Yankos, Ratcliffe, O'Connor, Watson, Mitchell, Kosmina, Murphy, Crino.

Melbourne, 4 December 1985, attendance 29,500
Australia (0)0
Scotland (0)0
Australia: Greedy; Davidson, Jennings, Yankos, Ratcliffe, Dunn (Farina), Murphy, Crino (Odzakov), Kosmina, Mitchell, Patikas.
Scotland: Leighton; Gough, Malpas, McLeish, Miller, Aitken, McAvennie, Souness, McStay, Speedie (Sharp), Cooper.

SCOTLAND QUALIFY

159

CHAPTER THREE

MEXICO 86 – THE GAME PLAN

Introduction

The competition will start with the twenty-four finalists arranged in six groups of four, with each group based in a different geographical location. Within each group, each team will play each other team once in a league system, with two points for a win, one point for a draw, and goal difference separating teams on the same number of points. If goal differences are identical, the team scoring more goals will be given precedence. If the teams still cannot be separated by this method, provisions will have to made for play-offs where necessary.

These first phase matches will be played betwen 31 May and 13 June, and then the top two teams from each group go forward to the second phase of the tournament, which is a knock-out competition. In order to make up the numbers to sixteen for the eighth-finals, the four best third-placed teams, based on points, goal difference and number of goals scored, will also go through. In the game plan which follows, the first phase league matches are laid out for you and you will be able to fill in the results as the competition progresses and construct the league tables at the end of the group matches.

The structure of the eighth-finals is only partially predictable, as we do not yet know which of the six groups will send their third-placed teams through to this stage, but this will become clear once the first stage has been completed. You will notice that each of the eighth-final matches has a number in brackets at the end of the first line, and these numbers relate to the pairings in the quarter-finals, where the numbers have been inserted in a pre-ordained sequence. The same principle applies to the transfer of quarter-final winners through to the semi-finals, except that the letters A,B,C,D are used. In the game plan for the first stage, the team named first in each heading is the seeded team. The term 'BST' in the headings refers to the kick-off time of the matches in British Summer Time.

GROUP A
Mexico City and Puebla

Italy, Bulgaria, Argentina, South Korea

Date/BST	Venue	Match	H-T F-T
31.5/7pm	Azteca	Bulgaria v Italy	0-1 , 1-1

Scorers: _Altobelli , Sirakhov ._

| 2.6/7pm | Olympic 68 | Argentina v South Korea | 2-0 3-1 |

Scorers: _(A) Valdano (2)_

| 5.6/7pm | Puebla | Italy v Argentina | 1-1 1-1 |

Scorers: _Altobelli (pen), Maradona_

| 5.6/11pm | Olympic 68 | South Korea v Bulgaria | 0-1 1-1 |

Scorers: _____

| 10.6/7pm | Puebla | South Korea v Italy | ___ ___ |

Scorers: _____

| 10.6/7pm | Olympic 68 | Argentina v Bulgaria | ___ ___ |

Scorers: _____

Final Table	P	W	D	L	F	A	Pts	GD
A1_____								
A2_____								
A3_____								
A4_____								

GROUP B
Mexico City and Toluca

Mexico, Belgium, Paraguay, Iraq

Date/BST	Venue	Match	H-TF-T
3.6/7pm	Azteca	Belgium v Mexico	1212

*Scorers:*_____

| 4.6/7pm | Toluca | Paraguay v Iraq | 1010 |

*Scorers:*_____

| 7.6/7pm | Azteca | Mexico v Paraguay | 1011 |

*Scorers:*_____

| 8.6/7pm | Toluca | Iraq v Belgium | 02 |

*Scorers:*_____

| 11.6/7pm | Azteca | Iraq v Mexico | __ __ |

*Scorers:*_____

| 11.6/7pm | Toluca | Paraguay v Belgium | __ __ |

*Scorers:*_____

Final Table	P	W	D	L	F	A	Pts	GD
B1_____								
B2_____								
B3_____								
B4_____								

GROUP C
Leon and Irapuato

France, Canada, USSR, Hungary

Date/BST	Venue	Match	H-TF-T
1.6/11pm	Leon	Canada v France	0 0 0 - 1

Scorers: _Papin_ .

| 2.6/7pm | Irapuato | USSR v Hungary | 3 0 - 6 0 |

Scorers: _____

| 5.6/7pm | Leon | France v USSR | __ __ |

Scorers: _____

| 6.6./7pm | Irapuato | Hungary v Canada | __ __ |

Scorers: _____

| 9.6/7pm | Leon | Hungary v France | __ __ |

Scorers: _____

| 9.6./7pm | Irapuato | USSR v Canada | __ __ |

Scorers: _____

Final Table	P	W	D	L	F	A	Pts	GD
C1								
C2								
C3								
C4								

GROUP D
Guadalajara

Brazil, Spain, Algeria, Northern Ireland

Date/BST	Venue	Match	H-TF-T
1.6/7pm	Jalisco	Spain v Brazil	00 0-1

Scorers: Socrates

| 3.6/7pm | 3 de Marzo | Algeria v N.Ireland | 01 1 1 |

Scorers: Whiteside , Zidane

| 6.6./7pm | Jalisco | Brazil v Algeria | __ __ |

Scorers: _____

| 7.6/7pm | 3 de Marzo | N.Ireland v Spain | 02 1 2 |

Scorers: _____

| 12.6/7pm | Jalisco | N.Ireland v Brazil | __ __ |

Scorers: _____

| 12.6/7pm | 3 de Marzo | Algeria v Spain | __ __ |

Scorers: _____

Final Table	P	W	D	L	F	A	Pts	GD
D1 _____								
D2 _____								
D3 _____								
D4 _____								

GROUP E
Queretaro and Nezahualcoyotl

West Germany, Uruguay, Scotland, Denmark

Date/BST	Venue	Match	H-TF-T
4.6/7pm	Queretaro	Uruguay v West Germany	1011

Scorers: *A Mofs*

| 4.6./11pm | Neza 86 | Scotland v Denmark | 0001 |

Scorers: *Elkjear (57)*

| 8.6/7pm | Queretaro | West Germany v Scotland | 1021 |

Scorers: *Strachen, Voller,*

| 8.6/11pm | Neza 86 | Denmark v Uruguay | 2161 |

Scorers: *Elkjear (3), Laudrup, lerby, Olsen, Frasicsoli*

| 13.6/7pm | Queretaro | Denmark v West Germany | __ __ |

Scorers:_____

| 13.6/7pm | Neza 86 | Scotland v Uruguay | __ __ |

Scorers:_____

Final Table	P	W	D	L	F	A	Pts	GD
E1								
E2								
E3								
E4								

GROUP F
Monterrey

Poland, Morocco, Portugal, England

Date/BST	Venue	Match	H-T F-T
2.6/11pm	Universitario	Morocco v Poland	00 10

Scorers: *Manuel.*

3.6/11pm	Tecnologico	Portugal v England	00 10

Scorers: *Manuel (85)*

6.6/11pm	Tecnologico	England v Morocco	00 00

Scorers:

7.6/11pm	Universitario	Poland v Portugal	00 10

Scorers:

12.6/11pm	Tecnologico	Portugal v Morocco	— —

Scorers:

12.6/11pm	Universitario	England v Poland	— —

Scorers:

Final Table	P	W	D	L	F	A	Pts	GD
F1								
F2								
F3								
F4								

EIGHTH-FINALS

Date	Venue	Match		
15.6	Azteca	B1_____	v A/C/D3_____	(8)

H-T___ F-T___ Scorers:_____

15.6	Leon	C1_____	v A/B/F3_____	(4)

H-T___ F-T___ Scorers:_____

16.6	Puebla	A1_____	v C/D/E3_____	(1)

H-T___ F-T___ Scorers:_____

16.6	Jalisco	D1_____	v B/E/F3_____	(5)

H-T___ F-T___ Scorers:_____

17.6	Olympic 68	A2_____	v C2_____	(6)

H-T___ F-T___ Scorers:_____

17.6	Universitario	F1_____	v E2_____	(7)

H-T___ F-T___ Scorers:_____

18.6	Azteca	F2_____	v B2_____	(2)

H-T___ F-T___ Scorers:_____

18.6	Queretaro	E1_____	v D2_____	(3)

H-T___ F-T___ Scorers:_____

QUARTER-FINALS

Date *Venue*   *Match*

21.6 Jalisco   (5)_____v (6)_____(C)

H-T___ F-T___ Scorers:_____

21.6 Universitario (7)_____v (8)_____(D)

H-T___ F-T___ Scorers:_____

22.6 Puebla   (3)_____v (4)_____(B)

H-T___ F-T___ Scorers:_____

22.6 Azteca   (1)_____v (2)_____(A)

H-T___ F-T___ Scorers:_____

SEMI-FINALS

Date *Venue*   *Match*

25.6 Azteca   (A)_____v (B)_____

H-T___ F-T___ Scorers:_____

25.6 Jalisco   (C)_____v (D)_____

H-T___ F-T___ Scorers:_____

THIRD PLACE PLAY-OFF

Date *Venue*   *Match*

28.6 Puebla   _____v_____

H-T___ F-T___ Scorers:_____

FINAL

Azteca Stadium, Mexico City, Sunday, 29 June 1986

_____v_____

H-T___ F-T___ Scorers:_____

_____

As four of the third-placed teams in the first phase of the finals
will go through to the knock-out stage, and there are six groups
in the first phase, it follows that there are fifteen possible
combinations of four groups which might produce third-placed
teams for the knock-out stages. The following table shows each
of the possible combinations of four groups (from A, B, C, D,
E, F), followed by the eighth-final pairings which such a
combination would produce.

Possible combination	A1 plays	B1 plays	C1 plays	D1 plays
A B C D	C3	D3	A3	B3
A B C E	C3	A3	B3	E3
A B C F	C3	A3	B3	F3
A B D E	D3	A3	B3	E3
A B D F	D3	A3	B3	F3
A B E F	E3	A3	B3	F3
A C D E	C3	D3	A3	E3
A C D F	C3	D3	A3	F3
A C E F	C3	A3	F3	E3
A D E F	D3	A3	F3	E3
B C D E	C3	D3	B3	E3
B C D F	C3	D3	B3	F3
B C E F	E3	C3	B3	F3
B D E F	E3	D3	B3	F3
C D E F	C3	D3	F3	E3

CHAPTER FOUR

WORLD CUP 1986 –
THE STADIA

Twelve stadia in nine cities are to be used for the 1986 World
Cup final tournament. This chapter gives details of the altitude and capacity of each stadium, the population of the city
in which each stadium is located, and the dates and group
details of each match which will be played there. There is also
a map showing the location of each of the nine cities involved.

MEXICO CITY
Population: 19,000,000. Altitude above sea level: 7,000ft
Azteca Stadium *Capacity:* 108,000. First phase matches in
Group B will be played here, as well as the opening match
involving the Champions. First phase matches are scheduled
for 31 May, 3 June, 7 June and 11 June. Host country Mexico
will be in Group B based in this stadium. The first eighth-final
will be held here on 15 June, as will one quarter-final on 22
June, one semi-final on 25 June and the final itself on 29 June.

Olympic 68 Stadium *Capacity:* 72,200. First phase matches in
Group A will be played here on 2 June, 5 June and 10 June,
as well as one eighth-final on 17 June.

GUADALAJARA
Population: 1,000,000. Altitude above sea level: 4,900ft
Jalisco Stadium *Capacity:* 66,200. First phase matches in
Group D will be played here on 1 June, 6 June, and 12 June.
There will be one eighth-final at Jalisco on 16 June, one
quarter-final on 21 June and one semi-final on 25 June.

Third of March Stadium *Capacity:* 40,000. Only first phase
matches are scheduled here, on 3 June, 7 June and 11 June in
Group D.

PUEBLA
Population: 1,000,000. Altitude above sea level: 6,600ft

Cuauhtemoc Stadium *Capacity:* 47,000. Two first phase matches in Group A are scheduled for this stadium, on 5 June and 10 June. It will also host an eighth-final on 16 June, a quarter-final on 22 June and the play-off for third place on 28 June, the eve of the final.

MONTERREY

Population: 1,700,000. Altitude above sea level: 1,700ft

Stadium Universitario *Capacity:* 45,000. In the first phase, Group F matches will be played here on 2 June, 7 June and 11 June. There will also be one eighth-final on 17 June and one quarter-final on 21 June.

Stadium Tecnologico *Capacity:* 40,000. Also in Group F, first phase matches are scheduled here for 3 June, 6 June and 12 June.

LEON

Population: 700,000. Altitude above sea level: 6,000ft

Stadium Nuevo Campo *Capacity:* 40,000. In Group C, first phase matches are scheduled here for 1 June, 5 June and 9 June. There will also be an eighth-final in Leon on 15 June, but no quarter-finals are scheduled for this venue in 1986!

TOLUCA

Population: 450,000. Altitude above sea level: 8,200ft

Bombonera Stadium *Capacity:* 40,000. In Group B with the Azteca Stadium, first phase matches are scheduled for the Bombonera Stadium on 4 June, 8 June and 11 June.

IRAPUATO

Population: 170,000. Altitude above sea level: 5,300ft

Revolucion Stadium *Capacity:* 40,000. In Group C, first phase matches are scheduled here on 2 June, 6 June, and 9 June.

NEZAHUALCOYOTL

Population: 250,000. Altitude above sea level: 5,900ft

Neza 86 Stadium *Capacity:* 40,000. First phase matches in Group E are scheduled here for 4 June, 8 June and 13 June.

QUERETARO

Population: 250,000. Altitude above sea level: 5,900ft

Corregidora Stadium *Capacity:* 40,000. The only stadium to be built specially for the 1986 final tournament, it will stage first phase matches in Group E on 4 June, 8 June and 13 June, and will also be used for an eighth-final on 18 June.

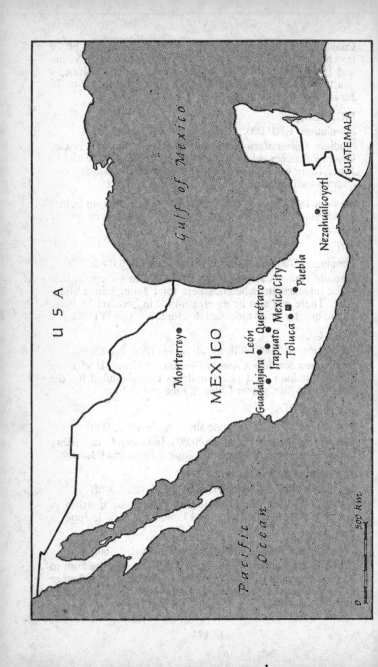

CHAPTER FIVE

MEXICO 86 –
THE BRITISH STARS

Introduction

For the second successive World Cup, three out of four of the British teams have qualified for the finals. The squads of twenty-two players which will be taken to Mexico from each country won't be announced until shortly before the finals are due to begin, but here are the pen-pictures of a likely selection of English, Scottish and Northern Irish players. The information was compiled as at 1 December 1985.

ROY AITKEN *Scotland*
A tall midfielder with Celtic, born in Irvine, he is a former Scotland Youth and Under-21 player who graduated from the ranks of the Celtic Boys' Club and turned professional in 1975. He made his League debut against Aberdeen in February 1976 and first played for Scotland against Peru in September 1979.

ARTHUR ALBISTON *Scotland*
Edinburgh-born Albiston is a defender with Manchester United, and a former Scottish Schools and Under-21 international. He made his League debut for United against Portsmouth in October 1974 and his international career started in Belfast when he played for Scotland against Northern Ireland in April 1982. In April 1985 he chalked up his 300th League appearance for Manchester United in the game against Leicester City.

VIV ANDERSON *England*
A Nottingham-born full-back who signed professional forms with Nottingham Forest in August 1974 and made his League debut against Sheffield Wednesday a month later. A former

England Under-21 international, he became the first black player to wear an England shirt when he made his full international debut against Czechoslovakia in November 1978. Made a total of 328 League appearances for Forest before transferring to Arsenal in a £200,000 move in the summer of 1984. Scored his first goal for England in the 8-0 rout of Turkey during the 1986 World Cup qualifying competition.

STEVE ARCHIBALD *Scotland*
A Glasgow-born striker who made his League debut for East Stirling against Brechin City in March 1974. He later moved on to Clyde, remaining a part-time player while he also worked as a Rolls Royce motor mechanic. In January 1978 he signed full professional forms with Aberdeen, and in May 1980 he moved on to Tottenham Hotspur for a fee of £800,000. A former Scotland Under-21 international, he made his full international debut against Portugal in March 1980, coming on as a substitute for Kenny Dalglish. Transferred to Barcelona in August 1984 to join up with Terry Venables and soon made a name for himself in the Spanish League.

GARY BAILEY *England*
Born in Ipswich in August 1958, goalkeeper Gary is the son of former Ipswich Town 'keeper Roy Bailey. Roy went to South Africa when he finished playing and it was there, in the Witts University team, that Gary was playing when he attracted the interest of Manchester United. He joined United in January 1978 and made his League debut against his father's old club in November that year. In March 1985 he made his full England debut in the friendly international against Eire at Wembley, although he has been considered as the number one understudy to Peter Shilton in the England goal for some time. Has made nearly 300 League appearances for United.

JOHN BARNES *England*
A tall and powerful Jamaican-born winger, John turned professional with Watford in July 1981 and made his League debut against Oldham two months later. One of very few international class wingers in the English game today, he could be a valuable asset in Mexico. In the summer of 1984 he scored a brilliant solo goal against Brazil in Rio de Janeiro to set up a rare England victory against the former World Champions. John is a former England Under-21 international.

JIM BETT *Scotland*
Born in Hamilton and now 26 years old, he started his League career with Rangers in Glasgow, making 104 League appearances for them before transferring to Belgian club Lokeren. Came back to Scottish football with Aberdeen in the summer of 1985, having scored an absolutely vital goal for Scotland against Iceland in the World Cup qualifier in Reykjavik a month earlier. He also got on the scoresheet in his first game for Aberdeen, against Hibernian in August 1985.

PAUL BRACEWELL *England*
A 23-year-old midfielder who was born in Stoke and signed professional forms with Stoke City in February 1980, making his League debut against Wolves a month later. In June 1983 he moved to Sunderland in a £225,000 transfer and a year later he moved on again, this time to Everton. He made his debut for England against West Germany in the summer tour of 1985 after his successful first season in the Championship-winning team at Goodison Park.

NOEL BROTHERSTON *Northern Ireland*
Belfast-born Noel can play either as a winger or a midfielder, and came to prominence in the national side when Northern Ireland won the British Championship in 1980. Made only one League appearance for his first League side, Tottenham, before transferring to Blackburn Rovers, where he has been a great success in more than 300 League games.

TERRY BUTCHER *England*
Born in Singapore in December 1958, Terry joined Ipswich Town straight from school in August 1976 and made his League debut against Everton in April 1978. A former England Under-21 international, he has played nearly 300 first team games for Ipswich and has developed into one of the most accomplished defenders in the country.

COLIN CLARKE *Northern Ireland*
Born in Newry, County Down, in October 1962, he started his career as an apprentice with Ipswich, but made his League debut with Peterborough. Had a period on loan with Gillingham, but really came to people's attention in 1984-85 when he scored twenty-two goals in the Fourth Division for Tranmere Rovers. In June 1985 he signed a three-year contract with Bournemouth, and is now being groomed as an international striker by Billy Bingham.

DAVIE COOPER *Rangers*

A 29-year-old Hamilton-born forward who started his career with Clydebank, transferring to Rangers for £100,000 in the summer of 1977. A former Scottish Under-21 international, he has become a regular choice for club and country and scored the vital penalty against Wales in September 1985 which earned Scotland the chance of a play-off against Australia.

KENNY DALGLISH MBE *Scotland*

One of the best-loved Scottish internationals of the past decade, and now player-manager of Liverpool. Started his career with Celtic, where he made 204 League appearances and scored 112 League goals before his £440,000 transfer in August 1977 to Liverpool - where he had once been rejected as a trialist! Has made well over 300 League appearances for the Anfield club and is the only man ever to score 100 or more League goals in both Scotland and England. Is likely to have topped the 100 mark in international games for Scotland by the time the World Cup finals start in Mexico, and could well have broken Denis Law's record of thirty international goals by then, too, because he had already equalled it as the 1985-86 season got under way.

KERRY DIXON *England*

Born in Luton in July 1961, he started his career on the books at White Hart Lane, but failed to make the first team there and slipped out of the League to Dunstable for a while before making his League debut with Reading in 1980. Was impressive as a goalscorer with the Berkshire club and transferred to Chelsea in the summer of 1983, since when he has continued to impress, and finished the 1984-85 League season as the First Division's leading scorer. His England debut came against Mexico on the summer tour of 1985, and he scored four goals in his first three internationals, so it looks as though he could be an important asset to England in the forthcoming tournament.

MAL DONAGHY *Northern Ireland*

Belfast-born 28-year-old defender who was playing for Larne Town when spotted by Luton scouts, and he signed for the Bedfordshire club in the summer of 1978 in a £20,000 transfer deal. Made his League debut against Oldham in August that year and has been a regular choice ever since. Was a member of the Northern Ireland team which beat Spain in the 1982 World Cup, and was the victim of what many people thought was an unfair decision when he was sent off in that game.

TERRY FENWICK *England*
A 26-year-old defender with Queen's Park Rangers, he started his League career with Crystal Palace, where he signed professional forms in December 1976 and made his debut a year later against Spurs. He followed manager Terry Venables to Rangers in December 1980 in a £100,000 transfer deal, since when he has played over 200 League games for the West London side. A former England Under-21 international, he made his full England debut when he came on as a substitute for Alvin Martin against Wales in May 1984.

TREVOR FRANCIS *England*
Born in April 1954, he is a skilful striker who was playing for Plymouth Schools when discovered by Birmingham City scouts, and made his League debut when aged only 16 in 1970. Stayed with City for nine seasons and also had a couple of summers in the North American Soccer League with Detroit before becoming the first £1 million player in Britain when he transferred to Nottingham Forest in February 1979. In September 1981 he moved on to Manchester City, and the following summer he went to Sampdoria in the Italian League, where he enjoyed great success. Made his full international debut for England against the Netherlands at Wembley in February 1977.

RICHARD GOUGH *Scotland*
A 23-year-old Stockholm-born defender who, like Manchester United goalkeeper Gary Bailey, was playing with Witts University in South Africa before being signed by Dundee United in March 1980. Soon established as a first-team regular, he made his international debut against Switzerland in March 1983. Scored the winning goal for Scotland against England in the inaugural Rous Cup game at Hampden Park in the summer of 1985.

ANDY GRAY *Scotland*
Glasgow-born Andy is a much-travelled striker who started his career with Dundee United. In October 1975 he moved to Aston Villa and four years later he became one of the most expensive footballers in British history when he was involved in a £1,500,000 transfer to Wolves. In November 1983, when

he moved to Everton, the price had dropped to £200,000, but he produced some of his best football at Goodison, and was instrumental in their League Championship victory in 1984-85. In the summer of 1985 he returned to his first English club, Aston Villa.

MARK HATELEY *England*

Son of sixties soccer star Tony Hateley, Mark, who was born in November 1961, started his career with Coventry City, where he made his League debut in the 1978-79 season. After five seasons at Highfield Road, he joined Portsmouth in the summer of 1983 in a £190,000 transfer, and things soon started to happen for him. After a 1983-84 season in which he scored 22 League goals in 38 games, he was taken on England's summer tour of South America, where he scored with a superb header against Brazil. He was immediately snapped up by AC Milan for a fee of £915,000, and has proved a great success in the defensively-minded Italian League.

GLENN HODDLE *England*

Now aged 28, Glenn was born in Hayes and served his football apprenticeship at White Hart Lane, where he turned professional in April 1975, making his League debut against Norwich City in August that year. Now seems to be fully recovered from a series of niggling injuries and established in the England side. He made his international debut against Bulgaria in November 1979, and when England played in Mexico City in the summer of 1985 he showed that his midfield talent could be a real trump card for England when the squad returns to those difficult conditions this summer.

PAT JENNINGS *Northern Ireland*

It is difficult to think of anything new to say about this supreme professional who seems to have been around forever. In fact he was born in Newry, County Down, on 12 June 1945, and so will celebrate his 41st birthday on the day when Northern Ireland are scheduled to play against Brazil in the 1986 World Cup. He made his League debut for Watford in the 1962-63 season, and moved on to Spurs in 1964. Soon established as one of the world's leading goalkeepers, he made 472 League appearances for Tottenham before following manager Terry Neill to Highbury in August 1977. Now semi-retired from pro football, he still plays in reserve football (now back with Tottenham) and when Northern Ireland drew 0-0 with England in November 1985, that was his 113th international cap - a world record for a goalkeeper. He had made his international debut in April 1964 against Wales - in the same match which saw the international debut of George Best!

MO JOHNSTON *Scotland*
A striker who started his League career with Partick Thistle, spent the 1983-84 season in English football with Watford and then transferred to Celtic in the autumn of 1984. In his first season back in his home town, he scored 14 League goals in 27 games. Now 22 years old, he made his international debut for Scotland against Wales in February 1984, coming on as a substitute and scoring the winning goal.

JIM LEIGHTON *Scotland*
After many years, Scotland at last seem to have solved the problem of finding a truly international class goalkeeper in Jim Leighton. Born in Johnstone and now aged 27, he was discovered playing non-League football with Dalry Thistle eight years ago, since when he has developed into the regular choice for club and country. A former Scottish Under-21 international, he made his full debut for Scotland against East Germany at Hampden Park in October 1982.

GARY LINEKER *England*
A 25-year-old Leicester-born striker who started his career with Leicester City, with whom he turned professional in December 1978 and made his League debut against Oldham in January the following year. He was City's leading scorer for three seasons before joining Everton in an £800,000 transfer deal upon his return from England's summer tour of Mexico and the USA in 1985. He made his full international debut for England against Scotland in May 1984, coming on as a substitute for Tony Woodcock. After the 5-0 drubbing of Turkey in October 1985 he was awarded the match ball to celebrate his first hat-trick for England.

MAURICE MALPAS *Scotland*
A 23-year-old defender, born in Dunfermline, he joined Dundee United from Leven Royals in 1979 and soon won caps at Under-21 level for Scotland. He completed a degree in electrical engineering before becoming a full-time professional footballer, and made his full international debut against France in Marseilles in June 1984.

ALVIN MARTIN *England*

A Bootle-born defender, now twenty-seven years old, he missed only two League games in 1984-85, having struggled with injuries the year before. Made his League debut for his only club, West Ham, against Aston Villa in March 1978, and by the summer of 1985 had made 245 League appearances for the club. Made his international debut in May 1981 against Brazil in a friendly match at Wembley.

FRANK McAVENNIE *Scotland*

A Glasgow-born striker who started in League football with St Mirren, joining them from Johnstone Burgh in 1980. In 1984-85 he was the Saints' top scorer with 16 League goals in 34 appearances, and then West Ham signed him in a £340,000 transfer deal. Has made a brilliant start to his spell in English football, and scored one of the all-important goals for Scotland against Australia at Hampden Park in the first leg of the World Cup play-off, in November 1985.

JOHN McCLELLAND *Northern Ireland*

In the past few seasons, John has played club football in England, Scotland and Wales, in addition to international football for Northern Ireland! His League career started with Cardiff, and he also played for Mansfield and Glasgow Rangers before Watford signed him in a £225,000 transfer deal during the 1984-85 season. He made his full international debut as a substitute against Scotland in May 1980.

DAVID McCREERY *Northern Ireland*

Now with Newcastle United, this 28-year-old Belfast-born midfielder is a former Northern Ireland Schools and Under-21 international who started his League career with Manchester United. Tommy Docherty signed him in a £200,000 transfer for Queen's Park Rangers in 1979, but after a year he left to join Tulsa Roughnecks in the NASL. When he returned to England, in 1982, he was signed by Newcastle for a fee of £75,000. He made his international debut against Scotland in May 1976, and won his fiftieth cap for his country in the World Cup qualifier against Rumania in Bucharest in October 1985.

ALAN McDONALD *Northern Ireland*

A young defender, Alan was spotted by Queen's Park Rangers scouts playing for Rathcoole School in his hometown of Belfast and was soon on the books at Loftus Road. His big brother, Roy, is a goalkeeper with Crusaders. He won Youth international honours for Northern Ireland, and has recently settled down into a regular spot in the QPR team. Made a great start to his full international career against Rumania in Bucharest in October 1985.

SAMMY McILROY *Northern Ireland*
The holder of Northern Ireland's record number of caps for an outfield player, he started his career with Manchester United, serving his apprenticeship at Old Trafford after being spotted by United's Irish scout, Bob Bishop. He won his first cap against Spain at Hull in 1972. After ten seasons at Old Trafford he moved to Stoke, but in May 1985 he signed a new two-year contract at Maine Road. Has served as captain of Northern Ireland in recent years in the absence of Martin O'Neill, and was in that position when they won the British Championship in 1980.

ALEX McLEISH *Scotland*
A Glasgow-born defender who joined Aberdeen from Glasgow University in 1976 as a midfielder, though he has since converted to the defence. A former Scotland Under-21 international, he made his full international debut against Portugal in March 1980, and by the end of the 1984-85 season had clocked up 37 caps.

BERNARD McNALLY *Northern Ireland*
Born in Shrewsbury in February 1963, Bernard is a midfielder who came to the attention of Billy Bingham when his eligibility for the Ulster squad was recognised (his father was from the province). Bingham watched him play in a testimonial match against Blackburn Rovers in May 1985 and Bernard was soon in the Northern Ireland squad. He joined Shrewsbury Town straight from school, signing professional forms at age eighteen, and at the time of writing is on the verge of full international honours.

PAUL McSTAY *Scotland*
A young midfielder, born in Hamilton, he came through the ranks of the Celtic Boys' Club to sign professional forms in 1977, and has now established himself as a regular for club and country. A former Scotland Under-21 player, he made his full international debut against Uruguay at Hampden Park in September 1983.

WILLIE MILLER *Scotland*
An experienced defender, Willie was born in Glasgow thirty years ago and joined Aberdeen from Eastercraigs in 1971. A former Scotland Youth, Under-21 and Under-23 international, he made his full international bow against Rumania in June 1975. Had chalked up 40 caps by the summer of 1985, and has enjoyed great success as captain of Aberdeen in their recent run of major trophies.

CHARLIE NICHOLAS *Scotland*
Born in Glasgow, this 24-year-old striker graduated through the junior ranks at Celtic, and soon established a reputation as a goalscorer with 48 goals in 74 League games. In June 1983 he was transferred to Arsenal for a fee of £750,000, and soon became the darling of the North Bank with his blend of cheek and skill. A former Under-21 player, he won his first full international cap for Scotland against Switzerland in March 1983 and celebrated the occasion with a goal.

JIMMY NICHOLL *Northern Ireland*
A much-travelled defender who was born in Hamilton, Ontario of Ulster parents twenty-nine years ago. He went straight from schools football in Belfast on to the books of Manchester United, and after appearing in 197 League games for them, he moved to Sunderland before returning to Canada for a spell with Toronto Blizzard. Back in Britain, he played for a time for Glasgow Rangers before joining West Bromwich Albion in the summer of 1984. Made his full international debut against Israel in Tel Aviv in March 1976.

STEVE NICOL *Scotland*
An Irvine-born defender who has chalked up over fifty League appearances for Liverpool since his transfer from Ayr United in the 1981-82 season. A former Scotland Under-21 international, he won his first full cap against Yugoslavia in a friendly match in September 1984.

JOHN O'NEILL *Northern Ireland*
Londonderry-born John, now aged twenty-seven, began his career with Derry Athletic, but was playing for Loughborough University when spotted by Leicester City scouts, and signed for them while still an undergraduate. He made his League debut against Burnley in August 1978, turned professional six months later, and was soon in the Northern Ireland Under-21 squad. He made his full international debut

against Israel in March 1980 in Tel Aviv. John is a true utility player, and has been used in a variety of positions by Billy Bingham.

JIM PLATT *Northern Ireland*
Now player-manager of Coleraine, this 33-year-old goalkeeper has had to live in the shadow of Pat Jennings since he made his international debut against Israel in Tel Aviv in March 1976. After playing for Middlesbrough for thirteen years, he returned to Northern Ireland, initially with Ballymena United before moving to Coleraine.

JIMMY QUINN *Northern Ireland*
Born in Belfast twenty-four years ago, Quinn is an exciting striker who came to England as a youngster and was playing in the Cheshire League with Oswestry Town before moving into League football with Swindon. After a transfer to Blackburn Rovers he made his full international debut against Israel in October 1984, and really shot to fame as the man who scored the all-important goal against Rumania in October 1985.

PAUL RAMSEY *Northern Ireland*
Joined Leicester City straight from Derry Athletic, his home-town club, and turned professional at Filbert Street in April 1980. In March 1981 he made his League debut when he came on as a substitute against Arsenal, and has developed into a powerful midfielder. He won his first cap against Austria in September 1983.

BRYAN ROBSON *England*
Widely-regarded as one of Britain's best all-round players, Robson was born in Chester-le-Street in January 1957 and made nearly 200 appearances for West Bromwich Albion before following manager Ron Atkinson to Old Trafford in October 1981 for a cool £1,500,000. Captain of club and country, he had chalked up 49 international caps before injury kept him out of England's last World Cup qualifier, against Northern Ireland in November 1985. He is therefore set to become the nineteenth player in England history to win fifty caps.

KENNY SANSOM *England*
Born in Camberwell in September 1958, he started his League career with Crystal Palace, where he made his League debut against Tranmere Rovers in May 1975. After turning

out in 172 League games for Palace, he moved to Arsenal in the exchange deal involving Clive Allen in August 1980, and is a regular for club and country. In fact he and Peter Shilton were England's only two ever-present players in the 1986 World Cup qualifying competition.

PETER SHILTON *England*
Born in Leicester in September 1949, he started his career as understudy to Gordon Banks at Leicester, where he made his League debut in the 1965-66 season. He moved to Stoke for £34,000 in November 1974, on to Nottingham Forest for £270,000 in September 1977, and finally to Southampton in August 1982 for £325,000. With over 900 first team games to his credit, he could well go on to beat Pat Jennings' record of 1084. When he won his 74th cap against Turkey in October 1985, he surpassed Gordon Banks as England's most-capped goalkeeper.

GRAEME SOUNESS *Scotland*
Born in Edinburgh in May 1953, he started his career on the books at Tottenham, but failed to make the first team there, and eventually made his League debut for Middlesbrough against Fulham in January 1973. Five years later, in January 1978, he was transferred to Liverpool for £325,000. A former Scottish Schools and Under-23 international, he made his full international debut for Scotland against East Germany in October 1974. Moved to Italian football with Sampdoria in the summer of 1984.

TREVOR STEVEN *England*
A midfielder, born in Berwick in September 1963, Trevor is a former England Youth international who made his League debut for Burnley against Huddersfield while still an apprentice, and moved on to Everton in a £300,000 transfer in June 1983. While at Goodison, he has earned FA Cup, League Championship and European Cup-Winners' Cup medals, and he made his full international debut against Northern Ireland in the World Cup qualifier at Belfast in February 1985.

GARY STEVENS *England*
A defender, Gary was born in Barrow in March 1963, and joined the staff as an apprentice at Goodison Park. He turned professional in April 1981 and made his League debut against West Ham in October that year. 1985 was a significant year for Gary, as he played his 100th League game for Everton v

Arsenal in March and won his first England cap in the match against Italy in Mexico City in June.

IAN STEWART *Northern Ireland*
Was playing youth football in his hometown of Belfast when Queen's Park Rangers scout Bill Smyth spotted him and sent him to Loftus Road after Everton declined to take up an option on him. In the Spring of 1983 he was loaned to Millwall, and he signed for Newcastle in September that year. He won his first full cap against France in March 1982, but was not selected for the 1982 World Cup squad, so he will be anxious to prove a point this time round.

GORDON STRACHAN *Scotland*
A 28-year-old midfielder, born in Edinburgh, he missed only one League game for Manchester United in the 1984-85 season, scoring fifteen goals in the process as well as two in the FA Cup. He started his career with Dundee, joined Aberdeen in 1977 and moved to Old Trafford in a £600,000 transfer deal in May 1984. Made his full international debut for Scotland against Northern Ireland in May 1980.

CHRIS WADDLE *England*
Was playing for Tow Law Town before Newcastle signed him up, and he made his League debut for them in 1981. Went on to make 170 League appearances for United before joining Spurs for £590,000 in June 1985 – a club record for Newcastle. Made his full international debut against the Republic of Ireland in March 1985, and scored his first goal for England in spectacular fashion against Turkey at Wembley in October.

DAVE WATSON *England*
Born in Liverpool in November 1961, he started his career at Anfield, but failed to make the first team there and transferred to Norwich in November 1980. The original fee of £50,000 went up to £100,000 when he became established in the first team, and £200,000 when he was first capped for England against Brazil in Rio de Janeiro in June 1984. Was captain of the Norwich side which won the Milk Cup in 1985.

NORMAN WHITESIDE *Northern Ireland*
Born in Belfast and still only twenty years old, he made his League debut for Manchester United against Brighton in April 1982 while still an apprentice, and that summer became the youngest player ever to appear in a World Cup final tournament, making his international debut against Yugo-

slavia in Zaragoza in June. Many honours have come his way already, and the highlight of the 1984-85 season for him was surely the winning goal in the FA Cup final against Everton.

RAY WILKINS *England*
Born in Hillingdon in September 1956, he is a vastly-experienced midfielder who started his career with Chelsea in season 1973-74 and went on to amass 177 League appearances for them before joining Manchester United in an £825,000 transfer in August 1979. Spent five seasons at Old Trafford before being lured to Italian football, joining AC Milan for £1,500,000 in June 1984. Made his full international debut for England against the Republic of Ireland at Wembley in September 1976, and is now the most capped outfield player in the current England squad.

TONY WOODCOCK *England*
A Nottingham-born forward who started his career with Nottingham Forest, making his League debut against Aston Villa in April 1974. Chalked up 129 League games for Forest, and also had spells on loan to Lincoln and Doncaster, before moving to 1FC Cologne for £650,000 in November 1979. After two seasons in the Bundesliga, he joined Arsenal in a £500,000 transfer in June 1982. Made his international debut for England against Northern Ireland in May 1978.

NIGEL WORTHINGTON *Northern Ireland*
Started his League career with Notts County, who signed him from his hometown club, Ballymena United, and he made 67 League appearances for County before joining Sheffield Wednesday in a £100,000 transfer in January 1984. Made his international debut against Wales at Swansea in May 1984. Plays on the left side of the field as a full-back or midfielder.

MARK WRIGHT *England*
A defender, born in Dorchester-on-Thames in August 1963, he started his career with Oxford United, making his League debut against Bristol City in October 1981. After only ten games for United, he joined Southampton in an exchange deal in November 1983. He made his full international debut for England at Wrexham against Wales in May 1984.

CHAPTER SIX

FORM GUIDE TO THE FINALISTS

Introduction

This chapter gives the results of all 'Category A' international matches played by the twenty-four finalists from the beginning of the European Championship finals in June 1984 until the end of the 1986 World Cup qualifying tournament in December 1985. Only games classified as 'Category A' matches by FIFA are included.

As well as the date, result (with the finalist's score given first), opponents and venue there is a code which classifies the match as a friendly international (F), a European Championship final tournament game (E) or a World Cup qualifying match (W). At the end of each set of results is a breakdown of the results similar to that found in a league table, but instead of a points column, which would be meaningless, there is the heading G.G.A., which refers to 'Goals per Game Average'. This is followed by a commentary on the prospects of each team for the World Cup finals in Mexico.

ALGERIA

Date	Score/Opponents	Code	Venue
10.10.84	2-5 v East Germany	F	Aue
31.3.85	0-0 v Angola	W	Luanda
19.4.85	3-2 v Angola	W	Algiers
1.5.85	0-1 v Tunisia	F	Tunis
13.7.85	2-0 v Zambia	W	Algiers
28.7.85	1-0 v Zambia	W	Lusaka
6.10.85	4-1 v Tunisia	W	Tunis
18.10.85	3-0 v Tunisia	W	Algiers

P	W	D	L	F	A	G.G.A.
8	5	1	2	15	9	1.875

Both Algeria and Morocco have qualified for the final tournament – the first time that any African nations have qualified for the World Cup finals for a second time. Algeria caused a major upset in 1982, when they beat West Germany 2-1. Later in the tournament, after adding the scalp of Chile to that of the West Germans, they were the victims of what most people considered to be an arranged game between West Germany and Austria, the result of which shut them out of the second stage on goal difference. They have been drawn in a tough group with Brazil, Spain and Northern Ireland, but soccer in Algeria continues to improve, and with Belloumi back from a broken leg and back in form, they could well surprise us again. Bensaoula and Madjer are still scoring regularly in the national side, and indeed each contributed one goal in the 2-0 defeat of the last surviving black African nation – Zambia – in July last year. They certainly won't be bothered by the heat in Mexico, so if they manage to acclimatise well to the altitude, they will have to be carefully watched, especially as they will feel relatively un-pressurised and know from past performances that they are capable of holding their own in the top flight.

ARGENTINA

Date	Score/Opponents	Code	Venue
17.6.84	0-0 v Brazil	F	Sao Paulo
18.7.84	0-1 v Uruguay	F	Montevideo
2.8.84	0-0 v Uruguay	F	Buenos Aires
24.8.84	0-1 v Colombia	F	Bogota
1.9.84	2-0 v Switzerland	F	Berne
5.9.84	2-0 v Belgium	F	Brussels
12.9.84	3-1 v West Germany	F	Dusseldorf
18.9.84	1-1 v Mexico	F	Monterrey
25.10.84	1-1 v Mexico	F	Buenos Aires
5.5.85	1-2 v Brazil	F	Salvador, Bahia
9.5.85	1-1 v Paraguay	F	Buenos Aires
14.5.85	2-0 v Chile	F	Buenos Aires
26.5.85	3-2 v Venezuela	W	San Cristobal
2.6.85	3-1 v Colombia	W	Bogota
9.6.85	3-0 v Venezuela	W	Buenos Aires
16.6.85	1-0 v Colombia	W	Buenos Aires
23.6.85	0-1 v Peru	W	Lima
30.6.85	2-2 v Peru	W	Buenos Aires

P	W	D	L	F	A	G.G.A.
18	8	6	4	25	14	1.389

This will be the ninth time that Argentina have competed in the World Cup final tournament. Winners in 1978 and runners-up in the first competition in 1930, they have, especially since 1974, been a leading force in world soccer, and number some great players in their ranks, including Diego Maradona, reckoned by many to be the world's finest player at present. In the matches listed above it can be seen that they had a string of indifferent results in their warm-up friendlies, but then turned it on when it mattered, putting together four straight wins before suffering a surprise defeat against Peru. In their final match, against Peru in Buenos Aires, they did enough to make sure of winning the group, and if they can keep their still-troublesome tempers in check at the moments of greatest pressure, they will have to be regarded as one of the favourites for the title in Mexico. Should qualify easily for the knock-out stages from a group including Bulgaria and South Korea.

BELGIUM

Date	Score/Opponents	Code	Venue
6.6.84	2-2 v Hungary	F	Brussels
13.6.84	2-0 v Yugoslavia	E	Lens
16.6.84	0-5 v France	E	Nantes
19.6.84	2-3 v Denmark	E	Strasbourg
5.9.84	0-2 v Argentina	F	Brussels
17.10.84	3-1 v Albania	W	Brussels
19.12.84	0-0 v Greece	W	Athens
22.12.84	0-2 v Albania	W	Tirana
27.3.85	2-0 v Greece	W	Brussels
1.5.85	2-0 v Poland	W	Brussels
11.9.85	0-0 v Poland	W	Chorzow
16.10.85	1-0 v Netherlands	W	Brussels
20.11.85	1-2 v Netherlands	W	Rotterdam

P	W	D	L	F	A	G.G.A
13	5	3	5	15	17	1.154

Belgium qualified for the finals – the fourth time they have done so since the war – by beating the Netherlands in a two-leg play-off on the away goals rule, so it can fairly be said that they scraped home. In Spain in 1982 they reached the second phase of the finals, where they were eliminated after defeats by Poland and the Soviet Union. They went on to qualify for the final stages of the European Championship in 1984 where, after making a bright start against the Yugoslavs, they suffered a heavy defeat at the hands of eventual winners France and were then eliminated by a Danish side which has since developed into one of the most stylish in Europe. Belgium's World Cup qualifying programme was not particularly impressive, but they lost only two out of eight matches on the way, and cannot be taken lightly by any of the other finalists. They will start the 1986 tournament in Group B with Mexico, Paraguay and Iraq, so should have no problems going through to the knock-out stage.

BRAZIL

Date	Score/Opponents	Code	Venue
10.6.84	0-2 v England	F	Rio De Janeiro
17.6.84	0-0 v Argentina	F	Sao Paulo
28.4.85	0-1 v Peru	F	Brasilia
2.5.85	2-0 v Uruguay	F	Recife
5.5.85	2-1 v Argentina	F	Salvador, Bahia
15.5.85	0-1 v Colombia	F	Bogota
21.5.85	1-2 v Chile	F	Santiago
2.6.85	2-0 v Bolivia	W	Santa Cruz
8.6.85	3-1 v Chile	F	Porto Alegre
16.6.85	2-0 v Paraguay	W	Asuncion
23.6.85	1-1 v Paraguay	W	Rio de Janeiro
30.6.85	1-1 v Bolivia	W	Sao Paulo

P	W	D	L	F	A	G.G.A.
12	5	3	4	14	10	1.167

Mexico 1986 will be the thirteenth World Cup tournament, and Brazil are the only country in the world to have taken part in all thirteen. Third in 1938, second in the final pool of 1950 and winners three times – the last in Mexico 1970 – the Brazilians have one of the finest records in the tournament and have produced a string of dazzlingly brilliant teams and players. Although it is now sixteen years since the Brazilians last won the World Cup, they were fourth in 1974, third in 1978 and were only eliminated in 1982 after a closely-fought second phase match against eventual champions Italy. Their 1986 qualifying programme was not inspiring – two wins and two draws – but they will relish the conditions in Mexico just as they did in 1970, and with players of the calibre of Zico, Eder, Socrates and the new scoring sensation Casagrande in the side, they have to be considered as favourites for the title for a record fourth time, and should get off to a good start in Group D alongside Spain, Algeria and Northern Ireland.

BULGARIA

Date	Score/Opponents	Code	Venue
6.9.84	0-1 v Portugal	F	Lisbon
29.9.84	0-0 v Yugoslavia	W	Belgrade
16.10.84	0-0 v Turkey	F	Istanbul
21.11.84	0-1 v France	W	Paris
5.12.84	4-0 v Luxembourg	W	Sofia
5.2.85	1-0 v Switzerland	F	Queretaro
6.2.85	2-2 v Poland	F	Queretaro
6.4.85	1-0 v East Germany	W	Sofia
17.4.85	1-4 v West Germany	F	Augsburg
2.5.85	2-0 v France	W	Sofia
1.6.85	2-1 v Yugoslavia	W	Sofia
27.8.85	1-1 v Mexico	F	Los Angeles
4.9.85	0-1 v Netherlands	F	Heerenveen
25.9.85	3-1 v Luxembourg	W	Luxembourg
16.10.85	2-0 v Greece	F	Salonika
16.11.85	1-2 v East Germany	W	Karl-Marx-Stadt

P	W	D	L	F	A	G.G.A.
16	7	4	5	20	14	1.250

Bulgaria have qualified for the fifth time for the World Cup final tournament. On none of the previous four occasions have they progressed beyond the first stage, and there is nothing in their recent performances to suggest that they will do so this time. Drawn in Group A in Puebla, they cannot be expected to beat Italy or Argentina, and although they have two chances in three of going through to the knock-out stage as one of the third-placed teams, their chances cannot be rated highly. The fact that Bulgaria qualified at all for the finals is somewhat surprising in light of the terrible problems that have plagued the domestic game in that country. For years, Bulgarian football has been riddled with bribery and corruption, and things came to a head at the end of last season when, after a particularly vicious cup final betwen CSKA and Levski Spartak, both clubs were disbanded, five players, including two internationals, were banned for life, and the whole club system was reorganised under the direct control of the government. Top goalkeeper Mikhailov and Footballer of the Year Nikolov are the two internationals we shall no longer be seeing. Maybe the pride of the remaining players will enable them to achieve more than we expect of them.

CANADA

Date	Score/Opponents	Code	Venue
25.7.84	0-0 v Chile	F	Edmonton
21.10.84	0-2 v Tunisia	F	Tunis
24.10.84	2-3 v Morocco	F	Rabat
31.10.84	0-0 v Cyprus	F	Nicosia
10.3.85	2-1 v Trinidad & Tobago	F	Port of Spain
13.3.85	1-1 v Jamaica	F	Montego Bay
21.3.85	0-1 v Costa Rica	F	San Jose
24.3.85	0-0 v Costa Rica	F	San Jose
13.4.85	2-0 v Haiti	W	Vancouver
20.4.85	2-1 v Guatemala	W	Vancouver
5.5.85	1-1 v Guatemala	W	Guatemala
8.5.85	2-0 v Haiti	W	Port-au-Prince
17.8.85	1-1 v Costa Rica	W	Toronto
25.8.85	1-0 v Honduras	W	Tegucigalpa
1.9.85	0-0 v Costa Rica	W	San Jose
14.9.85	2-1 v Honduras	W	St John's

P	W	D	L	F	A	G.G.A.
16	6	7	3	16	12	1.000

Canada, coached by Englishman Tony Waiters, have qualified for the World Cup finals for the first time in their history. They have an experienced team, which did so well in the 1984 Olympics, reaching the quarter-finals only to be knocked out by Brazil on penalties after a 1-1 draw, and they also have plenty of experience of playing in Central America, where many of their warm-up and qualifying matches took place. There is a tremendous team spirit in the Canadian camp, but they will have to do something exceptional to progress beyond the first stage in Mexico, having been drawn in Group C in Leon with France, Hungary and the Soviet Union. Most of the Canadian players will be familiar to followers of the North American Soccer League, including captain Bruce Wilson, goalkeeper Tino Lettieri, and others such as Bobby Lenarduzzi, Ian Bridge, Terry Moore, Randy Ragan, Mike Sweeney, David Norman, John Catliff, Igor Vrablic and George Pakos.

DENMARK

Date	Score/Opponents	Code	Venue
6.6.84	1-0 v Sweden	F	Gothenburg
12.6.84	0-1 v France	E	Paris
16.6.84	5-0 v Yugoslavia	E	Lyon
19.6.84	3-2 v Belgium	E	Strasbourg
24.6.84	1-1 v Spain	E	Lyon
12.9.84	3-1 v Austria	F	Copenhagen
26.9.84	1-0 v Norway	W	Copenhagen
17.10.84	0-1 v Switzerland	W	Berne
14.11.84	3-0 v Eire	W	Copenhagen
25.1.85	3-0 v Honduras	F	San Pedro Sula
27.1.85	0-1 v Honduras	F	Tegucigalpa
3.2.85	0-3 v El Salvador	F	San Salvador
8.5.85	4-1 v East Germany	F	Copenhagen
5.6.85	4-2 v USSR	W	Copenhagen
11.9.85	0-3 v Sweden	F	Copenhagen
25.9.85	0-1 v USSR	W	Moscow
9.10.85	0-0 v Switzerland	W	Copenhagen
16.10.85	5-1 v Norway	W	Oslo
13.11.85	4-1 v Eire	W	Dublin

P	W	D	L	F	A	G.G.A.
19	11	2	6	37	19	1.947

Although now recognised as one of the most stylish sides in
Europe, this is in fact the first time that Denmark have
qualified for the World Cup finals. English fans will be familiar
with the likes of Jan Molby (Liverpool) and Jesper Olsen
(Manchester United), while others such as Laudrup and
Elkjaer are making names for themselves in the Italian League.
English fans will also remember the night at Wembley in September 1983 when a 1-0 victory by Denmark put paid to England's chances of qualifying for the 1984 European
Championship finals. Denmark qualified for the finals comfortably enough along with the Soviet Union from UEFA's Group
6, and have been drawn in Group E for the finals, where they
will play against West Germany, Uruguay and Scotland in the
new Queretaro Stadium. It's a tough group, and Denmark's
results in their Central American tour early in 1985 were not
encouraging, but they could well go through in third place.

ENGLAND

Date	Score/Opponents	Code	Venue
2.6.84	0-2 v USSR	F	Wembley
13.6.84	0-2 v Uruguay	F	Montevideo
10.6.84	2-0 v Brazil	F	Rio de Janeiro
17.6.84	0-0 v Chile	F	Santiago
12.9.84	1-0 v East Germany	F	Wembley
17.10.84	5-0 v Finland	W	Wembley
14.11.84	8-0 v Turkey	W	Istanbul
27.2.85	1-0 v Northern Ireland	W	Belfast
26.3.85	2-1 v Eire	F	Wembley
1.5.85	0-0 v Rumania	W	Bucharest
22.5.85	1-1 v Finland	W	Helsinki
25.5.85	0-1 v Scotland	F	Glasgow
6.6.85	1-2 v Italy	F	Mexico City
9.6.85	0-1 v Mexico	F	Mexico City
12.6.85	3-0 v West Germany	F	Mexico City
16.6.85	5-0 v USA	F	Los Angeles
11.9.85	1-1 v Rumania	W	Wembley
16.10.85	5-0 v Turkey	W	Wembley
13.11.85	0-0 v Northern Ireland	W	Wembley

P	W	D	L	F	A	G.G.A.
19	9	5	5	35	11	1.842

The only team to qualify from Europe without being beaten, England now face the difficulties of playing in extreme heat in the venue they least wanted – Monterrey. The opposition doesn't seem strong enough to prevent England going through to the knock-out stages, but they will have to continue training at altitude outside Monterrey in order not to negate the benefit of their pre-World Cup warm-up programme in Colorado and Mexico. An injury-free England squad will be formidable opposition for anybody in the finals, but they will have to improve on the form they showed in South and Central America in the past two summers. The squad scored plenty of goals in the qualifying matches, but the opposition, especially after the first phase, will be stiffer once they get to Mexico. In the first stage, Morocco are a talented side, who should nevertheless be beaten by England, while Portugal (the 1966 semi-final) and Poland (England's elimination in 1973) are old World Cup adversaries.

FRANCE

Date	Score/Opponents	Code	Venue
1.6.84	2-0 v Scotland	F	Marseilles
12.6.84	1-0 v Denmark	E	Paris
16.6.84	5-0 v Belgium	E	Nantes
19.6.84	3-2 v Yugoslavia	E	St Etienne
23.6.84	3-2 v Portugal	E	Marseilles
27.6.84	2-0 v Spain	E	Paris
13.10.84	4-0 v Luxembourg	W	Luxembourg
21.11.84	1-0 v Bulgaria	W	Paris
8.12.84	2-0 v East Germany	W	Paris
3.4.85	0-0 v Yugoslavia	W	Sarajevo
2.5.85	0-2 v Bulgaria	W	Sofia
21.8.85	2-0 v Uruguay	*	Paris
11.9.85	0-2 v East Germany	W	Leipzig
30.10.85	6-0 v Luxembourg	W	Paris
16.11.85	2-0 v Yugoslavia	W	Paris

Match for the Artemio Franchi Trophy between the European and South American Champions.

P	W	D	L	F	A	G.G.A.
15	12	1	2	33	8	2.200

Fourth-placed team in the 1982 World Cup and current European Champions, France are certainly among the top teams in the 1986 World Cup, and have been seeded in Group C, based in Leon, where they will face opposition from the Soviet Union, Hungary and Canada. The Canadians must be considered as rank outsiders, but the other two sides, both European, will not make it easy for the French, led by their inspirational captain, Michel Platini. European Footballer of the Year for 1983 and 1984, and recently voted World Footballer of the Year, he has been the architect of the revival in French football fortunes over the past five years. However, French form in the qualifying tournament was not too consistent, especially away from home, where the only victory they gained was against Luxembourg. In view of this, it will be interesting to see how well the French play in Mexico. All the praise attracted to French football in the past few seasons has been won in Europe, but they will have to prove themselves all over again in the cauldron of Central America.

HUNGARY

Date	Score/Opponents	Code	Venue
6.6.84	2-2 v Belgium	F	Brussels
22.8.84	3-0 v Switzerland	F	Budapest
25.8.84	0-2 v Mexico	F	Budapest
26.9.84	3-1 v Austria	W	Budapest
17.10.84	2-1 v Netherlands	W	Rotterdam
17.11.84	2-1 v Cyprus	W	Nicosia
29.1.85	1-0 v West Germany	F	Hamburg
3.4.85	2-0 v Cyprus	W	Budapest
17.4.85	3-0 v Austria	W	Vienna
14.5.85	0-1 v Netherlands	W	Budapest
16.10.85	0-0 v Wales	F	Cardiff

P	W	D	L	F	A	G.G.A.
11	7	2	2	18	8	1.636

Twice runners-up in the World Cup (1938 and 1954), the Hungarians have a proud tradition in international football, but that will count for nothing as they step into the cauldron of Mexico in the summer of 1986. What will count is that Hungary has an exciting young team, coached by Gyorgy Mezey and captained by the experienced Tibor Nyilasi. They stormed through the qualifying competition, winning five of their six fixtures and slipping up only against the Netherlands in the last game, when the result was academic. In Mexico they will start their programme in Group C in Leon, alongside France, the Soviet Union and lowly Canada, and should be looking forward with some confidence to progressing into the knock-out stage which follows. This will be Hungary's third successive World Cup final tournament. In Argentina in 1978 they had an unhappy time, losing all three of their first phase matches, but in Spain they were desperately unlucky not to go through to the second phase after opening their campaign with a 10-1 win over El Salvador. After defeat by Argentina, a draw against Belgium was not enough, but this time they should make it. Whether the talents of the youngsters in the side will be enough to take them much further in conditions which are unfavourable to all Europeans remains to be seen, but this competition will probably mark Nyilasi's last appearance on the world stage, and he will be driving them on with all the skill and experience he can muster.

IRAQ

Date	Score/Opponents	Code	Venue
29.3.85	3-2 v Jordan	W	Amman
5,4,85	0-3 v Qatar	W	Doha
19.4.85	2-0 v Jordan	W	Kuwait
5.5.85	2-1 v Qatar	W	Calcutta
2.9.85	3-2 v UAE	W	Dubai
27.9.85	1-2 v UAE	W	Taif, Saudi Arabia
15.11.85	0-0 v Syria	W	Damascus
29.11.85	3-1 v Syria	W	Taif, Saudi Arabia

P	W	D	L	F	A	G.G.A.
8	5	1	2	14	11	1.750

Very much an unknown quantity in international football, Iraq qualified for the 1986 finals against all the odds, being forced to play all their home ties on neutral territory because of the disruption caused at home by the war with Iran. Iran had been required to do the same, but withdrew from the competition altogether. The 1986 finals will be the first that Iraq have qualified for, and they cannot be considered as anything other than rank outsiders. Their current enemies, Iran, qualified in 1978, where they managed a 1-1 draw with Scotland but did not progress beyond the first stage. If Iraq do have any surprises up their sleeves for us in these finals, they have at least been drawn in Group B in Mexico City, where their opposition of Mexico, Belgium and Paraguay cannot be considered as particularly strong, but it is unlikely that they will in the running once their first stage matches have been completed on 11 June .

ITALY

Date	Score/Opponents	Code	Venue
26.9.84	1-0 v Sweden	F	Milan
3.11.84	1-1 v Switzerland	F	Lausanne
8.12.84	2-0 v Poland	F	Pescara
5.2.85	2-1 v Eire	F	Dublin
13.3.85	0-0 v Greece	F	Athens
3.4.85	2-0 v Portugal	F	Ascoli
2.6.85	1-1 v Mexico	F	Mexico City
6.6.85	2-1 v England	F	Mexico City
25.9.85	1-2 v Norway	F	Lecce

P	W	D	L	F	A	G.G.A.
9	5	3	1	12	6	1.333

World Champions Italy have been seeded in Group A, based at
Puebla, where they will face Bulgaria, Argentina and South
Korea in the first stage of the 1986 finals. The Italians have
been involved in every World Cup final tournament except
1958, and have appeared in four finals, winning three. The only
time they have ever lost a final was against Brazil on the last
occasion the finals were held in Mexico, in 1970, and so they
know they have the pedigree to go far enough to defend their
title. Still managed by Enzo Bearzot, who guided them to
victory in 1982, they have retained some of that squad in 1986,
not least Paulo Rossi, who has recently rediscovered his goal-
scoring form in the Italian League. One echo of past disasters
will be the presence of the Koreans in Puebla, although it's
South Korea this time, while North Korea did the damage in
1966. After winning in 1982, the *azzuri* suffered a bad loss of
form, and failed to qualify for the final stages of the 1982
European Championship, but since then their results have
improved, losing only one match in the nine listed above, and
they certainly can't be dismissed as possible winners this time.
At least they should get through the first stage without too
much trouble, and if they follow the 1982 pattern of improving
with every match, they could be very difficult to separate from
the trophy which they have held for the past four years.

MEXICO

Date	Scorer/Opponents	Code	Venue
22.7.84	3-1 v Guatemala	F	Guatemala
8.8.84	0-0 v Eire	F	Dublin
11.8.84	1-1 v East Germany	F	East Berlin
16.8.84	3-0 v Finland	F	Helsinki
19.8.84	0-3 v USSR	F	Leningrad
22.8.84	1-1 v Sweden	F	Malmo
25.8.84	2-0 v Hungary	F	Budapest
18.9.84	1-1 v Argentina	F	Monterrey
9.10.84	1-0 v Colombia	F	Los Angeles
11.10.84	1-0 v El Salvador	F	Los Angeles
25.10.84	1-1 v Argentina	F	Buenos Aires
28.10.84	0-1 v Chile	F	Santiago
31.10.84	1-1 v Uruguay	F	Montevideo
11.11.84	2-0 v Trinidad & Tobago	F	Port of Spain
5.2.85	5-0 v Poland	F	Queretaro
26.2.85	2-1 v Finland	F	Acapulco
2.6.85	1-1 v Italy	F	Mexico City
9.6.85	1-0 v England	F	Mexico City
15.6.85	2-0 v West Germany	F	Mexico City
27.8.85	1-1 v Bulgaria	F	Los Angeles
20.9.85	0-0 v Peru	F	Los Angeles

P	W	D	L	F	A	G.G.A.
21	10	9	2	29	13	1.381

The Mexican squad have been training together continuously since May 1985, obviously keen to make a better impression than they have in their previous eight final tournament appearances. Unfortunately for them, the preparation does not seem to be paying off. Of the victories in the above list, those against England, West Germany, Poland and Hungary can be dismissed as the sort of results which often occur in meaningless friendlies, and there was serious concern towards the end of 1985 when the squad embarked on a series of unofficial internationals in the middle east, where they managed to beat North Yemen, but lost to Libya and Egypt and could only draw with Jordan, the UAE and Kuwait. Criticism at home was harsh, some people calling for the resignation of manager Bora Milutinovic, and although artificial pitches and intense heat were blamed by squad officials for the poor results, it seems that Mexico are unlikely to cause too many upsets when the chips are down.

MOROCCO

Date	Score/Opponents	Code	Venue
30.6.84	1-0 v Sierra Leone	W	Freetown
15.7.84	4-0 v Sierra Leone	W	Rabat
7.4.85	2-0 v Malawi	W	Rabat
21.4.85	0-0 v Malawi	W	Lilongwe
12.7.85	0-0 v Egypt	W	Cairo
28.7.85	2-0 v Egypt	W	Casablanca
6.10.85	3-0 v Libya	W	Rabat
18.10.85	0-1 v Libya	W	Benghazi

P	W	D	L	F	A	G.G.A.
8	5	2	1	12	1	1.500

Like Algeria, Morocco have qualified for the finals for a second time, their other appearance being in 1970 when they were eliminated after defeats by West Germany and Peru. North Africa is slowly emerging as a footballing area in its own right, and although many people will be sorry to see how long it seems to be taking black African nations to emerge in the context of international football, especially given their tremendous enthusiasm for the game, both Algeria and Morocco are examples of talented and well-organised sides which can no longer be dismissed as cannon fodder for the more recognised exponents of the sport. This will be of particular interest to England in 1986, as Morocco have been drawn along with England, Poland and Portugal in Group F. Given that there is no altitude problem in Monterrey, and that the heat will not bother the North Africans unduly, they will have to taken seriously, but having said that, the Moroccans will have to really turn it on if they want to progress beyond the first phase of the competition.

NORTHERN IRELAND

Date	Score/Opponents	Code	Venue
27.5.84	0-1 v Finland	W	Pori
12.9.84	3-2 v Rumania	W	Belfast
16.10.84	3-0 v Israel	F	Belfast
14.11.84	2-1 v Finland	W	Belfast
27.2.85	0-1 v England	W	Belfast
27.3.85	0-0 v Spain	F	Palma
1.5.85	2-0 v Turkey	W	Belfast
11.9.85	0-0 v Turkey	W	Izmir
16.10.85	1-0 v Rumania	W	Bucharest
13.11.85	0-0 v England	W	Wembley

P	W	D	L	F	A	G.G.A.
10	5	3	2	11	5	1.100

Northern Ireland have qualified for the World Cup finals for only the third time, but on both previous occasions, in 1958 and 1982, they surprised everybody by their ability to lift their game and upset more highly-rated opponents. For the 1986 tournament they have been drawn in Group D, based in Guadalajara, and manager Billy Bingham has described the draw as 'absolutely excellent'. Whether this optimism is well-founded remains to be seen, but there are some factors in his side's favour. Bingham was involved in the World Youth Cup in Guadalajara a couple of years ago, and so knows what to expect in terms of playing conditions. As far as Northern Ireland's opponents are concerned, Spain have failed to beat Northern Ireland in their previous three meetings, including the classic encounter in the 1982 finals, and the most difficult opposition, Brazil, will not be encountered until the last match of the initial series, on June 12, by which time Northern Ireland may have done enough to go through in either second or third place, especially if they get a good result against the Algerians. There's plenty of talent in the Irish side, and the evergreen Pat Jennings in goal could well turn in some brilliant performances on what will surely be his last appearances in first class competition.

PARAGUAY

Date	Score/Opponents	Code	Venue
3.2.85	0-1 v Uruguay	F	Montevideo
6.2.85	0-1 v Chile	F	Vina del Mar
10.2.85	1-3 v Uruguay	F	Asuncion
28.2.85	0-3 v Colombia	F	Asuncion
17.4.85	0-2 v Colombia	F	Pereira
9.5.85	1-1 v Argentina	F	Buenos Aires
26.5.85	1-1 v Bolivia	W	Santa Cruz
9.6.85	3-0 v Bolivia	W	Asuncion
16.6.85	0-2 v Brazil	W	Asuncion
23.6.85	1-1 v Brazil	W	Rio de Janeiro
27.10.85	3-0 v Colombia	W	Asuncion
3.11.85	1-2 v Colombia	W	Cali
10.11.85	3-0 v Chile	W	Asuncion
17.11.85	2-2 v Chile	W	Santiago

P	W	D	L	F	A	G.G.A.
14	3	4	7	16	19	1.143

This is the first time that Paraguay have qualified for the World Cup finals since 1958, when they did not survive the first round, having been thrashed by France, drawn against Yugoslavia and beaten Scotland 3-2. Prior to that, they were briefly involved in the 1930 and 1950 tournaments. They do not appear to be among the more impressive South American sides at the moment, if recent results are anything to go by. Their warm-up matches prior to the 1986 qualifying competition resulted in a string of five consecutive defeats, although they did manage a draw with Argentina in Buenos Aires in the final fixture. Having been drawn in the same qualifying group as Brazil, they then had to rely on qualifying from play-off matches against Colombia and Chile, and this they did by scoring two wins and a draw to secure their place. Having got to the finals in such a lacklustre fashion, they may well progress beyond the first stage, because they have been drawn in Group B, based in Mexico City. Here they will face Iraq, against whom they should get a result, and Mexico and Belgium, where anything could happen. After that, however, their progress is likely to be distinctly limited.

POLAND

Date	Score/Opponents	Code	Venue
29.8.84	1-1 v Norway	F	Dramman
12.9.84	2-0 v Finland	F	Helsinki
26.9.84	2-0 v Turkey	F	Slupsk
17.10.84	3-1 v Greece	W	Zabrze
31.10.84	2-2 v Albania	W	Mielec
8.12.84	0-2 v Italy	F	Pescara
5.2.85	0-5 v Mexico	F	Queretaro
6.2.85	2-2 v Bulgaria	F	Queretaro
10.2.85	2-1 v Colombia	F	Bogota
14.2.85	0-1 v Colombia	F	Cali
27.3.85	0-0 v Rumania	F	Sibiu
17.4.85	2-1 v Finland	F	Opole
1.5.85	0-2 v Belgium	W	Brussels
19.5.85	4-1 v Greece	W	Athens
30.5.85	1-0 v Albania	W	Tirana
21.8.85	0-1 v Sweden	F	Malmo
4.9.85	1-3 v Czechoslovakia	F	Brno
11.9.85	0-0 v Belgium	W	Chorzow

P	W	D	L	F	A	G.G.A.
18	7	5	6	22	23	1.222

Poland played one game in the 1938 World Cup finals, losing 5-6 to Brazil, and did not re-appear in the finals until 1974. On that occasion they came third. In 1978 they progressed to the second phase, and in 1982 they again came third, so they have a good record in World Cup football over the past decade. This record led to them being seeded at the head of Group F in Monterrey, but their qualification for the 1986 finals was not without its problems. They registered three wins in six games, and only just shaded Belgium into second place. Both teams had identical points and goal differences, but Poland went through on account of having scored more goals. Belgium subsequently qualified after a two-leg play-off against the Netherlands. In Monterrey they will have to deal with Morocco, a much-improved Portugal, and England, who they have not met since that fateful night at Wembley in October 1973 which saw a 1-1 draw, England's elimination from the World Cup, and the end of Sir Alf Ramsey's reign as England manager. The match at the University Stadium on 11 June will be full of memories.

PORTUGAL

Date	Score/Opponents	Code	Venue
2.6.84	2-3 v Yugoslavia	F	Lisbon
9.6.84	2-1 v Luxembourg	F	Luxembourg
14.6.84	0-0 v West Germany	E	Strasbourg
17.6.84	1-1 v Spain	E	Marseilles
20.6.84	1-0 v Rumania	E	Nantes
23.6.84	2-3 v France	E	Marseilles
6.9.84	1-0 v Bulgaria	F	Lisbon
12.9.84	1-0 v Sweden	W	Stockholm
14.10.84	2-1 v Czechoslovakia	W	Oporto
14.11.84	1-3 v Sweden	W	Lisbon
30.1.85	2-3 v Rumania	F	Lisbon
11.2.85	3-1 v Malta	W	Valletta
24.2.85	1-2 v West Germany	W	Lisbon
3.4.85	0-2 v Italy	F	Ascoli
25.9.85	0-1 v Czechoslovakia	W	Prague
12.10.85	3-2 v Malta	W	Lisbon
16.10.85	1-0 v West Germany	W	Stuttgart

P	W	D	L	F	A	G.G.A.
17	8	2	7	23	22	1.353

On their only other appearance in the World Cup finals, when they were led by the brilliant Eusebio in England in 1966, Portugal came third in the tournament. For the 1986 finals, they qualified mainly by virtue of a surprising win against West Germany in Stuttgart, without which they would certainly have been eliminated. However, they played well in the 1984 European Championship and will be a threat to the other teams in Group F, including, of course, England. Their attack is led by one of Europe's leading goalscorers, Fernando Gomes, and although another of their outstanding players, left-winger Chalana, has been handicapped by a series of injuries, they are a much-revived force to be reckoned with. The England v Portugal clash in Monterrey on 3 June will be the first fixture of the tournament for both sides, and as England have failed to beat the Portuguese on their last three meetings, it should be an interesting encounter.

SCOTLAND

Date	Score/Opponents	Code	Venue
1.6.84	0-2 v France	F	Marseilles
12.9.84	6-1 v Yugoslavia	F	Glasgow
17.10.84	3-0 v Iceland	W	Glasgow
14.11.84	3-1 v Spain	W	Glasgow
27.2.85	0-1 v Spain	W	Seville
27.3.85	0-1 v Wales	W	Glasgow
25.5.85	1-0 v England	F	Glasgow
28.5.85	1-0 v Iceland	W	Reykjavik
10.9.85	1-1 v Wales	W	Cardiff
16.10.85	0-0 v East Germany	F	Glasgow
20.11.85	2-0 v Australia	W	Glasgow
4.12.85	0-0 v Australia	W	Melbourne

P	W	D	L	F	A	G.G.A.
12	6	3	3	17	7	1.417

Scotland qualified for their fourth consecutive World Cup finals after finishing second in the European Group 7 behind Spain and then winning a two-leg play-off against Australia by an aggregate score of 2-0. Sadly, their final Group 7 match, against Wales at Cardiff, was marred by the sudden death of manager Jock Stein from a heart attack suffered shortly before the final whistle. His place was taken by his assistant, Aberdeen manager Alex Ferguson, who now faces the unenviable task of steering Scotland through the first stage in Mexico in what many people consider to be the toughest group of them all. Centred on the new stadium at Queretaro, Scotland will have to play against West Germany, twice World Cup winners and twice runners-up, South American Champions Uruguay and the team which has recently emerged as one of the best in Europe – Denmark. No easy matches here, but, as Ferguson was quick to remind people when the draw was announced, at least Scotland will not make the trip to Mexico over-burdened with optimism. Scotland haven't beaten West Germany since 1959, and the Uruguayan team which they will have to face will be a very different proposition from the poor side which lost in Hampden Park in September 1983. In all, a very difficult task for the Scots, but they have class players at their disposal and anything could happen.

SOUTH KOREA

Date	Score/Opponents	Code	Venue
30.9.84	1-2 v Japan	F	Seoul
2.3.85	2-1 v Nepal	W	Kathmandu
7.3.85	5-1 v Bahrain	F	Bahrain
10.3.85	0-1 v Malaysia	W	Kuala Lumpur
6.4.85	4-0 v Nepal	W	Seoul
19.5.85	2-0 v Malaysia	W	Seoul
21.7.85	2-0 v Indonesia	W	Seoul
30.7.85	4-1 v Indonesia	W	Jakarta
26.10.85	2-1 v Japan	W	Tokyo
3.11.85	1-0 v Japan	W	Seoul

P	W	D	L	F	A	G.G.A.
10	8	0	2	23	7	2.300

This is the second time that South Korea have qualified for the World Cup finals. The last time was in 1954 when they were duly trounced 9-0 by Hungary and 7-0 by Turkey before making the long trip home. No doubt this time they will be a little more difficult to beat, but beyond that very little is known about them. In 1966, of course, very little was known about their neighbours North Korea, but they went into the quarter-finals on the strength of a splendid victory over Italy and looked certain to be in the semi-finals when they were 3-0 up against Portugal after twenty minutes, before Eusebio turned the game and Portugal eventually won 5-3. In Mexico, the South Koreans have been drawn in Group A, which is based at Puebla, and will play Argentina, Bulgaria and – ironically – Italy. It can be assumed that the Koreans will be small of stature, fast on their feet, and tremendously enthusiastic. Also, they have mountains on the eastern coast of their own country which rise to just above 4000 feet, and they are used to heat, so they should be fairly well prepared. Whether they will give us as much pleasure and entertainment as the North Koreans did twenty years ago remains to be seen, but, just as happened in 1966, they are scheduled to play their last game in Group A against Italy, on 10 June, and the match is certain to generate a great deal of interest.

SPAIN

Date	Score/Opponents	Code	Venue
7.6.84	0-1 v Yugoslavia	F	La Linea
14.6.84	1-1 v Rumania	E	St Etienne
17.6.84	1-1 v Portugal	E	Marseilles
20.6.84	1-0 v West Germany	E	Paris
24.6.84	1-1 v Denmark	E	Lyon
27.6.84	0-2 v France	E	Paris
17.10.84	3-0 v Wales	W	Seville
14.11.84	1-3 v Scotland	W	Glasgow
23.1.85	3-1 v Finland	F	Alicante
27.2.85	1-0 v Scotland	W	Seville
27.3.85	0-0 v Northern Ireland	F	Palma
30.4.85	0-3 v Wales	W	Wrexham
26.5.85	0-0 v Eire	F	Cork
12.6.85	2-1 v Iceland	W	Reykjavik
25.9.85	2-1 v Iceland	W	Seville

P	W	D	L	F	A	G.G.A.
15	6	5	4	16	15	1.066

It is perhaps surprising that a country with as much footballing talent and tradition as Spain has never won the World Cup. Their clubs have a proud record in European competition, but their national squad have never quite seemed to make it. They won the European Nations' Cup, as it was then called, by beating the Soviet Union 2-1 in 1964, when the final was held in Madrid, and were runners-up to France in the re-named version – the European Championship, in 1984, but they have never been in a World Cup final, and their best position was fourth in 1950. When they hosted the World Cup in 1982 they stuttered through the first round with a draw, a win, and a defeat at the hands of Northern Ireland, only to be beaten by West Germany in the second phase before a goalless draw with England sealed their fate. Now, drawn in Group D in Guadalajara, they must face the favourites, Brazil, the ever-improving Algerians and the side which must by now be taking on the aspect of a bogey-team for the Spanish – Northern Ireland, who they have failed to beat in their last three encounters. To add to their troubles, they could be without first-choice goalkeeper Luis Miguel Arconada, who suffered a terrible knee injury at the start of the 1985-86 domestic season, but they should at least go through to the knock-out stages.

URUGUAY

Date	Score/Opponents	Code	Venue
13.6.84	2-0 v England	F	Montevideo
18.7.84	1-0 v Argentina	F	Montevideo
2.8.84	0-0 v Argentina	F	Buenos Aires
19.9.84	2-0 v Peru	F	Montevideo
3.10.84	3-1 v Peru	F	Lima
31.10.84	1-1 v Mexico	F	Montevideo
29.1.85	3-0 v East Germany	F	Montevideo
3.2.85	1-0 v Paraguay	F	Montevideo
6.2.85	1-0 v Bolivia	F	Cochabamba
10.2.85	3-1 v Paraguay	F	Asuncion
14.2.85	2-1 v Finland	F	Montevideo
24.2.85	3-0 v Colombia	F	Montevideo
27.2.85	2-2 v Peru	F	Montevideo
10.3.85	2-1 v Ecuador	W	Montevideo
24.3.85	0-2 v Chile	W	Santiago
31.3.85	2-0 v Ecuador	W	Quito
7.4.85	2-1 v Chile	W	Montevideo
23.4.85	1-2 v Peru	F	Lima
28.4.85	1-2 v Colombia	F	Bogota
2.5.85	0-2 v Brazil	F	Recife
21.8.85	0-2 v France	*	Paris

Match for the Artemio Franchi Trophy between the European and South American Champions.

P	W	D	L	F	A	G.G.A.
21	13	3	5	32	18	1.524

South American Champions Uruguay, who won the World Cup in 1930 and 1950 and finished fourth in 1954 and 1970, have qualified for the final tournament for the first time since 1974, when they were eliminated after failing to register a victory in the first stage of the competition. When they last played in Britain – a friendly against Scotland in 1983 – they didn't look particularly impressive, and they also lost the Europe v South America clash with France in August 1985, but they have been improving steadily over the past eighteen months and look likely to justify the bookmakers' view of them as third favourites to take the title. Their match against Scotland on 13 June is more likely to reawaken the memories of the 7-0 defeat which the Uruguayans inflicted in the 1954 finals than Scotland's 2-0 win in 1983.

USSR

Date	Score/Opponents	Code	Venue
2.6.84	2-0 v England	F	Wembley
19.8.84	3-0 v Mexico	F	Leningrad
27.3.85	2-0 v Austria	F	Tbilisi
7.8.85	2-0 v Rumania	F	Moscow
28.8.85	1-0 v West Germany	F	Moscow
12.9.84	0-1 v Eire	W	Dublin
10.10.84	1-1 v Norway	W	Oslo
17.4.85	2-2 v Switzerland	W	Berne
2.5.85	4-0 v Switzerland	W	Moscow
5.6.85	2-4 v Denmark	W	Copenhagen
25.9.85	1-0 v Denmark	W	Moscow
16.10.85	2-0 v Eire	W	Moscow
30.10.85	1-0 v Norway	W	Moscow

P	W	D	L	F	A	G.G.A.
13	9	2	2	23	8	1.769

The Soviet Union are in the World Cup finals for the sixth time, having qualified in second place behind Denmark in European Group 6. As we have come to expect from Soviet teams, they are well-organised in all departments and their star striker, Oleg Blokhin, although thirty-two years old, has recently regained his best form. Immediately after the draw was announced, with the Soviet Union placed in Group C along with France, Canada and Hungary, the bookmakers quoted them at 25-1 ninth favourites – the same category as England. They are sure to be well-prepared for the finals, but whether they have the flair to progress any further than they have in previous South American-based World Cup tournaments is open to doubt. In 1970 they were beaten in the quarter-finals by Uruguay, and it looks unlikely that they will do much better this time, especially as they are still prone to disappointing results in major competitions. In the 1984 European Championship, they failed to qualify for the final stages from a group that included Poland, Portugal and Finland, and in the 1986 World Cup qualifying competition, they scored only twice against Norway in two games. They cannot be written off, as they are always difficult to beat, but in terms of looking for winners, the bookmakers are probably being a bit mean with their odds.

WEST GERMANY

Date	Score/Opponents	Code	Venue
14.6.84	0-0 v Portugal	E	Strasbourg
17.6.84	2-1 v Rumania	E	Lens
20.6.84	0-1 v Spain	E	Paris
12.9.84	1-3 v Argentina	F	Dusseldorf
17.10.84	2-0 v Sweden	W	Cologne
16.12.84	3-2 v Malta	W	Valletta
29.1.85	0-1 v Hungary	F	Hamburg
24.2.85	2-1 v Portugal	W	Lisbon
27.3.85	6-0 v Malta	W	Saarbrucken
17.4.85	4-1 v Bulgaria	F	Augsburg
1.5.85	5-1 v Czechoslovakia	W	Prague
12.6.85	0-3 v England	F	Mexico City
15.6.85	0-2 v Mexico	F	Mexico City
28.8.85	0-1 v USSR	F	Moscow
25.9.85	2-2 v Sweden	W	Malmo
16.10.85	0-1 v Portugal	W	Stuttgart
17.11.85	2-2 v Czechoslovakia	W	Munich

P	W	D	L	F	A	G.G.A.
17	7	3	7	29	22	1.706

The West Germans were not allowed to take part in the 1950 World Cup, but they were re-admitted to FIFA in time for the 1954 tournament, which they promptly won. They have taken part in every final tournament since then, winning twice, finishing second twice, and also registering third and fourth places. Now under the managership of their greatest post-war player, Franz Beckenbauer, they are still a very strong team and qualified at the head of Group 2 in Europe, ahead of Portugal. The only blot on the German record book was that on October 16 1985 they lost a World Cup qualifying match for the first time in their history when Portugal beat them 1-0 in Stuttgart. The Germans have often been criticised for only playing at their best when something is at stake, which may explain the lapse against Portugal (the Germans were already sure of qualifying) and the indifferent performances in Mexico last summer, but in Mexico 1986 a great deal will be at stake, and Karl-Heinz Rummenigge and his merry men will be a formidable barrier to Denmark, Uruguay and Scotland at Queretaro when business starts in earnest.

CHAPTER SEVEN

WORLD CUP QUIZ

Questions

(Answers start on page 221)

1.
In which year was the first World Cup tournament held?

2.
Who was the first British President of FIFA?

3.
What was the reason for the British withdrawl from FIFA in 1920?

4.
In which year did the British Associations withdraw from FIFA for a second time, and what was their reason?

5.
How many national associations were present at the first meeting of FIFA in 1904, and where did the meeting take place?

6.
To 1982, how many times has the host nation won the World Cup, and can you name them?

7.
In which year was the World Cup final tournament organised on a league basis throughout, with no knock-out games?

8.
Which was the first country to play against England in a World Cup match?

9.
What is the significance of the Brazilian town of Belo
Horizonte to English football?

10.
How many countries entered the first World Cup
tournament?

11.
Who scored West Germany's dramatic last-minute equaliser
in the 1966 World Cup final?

12.
In which year did the USA reach the World Cup semi-finals?

13.
Who was the overall leading goalscorer in the 1966 World
Cup final tournament?

14.
Which city hosted the 1974 World Cup final?

15.
Who scored West Germany's goal in the 1982 World Cup
final against Italy?

16.
Which country was originally chosen to host the 1986 World
Cup finals?

17.
Which country will host the 1990 World Cup final
tournament?

18.
What's the connection between Dino Zoff and Gianpiero
Combi?

19.
Who won a World Cup winners' medal and later managed a
World Cup winning side?

20.
In which year were substitutes first used in a World Cup final
tournament?

21.
The attendance record for any World Cup match is 200,000
(officially 199,580). Which two teams were playing, and in
which year was the game played?

22.
Who did Brazil beat in the final to take their second World Cup in 1962?

23.
Who beat El Salvador 10-1 in the 1982 World Cup finals, but still failed to qualify for the second phase?

24.
What was the name of the town where England were eliminated from the 1970 World Cup final tournament?

25.
Who finished in third place in the 1982 World Cup tournament?

26.
Where did England play their first phase games in the 1982 World Cup finals?

27.
In which year did Wales qualify for the World Cup finals for the one and only time?

28.
Who were the winners of the 1954 World Cup, and who did they beat in the final?

29.
Which is the only country to have appeared in every World Cup final tournament?

30.
Can you name the only player to have scored in successive World Cup finals?

31.
Who holds the record for appearing in the greatest number of World Cup final tournaments?

32.
Who holds the record for appearing in the greatest number of World Cup final tournament matches?

33.
Who holds the record for scoring the greatest number of goals in a single World Cup final tournament?

34.
Apart from Just Fontaine, only one other player has scored in

every game in a World Cup final tournament. Who is he?

35.
Who is the oldest player to have played on the winning side in a World Cup final?

36.
Who is the youngest player to have appeared in a World Cup final tournament?

37.
Who was the leading scorer in the 1982 World Cup final tournament in Spain?

38.
In what year was the World Cup final tournament held in France?

39.
England finished second in their qualifying group for the 1982 World Cup finals. Who headed the group?

40.
Who was the leading scorer in the 1970 World Cup final tournament in Mexico?

41.
Who scored England's first goal in the 1966 World Cup final tournament?

42.
To 1982, when was the only occasion on which the World Cup was won by a team not playing on their home continent?

43.
Who holds the record for the most goals in World Cup final tournaments in aggregate?

44.
Who beat Fiji 13-0 in a World Cup qualifying match on 15 August 1981?

45.
Which country knocked England out at quarter-final stage in the 1954 World Cup?

46.
Who scored England's first-ever goal in a World Cup final tournament match?

47.
Who scored England's last goal in the 1982 World Cup finals in Spain?

48.
Which country beat England in a play-off to go through to the quarter-finals in 1958?

49.
Who beat Northern Ireland in the quarter-finals of the 1958 World Cup?

50.
Who did Brazil beat in the 1970 World Cup final?

51.
Which World Cup final tournament, to 1982, produced the highest average number of goals per game?

52.
Which World Cup final tournament, to 1982, produced the lowest average number of goals per game?

53.
Who was President of FIFA from 1921 to 1954, and what was his particular connection with the World Cup?

54.
What was the name of the new stadium which was built in Montevideo for the first World Cup tournament in 1930?

55.
How did Alex Villaplane, captain of the French team in the 1930 World Cup, ultimately meet his death?

56.
Who was Abel Lafleur?

57.
Who was the manager of the Italian teams which won the World Cup in 1934 and 1938?

58.
Which country qualified for the 1938 World Cup final tournament, but had to withdraw because they had been overrun by Germany before the tournament started?

59.
Who did Italy beat in the semi-finals of the 1970 World Cup, and what was the score?

60.
Kempes scored two of Argentina's three goals in the 1978 World Cup final. Who scored the other?

61.
Who scored for the Netherlands from a penalty in the first minute of the 1974 World Cup final?

62.
Who surprisingly joined New York Cosmos in April 1977 for $2,500,000, thus taking himself out of the 1978 World Cup arena?

63.
North Korea provided the biggest shock of the 1966 World Cup finals, beating Italy 1-0 in the first phase matches, but who knocked the Koreans out at the quarter-final stages?

64.
Who did Northern Ireland beat in a play-off to win through to the quarter-finals in 1958?

65.
What was the venue for the first World Cup tournament to be held after the Second World War?

66.
Who knocked England out of the 1962 World Cup at the quarter-final stage?

67.
Where was the World Cup hidden for most of the Second World War?

68.
On what basis did England qualify for the World Cup final tournaments of 1950 and 1954?

69.
Which was the only World Cup final tournament for which all four home countries qualified?

70.
England suffered three defeats on the way to qualifying for the 1982 World Cup finals. Norway and Switzerland inflicted two of them, but can you name the third?

71.
Northern Ireland qualified for the 1982 World Cup finals by finishing second in their group. Who won the group?

72.
Who were the representatives from the Oceania confederation at the 1982 World Cup finals?

73.
Italy drew all three of her first phase matches in the 1982 World Cup final tournament. Two of her opponents were Poland and Peru, but can you name the third?

74.
Which two teams were involved in a 1-0 result in Spain in 1982, which was widely suspected of being 'rigged'?

75.
In qualifying for the 1986 finals, England were in a group which included Northern Ireland, Rumania, Turkey and who else?

76.
When England beat Turkey 8-0 in a World Cup qualifying match on 14 November 1984, one player scored a hat-trick. Can you name him?

77.
Who were the first team to qualify (not including automatic qualification) for the 1986 finals?

78.
Which two teams were involved in the 'Battle of Santiago' in 1962, and who won the match?

79.
Who was in charge of the England team in the 1950 World Cup?

80.
What was the name of the Argentinian captain sent off in a 1966 World Cup quarter-final?

81.
Who once described Martin Peters as being 'ten years ahead of his time'?

82.
What offer did Uruguay make to clinch their selection as hosts for the first World Cup finals?

83.
Who beat Brazil 1-0 to win third place in the 1974 World Cup?

84.
In the context of World Cup finals, what do Hungary and Czechoslovakia have in common?

85.
Which two teams have played in four World Cup finals?

86.
Which two London stadiums were used in the 1966 World Cup final tournament?

87.
Can you remember the name of the North Korean player who scored the goal which beat Italy in the 1966 finals?

88.
Who scored the only goal of the game between England and Brazil in the 1970 World Cup finals?

89.
In which city was Bobby Moore falsely accused of stealing a bracelet just before the 1970 final tournament?

90.
Who were the two scorers of England's goals in the 1970 quarter-final against West Germany?

91.
What was the name given to the deeply negative, defensive style of play for which Italian teams in the 1960s and early 1970s became famous?

92.
After beating Zaire 2-0 in their opening game in the 1974 World Cup finals, Scotland went on to register two draws before being eliminated undefeated. Who were their opponents in those drawn games?

93.
Who was Scotland's manager in the 1974 World Cup campaign?

94.
Who was manager of the victorious Argentinian team in 1978?

95.
Which two teams were involved in a thrilling 12-goal quarter-final in the 1954 World Cup?

96.
Who beat Scotland 7-0 in the 1954 World Cup final tournament?

97.
Only four European sides made the long trip to Uruguay for the first World Cup tournament in 1930. Can you name two of them?

98.
Which decision, taken by the FIFA organising committee in Paris in February 1950, led to the withdrawal of the Indian team from the 1950 World Cup?

99.
Who was Larry Gaetjens?

100.
Including the qualifying tournament, who was England's top goalscorer in the 1982 World Cup?

Answers

1.
1930.

2.
D.B.Woolfall of the FA. Elected in 1906-07, he served in the post until his death in 1918.

3.
The British Associations refused to be associated with countries who had been enemies during the Great War of 1914-18, or had remained neutral.

4.
1928. Because FIFA had decided that 'broken time' payments (i.e. payments for loss of earnings) should be made to amateur players in addition to the accepted payment of expenses for travel and accommodation.

5.
Seven - Belgium, Denmark, France, the Netherlands, Spain, Sweden and Switzerland. The meeting took place in Paris.

6.
Five times - Uruguay 1930, Italy 1934, England 1966, West Germany 1974 and Argentina 1978.

7.
1950 in Brazil.

8.
Chile. England won 2-0 in Rio de Janeiro.

9.
It was the venue for England's shock 1-0 defeat by the USA in the 1950 World Cup.

10.
Thirteen - Argentina, Belgium, Bolivia, Brazil, Chile, France, Mexico, Paraguay, Peru, Rumania, Uruguay, USA, Yugoslavia.

11.
Weber. Haller scored the first and England's scorers were Hurst (3) and Peters.

12.
1930. They beat Paraguay and Belgium to get there, but were beaten 6-1 by Argentina in the semi-final.

13.
Eusebio of Portugal with nine goals.

14.
Munich.

15.
Breitner.

16.
Colombia.

17.
Italy.

18.
They are both Italians, both goalkeepers, and both captained their sides to World Cup victory - Combi in 1934, Zoff in 1982.

19.
Mario Zagalo. He played in the Brazilian winning teams of 1958 and 1962 and managed the Brazilians to victory in 1970.

20.
1970, in Mexico.

21.
Uruguay and Brazil in the final game of the 1950 tournament. The match was staged in the Maracana Stadium in Rio de Janeiro.

22.
Czechoslovakia, by a score of 3-1.

23.
Hungary. Belgium and Argentina qualified from that group.

24.
Leon.

25.
Poland, who beat France 3-2 in the third place play-off.

26.
Bilbao.

27.
1958. They were knocked out 1-0 by Brazil at the quarter-final stage.

28.
West Germany beat Hungary 3-2 in the final.

29.
Brazil. Including 1982 they had played fifty-seven final tournament matches, winning thirty-seven, drawing ten and losing ten.

30.
Vava of Brazil. Real name Edwaldo Izidio Neto, he scored

two against Sweden in the 1958 final and one against
Czechoslovakia in 1962.

31.
Antonio Carbajal, who kept goal for Mexico in 1950, 1954,
1958, 1962 and 1966, playing eleven games in all.

32.
Uwe Seeler of West Germany, who made twenty-one
appearances in final tournament matches between 1958 and
1970.

33.
Just Fontaine of France, who scored thirteen goals in the 1958
finals in Sweden.

34.
Jairzinho of Brazil, who scored seven goals in six matches in
1970.

35.
Dino Zoff of Italy, who was forty years old in the 1982
tournament in Spain.

36.
Norman Whiteside, who turned out for Northern Ireland at
the age of seventeen in 1982 after only two first team
appearances for Manchester United.

37.
Paulo Rossi of Italy, who scored six in 1982.

38.
1938.

39.
Hungary, with ten points to England's nine. Rumania
amassed eight, Switzerland seven and Norway six.

40.
Gerd Müller of West Germany, with ten goals.

41.
Bobby Charlton, against Mexico.

42.
1958, when Brazil won in Sweden.

43.
Gerd Müller of West Germany, with ten in 1970 and four

more in 1974.

44.
New Zealand.

45.
Uruguay, by a score of 4-2 in Basle.

46.
Stan Mortensen, against Chile in 1950.

47.
Trevor Francis, who scored the only goal of England's last
Phase One match, against Kuwait.

48.
USSR.

49.
France, by a score of 4-0.

50.
Italy, by a score of 4-1.

51.
Switzerland, in 1954. There were twenty-six matches and 140
goals, giving an average of 5.38 goals per game.

52.
West Germany, in 1974. There were thirty-eight games and
ninety- seven goals, for an average of 2.55 goals per game.

53.
Jules Rimet. The first World Cup trophy was named after
him.

54.
The Centenary Stadium.

55.
He was shot by the French Resistance for collaborating with
the Nazis.

56.
The French sculptor who designed the original World Cup.

57.
Vittorio Pozzo.

58.
Austria.

59.
West Germany, by 4-3.

60.
Bertoni.

61.
Neeskens.

62.
Franz Beckenbauer.

63.
Portugal, by 5-3 after trailing 0-3 at one stage.

64.
Czechoslovakia, by 2-1.

65.
Brazil in 1950.

66.
Brazil by 3-1.

67.
Under Jules Rimet's bed in German-occupied Paris.

68.
By winning the British Championship. Scotland also qualified by virtue of being runners-up, but declined to take part in 1950.

69.
1958.

70.
Rumania.

71.
Scotland.

72.
New Zealand.

73.
Cameroon.

74.
West Germany and Austria.

75.
Finland.

76.
Bryan Robson. The other scorers were Woodcock and Barnes with two apiece, and Anderson.

77.
Uruguay, who beat Chile 2-1 in their final qualifying game on 7 April 1985.

78.
Chile and Italy. Chile won 2-0.

79.
Walter Winterbottom.

80.
Rattin.

81.
Ron Greenwood, then Peters' manager at West Ham.

82.
They offered to pay the travelling and accommodation expenses for all participating countries.

83.
Poland.

84.
They have both been losing finalists twice. Hungary lost to Italy in 1938 and West Germany in 1954, while Czechoslovakia lost to Italy in 1934 and Brazil in 1962.

85.
Italy and West Germany. Italy won in 1934, 1938 and 1982 and lost in 1970. West Germany won in 1954 and 1974, losing in 1966 and 1982. Brazil have appeared in three finals, winning them all (1958, 1962, 1970) and although they also played in what amounted to a final against Uruguay in 1950, that tournament was decided on a league basis throughout, and so the match cannot be counted as a final.

86.
Wembley and White City. Only one match - the first stage game between Uruguay and France - was played at the White City stadium.

87.
Pak Doo Ik.

88.
Jairzinho.

89.
Bogota, Colombia.

90.
Alan Mullery and Martin Peters.

91.
Catenaccio.

92.
Brazil (0-0) and Yugoslavia (1-1).

93.
Willie Ormond.

94.
Cesar Luis Menotti.

95.
Austria 7, Switzerland 5.

96.
Uruguay. Scotland had already lost 0-1 to Austria, and were therefore eliminated.

97.
The four were France, Belgium, Rumania and Yugoslavia.

98.
That nobody would be allowed to play barefoot.

99.
The Haitian-born United States forward who scored the goal which defeated England at Belo Horizonte in the 1950 World Cup.

100.
Paul Mariner, who scored three in the qualifying matches and two more in the finals.

CHAPTER EIGHT

WORLD CUP MISCELLANY
MEXICO – MAKING THE BIGGEST EFFORT

The 1986 final tournament will be the ninth that Mexico have taken part in, but their record in the previous eight tournaments has been dismal - Played twenty-four, Won three, Drawn four, Lost seventeen, Goals For twenty-one, Goals Against sixty-two. They didn't register their first win in a final tournament until 1962 when they beat eventual finalists Czechoslovakia 3-1 in a meaningless final game in the first round, and the only time they have ever progressed beyond the first round was on the last occasion the final tournament was held in their own country. In 1970 they got through to the quarter-finals, only to be crushed 4-1 by Italy.

Despite this uninspiring record, they are taking the 1986 finals very seriously indeed, as is shown by their preparations. Clubs are required – they have no choice – to make their best players available, and those players were formed into a squad as soon as the 1984-85 League season had finished in May 1985. From that point onwards, the entire squad remained at the disposal of their Yugoslavian manager, Bora Milutinovich, for more than a year - right through to the final tournament in the summer of 1986.

Meanwhile, the League Championship 1985-86 went ahead, but with one important difference – there would be no relegation, thus removing the fear that might otherwise have afflicted the weakened teams. An object lesson here for certain other Leagues who are unwilling even to postpone one match! During their year-long exile, the Mexican team will play more than twenty practice games against the best opposition they can find. It will be interesting to see if these preparations will pay dividends when the competition starts in earnest.

French Celebrations

The first ever World Cup goal was scored by Louis Laurent for France against Mexico in Montevideo. France went on to win the match 4-1. The date was 13 July 1930 – and by the time the news reached France it was 14 July, Bastille Day.

Grand Achievement

When Robbie Rensenbrink scored from the penalty spot against Scotland in 1978, it was the 1,000th goal in World Cup final tournaments.

A Field Day for Paddy

Paddy Moore, of the Republic of Ireland, became the first player to score four goals in a World Cup game when he scored all four for Ireland in their 4-4 draw with Belgium in a World Cup qualifying match in Dublin on 25 February 1934.

Quick Off the Mark

England captain Bryan Robson registered the fastest-ever World Cup goal when he scored against France after only twenty-seven seconds in England's opening game in the 1982 World Cup finals. England went on to win the match 3-1. Coincidentally, the match was held on 16 June 1982, exactly forty-four years to the day after Olle Nyberg of Sweden had set the previous record, scoring after 30 seconds against Hungary in Paris.

Manager of the Century?

Helmut Schoen retired after the 1978 World Cup finals, having spent fourteen years in charge of the West German national team. During that period his team finished as runners-up in the 1966 World Cup, came third in 1970 and won in 1974. They also won the European Championship in 1972 and were runners-up in 1976.

Kiwi Keeper

During the 1982 World Cup qualifying competition, New Zealand played an unprecedented fifteen games to reach the finals. During these matches, goalkeeper Richard Wilson played for fifteen hours and twenty minutes without conceding a goal.

Unlikely Lads

Of the fifty-three countries who had participated in World Cup final tournaments up to and including 1982, only one - Cameroon - remains undefeated. They qualified in 1982 and drew all three of their opening phase matches, 0-0 v Peru, 0-0 v Poland and 1-1 v Italy.

Hat-trick Hero

Geoff Hurst is the only player to have registered a hat-trick in a World Cup final. He did it for England against West Germany in 1966, though one of his goals in extra time remains the most controversial ever scored in a World Cup final.

The First Penalty to be Missed

In the 1982 World Cup final between Italy and West Germany, Antonio Cabrini missed a penalty for Italy. The mistake didn't make any difference to the final outcome, but it was the first time a penalty had ever been missed in a World Cup final.

Shoot-out

The 1982 World Cup semi-final between France and West Germany, played in Seville on 8 July 1982, was the first match in a World Cup series to be decided on penalties. After a 3-3 draw, West Germany went through 5-4 on spot-kicks.

Second-half Improvement

In August 1981 Fiji lined up to play New Zealand in a World Cup qualifier. Their goalkeeper Akuila Nataro Rovono let in seven goals in the first half, and so at half-time he was replaced by Semi Bai. The improvement was immediate - Fiji only conceded six goals in the second half! Fiji were later suspended from international competition for a year by FIFA because of repeated rioting amongst their supporters.

England spoil the Party

When Garaba scored for Hungary against England in a World Cup qualifier in Budapest on 6 June 1981, it was Hungary's one hundredth goal in World Cup games, but goals from Brooking (2) and Keegan (penalty) gave the points to the visitors.

Incentive Scheme, Kuwaiti Style

Kuwait's qualification for the 1982 World Cup finals was greeted enthusiastically by Crown Prince Sheik Saad Abdullah Al Sabah. He presented each of the twenty-four players in the squad with a Cadillac, a luxury villa, a plot of land, a gold watch and a speedboat!

England win the First World Cup!

Mention has been made in the History of the World Cup *(Chapter One)* of Sir Thomas Lipton, the tea millionaire who presented the Lipton Trophy as the prize for the annual match between Uruguay and Argentina. However, Sir Thomas was also responsible for the first World Cup tournament, held in 1910.

Glasgow-born Sir Thomas had been made a Knight of the Grand Order of Italy, and in gratitude he set the tournament up in 1910, presenting the trophy himself and stipulating that if anybody won it twice in succession, they should keep the trophy outright.

We have seen in the History of the World Cup how insular and pompous the English football authorities were towards international competitions in those days, and Sir Thomas was unsuccessful in his attempt to get any sort of official England team to take part in the tournament, to be held in Italy. He therefore invited West Auckland, third from bottom in the Northern Amateur League at the time, to represent England!

The team, consisting mostly of miners, was so keen to take part that they were prepared to lose money at the pit and even sell personal furniture and other items to raise the money for the trip. Their enthusiasm was rewarded when, after beating Red Star Zurich and Stuttgart to reach the final, they overcame the mighty Juventus 2-0 in Turin to take the cup. The following year they returned to Turin and again beat Juventus in the final, so winning the Lipton World Cup outright! In 1982 the events of those marvellous years were turned into a film by Tyne Tees TV. Called *The World Cup: A Captain's Tale* it starred Dennis Waterman and Nigel Hawthorne.

England's Top Trio

Three Englishmen have been Presidents of FIFA over the years. The first was D.B. Woolfall, who held the post from 4

June 1906 until his death on 24 October 1918; the second was Arthur Drewry, who served from 9 June 1956 until 25 March 1961; the third was Sir Stanley Rous, President from 28 September 1961 until 11 June 1974. Sir Stanley was succeeded by the only South American to hold the post, current President João Havelange of Brazil.

Healing Old Wounds

The 1982 World Cup saw the resumption of matches between Honduras and El Salvador. In 1969, a qualifying game between these two countries had sparked off a four-day war!

Back in Winning Ways

On 23 November 1980, in a World Cup qualifying match in Fort Lauderdale, Florida, the United States beat Mexico 2-1 - the first victory by the USA over Mexico since the 1934 World Cup, when they beat them 4-2 in a preliminary play-off in Rome. The 1980 victory was less useful, however, as the States had already been eliminated.

Odd One Out

The Israeli team which played in the European Group Six of the 1982 World Cup qualifying competition included an Arab player - Rifat Turk. He was a midfielder from Hapoel Tel Aviv.

Deyna's Disappointment

Poland's Kazimierz Deyna made his hundredth international appearance for Poland against Argentina in the 1978 final tournament, but it wasn't a happy day for him. His team lost 2-0 and he had a penalty saved by Argentine 'keeper Ubaldo Fillol.

Maier the Magnificent

Josef 'Sepp' Maier, West Germany's goalkeeper, kept a clean sheet for a continuous spell of 475 minutes in World Cup final games - a record. He conceded a penalty in the first minute of the 1974 final against the Netherlands and was not beaten again until the same team scored against West Germany in the 1978 finals.

Brazilian Sympathy

After England's disastrous defeat by the United States at Belo Horizonte during the 1950 World Cup, the Rio de Janeiro evening newspaper *A Noite* wrote: 'Goals are decisive, that cannot be denied, but who would not admit that it was a spectacle well worth seeing to watch the English playing – they are still the Kings'.

More Brazilian Compliments

In the first phase matches of the 1950 World Cup, Brazil drew one of their matches – 2-2 against Switzerland – and were not pleased with the performance of the Spanish referee, Azon. As a consequence, the Editor of the *Gazeta Esportiva* in São Paulo wrote the following: 'We must strongly demand that Brazil shall not take the field again in this World Championship if a British referee is not in charge. . . . Even should we finally meet the English we shall still demand a British referee and have full confidence in him.' Unfortunately, the opportunity did not arise, although all three of Brazil's games in the final pool matches were refereed by Englishmen - messrs Ellis, Leafe and Reader.

The Last to Go

Ernesto Mascheroni, the last survivor of the Uruguayan team which won the first World Cup in 1930, died on 3 July 1984, aged seventy-six. He started his career with Olimpia, then played for Peñarol, finishing his playing days with the Italian club Ambrossiana, for whom he played until his mid-thirties.

TV Record Broken

The 1982 World Cup final between Italy and West Germany was watched by a television audience of two billion - the highest figure ever registered.

Kissinger's Comeback

In September 1984 it was announced that former US Secretary of State Henry Kissinger had been appointed Chairman of an advisory board to the United States Soccer Federation, the main aim of which is to secure the candidacy of the United States for hosting a future World Cup final tournament.

Pressed Too Far

In October 1984 FIFA announced that Press accreditation for the 1986 World Cup finals in Mexico would be limited to 5,000. This follows from the ridiculous scenes at the 1982 final where over 7,000 Press passes were issued, thus taking up a substantial portion of the stadium, and many seats were unclaimed. Press accreditation had risen from 1,777 in 1966 to 7,290 in 1982!

The Price is Right

Admission prices for World Cup games in Mexico have been set at between US$3 and US$50 per seat, equivalent to approximately £2 to £35 sterling at the time of going to press.

It's Still Kaiser Franz

Franz Beckenbauer, one of Europe's most gifted players for more than a decade in the sixties and seventies, is now manager of the West German national squad. His dominant qualities on the field of play earned him the nickname 'Kaiser Franz' - a tag which is sure to stay with him if he continues in the successful manner of his predecessor, Helmut Schoen.

Super Start for New Stadium

The new Queretaro Stadium in Mexico - the only one built specially for the 1986 World Cup - was opened on 5 February 1985 by the Mexican Head of State, President Miguel de la Madrid and, in the presence of many FIFA dignitaries including President João Havelange, Mexico celebrated the occasion by trouncing Poland 5-0 in front of a capacity 40,000 crowd.

Recycling Rules OK

A remarkable project has been carried out at Mexico's Puebla Stadium in preparation for the 1986 World Cup. Any rain which falls on the stadium is drained into a 7,000 cubic metre underground reservoir, where it is purified and recycled for general use in the stadium, including showers for the teams!

Iran Kicked Out

It was reported by FIFA in March 1985 that Iran has been excluded from the 1986 World Cup qualifying tournament because the national football association refused to play their qualifying matches on neutral territory. The original decision that neutral venues should be used was taken because of the war between Iraq and Iran. The same limitations were placed on Iraq and Lebanon, who accepted them. However, Lebanon subsequently withdrew from the competition of their own accord because of the domestic situation.

First Past the Post

The first country to qualify for the 1986 World Cup final tournament (apart from the hosts and the champions, who qualify automatically) was Uruguay. They defeated Chile 2-1 in the final match of South America Group Two, and so the Champions of 1930 and 1950 are back in the finals for the first time since 1974.

Record Entry

The 1986 World Cup attracted a record number of 123 entries out of the 150 countries affiliated to FIFA. Exactly one year before the kick-off, in May 1985, FIFA announced that the qualifying tournament so far had thrown up the following statistics: 197 matches played, in front of approximately 4.5 million spectators; 541 goals scored; 106 home victories, thirty-six draws, fifty-five away wins; 345 yellow cards shown, ten players sent off.

Big Day for Michel

29 April 1985 was a big day for Michel Platini. In the morning he was taken to see his waxwork effigy in the Parisian 'Musée Grevin', in the afternoon President Mitterand conferred upon him the knighthood of the 'Legion d'Honneur' and in the evening he was presented with the 'Ballon d'Or' to mark his election as European Footballer of the Year 1984.

Rous Cup to be Extended

On the occasion of the 90th birthday of football's elder statesman, Sir Stanley Rous, Honorary Life President of FIFA, on 25 April 1985, the Rous Cup was announced by João

Havelange. Initially the cup was awarded to the winners of the annual England v Scotland match, but it was also stated that in future a third, non-British, participant would be invited.

It Can't be True!

When the scoreline of 1-0 was transmitted to the British Press agencies after England's defeat by the USA in Belo Horizonte in the 1950 World Cup, one agency assumed that it was a mistake and printed the result as 1-10 in England's favour!

Fortress Wembley

Nobody should have been surprised when England won the World Cup in 1966. They played all six of their matches at Wembley, and history dictated that they were likely to win. They had, to that point, lost only three times against non-British opposition at Wembley - to Hungary in 1953, Sweden in 1959 and Austria in 1965. None of the six countries England faced in 1966 had even managed a draw at Wembley, and West Germany had never beaten England anywhere.

CHAPTER NINE

WORLD CUP 1930–1982

Merit Table

A league table compilation of all matches played in World Cup final tournaments between 1930 and 1982.

	P	W	D	L	F	A	% Wins	Goal Diff.	No.of finals
Brazil	57	37	10	10	134	62	64.9	+72	12
West Germany*	54	31	11	12	122	78	57.4	+44	10
Italy	43	24	9	10	74	46	55.8	+28	10
Argentina	34	16	5	13	63	50	47.0	+13	8
England	29	13	8	8	40	29	44.8	+11	7
Uruguay	29	14	5	10	57	39	48.3	+18	7
Hungary	29	14	3	12	85	48	48.3	+37	5
USSR	24	12	5	7	37	25	50.0	+12	5
Poland	21	12	4	5	38	22	57.1	+16	4
Yugoslavia	28	12	4	12	47	36	42.9	+11	7
Sweden	28	11	6	11	48	46	39.3	+2	7
France	27	11	3	13	59	50	40.8	+9	8
Austria	23	11	2	10	38	40	47.8	−2	5
Spain	23	8	5	10	26	30	34.8	−4	6
Czechoslovakia	25	8	5	12	34	40	32.0	−6	7
Netherlands	16	8	3	5	32	19	50.0	+13	4
Chile	21	7	3	11	26	32	33.3	−6	6
Switzerland	18	5	2	11	28	44	27.8	−16	6
Scotland	14	3	5	6	20	29	21.4	−9	5
Peru	15	4	3	8	19	31	26.7	−12	4
Portugal	6	5	0	1	17	8	83.3	+9	2
Northern Ireland	10	3	4	3	11	17	30.0	−6	2
Mexico	24	3	4	17	21	62	12.5	−41	8
Belgium	14	3	2	9	15	30	21.4	−15	6
East Germany	6	2	2	2	5	5	33.3	0	1
Paraguay	7	2	2	3	12	19	28.6	−7	3

USA	7	3	0	4	12	21	42.9	−9	3
Wales	5	1	3	1	4	4	20.0	0	1
Rumania	8	2	1	5	12	17	25.0	−5	4
Algeria	3	2	0	1	5	5	66.7	0	1
Bulgaria	12	0	4	8	9	29	0	−20	4
Tunisia	3	1	1	1	3	2	33.3	+1	1
Cameroon	3	0	3	0	1	1	0	0	1
Cuba	3	1	1	1	5	12	33.3	−7	1
North Korea	4	1	1	2	5	9	25.0	−4	1
Turkey	3	1	0	2	10	11	33.3	−1	1
Honduras	3	0	2	1	2	3	0	−1	1
Israel	3	1	0	2	1	3	33.3	−2	1
Kuwait	3	0	1	2	2	6	0	−4	1
Morocco	3	0	1	2	2	6	0	−4	1
Australia	3	0	1	2	0	5	0	−5	1
Colombia	3	0	1	2	5	11	0	−6	1
Iran	3	0	1	2	2	8	0	−6	1
Norway	1	0	0	1	1	2	0	−1	1
Egypt	1	0	0	1	2	4	0	−2	1
Dutch East Indies	1	0	0	1	0	6	0	−6	1
South Korea	2	0	0	2	0	16	0	−16	1
New Zealand	3	0	0	3	2	12	0	−10	1
Haiti	3	0	0	3	2	14	0	−12	1
Zaire	3	0	0	3	0	14	0	−14	1
Bolivia	3	0	0	3	0	16	0	−16	1
El Salvador	6	0	0	6	1	22	0	−21	2

Includes Germany 1934−38

World Cup Attendances & Goals 1930–1982

Year	Venue	Games	Attendance	(Av.)	Goals	(Av.)
1930	Uruguay	18	434,500	(24,139)	70	(3.9)
1934	Italy	17	395,000	(23,235)	70	(4.1)
1938	France	18	483,000	(26,833)	84	(4.7)
1950	Brazil	22	1,337,000	(60,772)	88	(4.0)
1954	Switzerland	26	943,000	(36,270)	140	(5.4)
1958	Sweden	35	868,000	(24,800)	126	(3.6)
1962	Chile	32	776,000	(24,250)	89	(2.8)
1966	England	32	1,614,677	(50,458)	89	(2.8)
1970	Mexico	32	1,673,975	(52,312)	95	(2.9)
1974	West Germany	38	1,774,022	(46,685)	97	(2.6)
1978	Argentina	38	1,610,215	(42,374)	102	(2.7)
1982	Spain	52	1,766,277	(33,967)	146	(2.8)

World Cup Leading Scorers 1930–1982

Year	Name	Country	Goals
1930	Guillermo Stabile	Argentina	8
1934	Angelo Schiavio	Italy	4
	Oldrich Nejedly	Czechoslovakia	4
	Edmund Cohen	Germany	4
1938	Leonidas da Silva	Brazil	8
1950	Ademir	Brazil	9
1954	Sandor Kocsis	Hungary	11
1958	Just Fontaine	France	13
1962	Drazen Jerkovic	Yugoslavia	5
1966	Eusebio	Portugal	9
1970	Gerd Müller	West Germany	10
1974	Grzegorz Lato	Poland	7
1978	Mario Kempes	Argentina	6
1982	Paulo Rossi	Italy	6

CHAPTER TEN

WORLD CUP FINAL TOURNAMENT RESULTS

Country-by-Country Guide

Key: W=Winners; L=Losing Finalists; T=Third; F=Fourth;
P=Play-off; R=Replay; *=Won on Penalties; +=Lost on Penalties.

ALGERIA

1982
West Germany 2-1
Austria 0-2
Chile 3-2

ARGENTINA

1930
France 1-0
Mexico 6-3
Chile 3-1
USA 6-1
Uruguay 2-4 (L)

1934
Sweden 2-3

1958
West Germany 1-3
Northern Ireland 3-1
Czechoslovakia 1-6

1962
Bulgaria 1-0
England 1-3
Hungary 0-0

1966
Spain 2-1
West Germany 0-0
Switzerland 2-0
England 0-1

1974
Poland 2-3
Italy 1-1
Haiti 4-1
Netherlands 0-4
Brazil 1-2
East Germany 1-1

1978
Hungary 2-1
France 2-1

Italy 0-1
Poland 2-0
Brazil 0-0
Peru 6-0
Netherlands 3-1 (W)

1982
Belgium 0-1
Hungary 4-1
El Salvador 2-0
Italy 1-2
Brazil 1-3

AUSTRALIA

1974
East Germany 0-2
West Germany 0-3
Chile 0-0

AUSTRIA

1934
France 3-2
France 2-1
Italy 0-1
Germany 2-3 (F)

1954
Scotland 0-1
Czechoslovakia 5-0
Switzerland 7-5
West Germany 1-6
Uruguay 3-1 (T)

1958
Brazil 0-3
USSR 0-2
England 2-2

1978
Spain 2-1
Sweden 1-0
Brazil 0-1
Netherlands 1-5
Italy 0-1

West Germany 3-2

1982
Chile 1-0
Algeria 2-0
West Germany 0-1
France 0-1
Northern Ireland 2-2

BELGIUM

1930
USA 0-3
Paraguay 0-1

1934
Germany 2-5

1938
France 1-3

1954
England 4-4
Italy 1-4

1970
El Salvador 3-0
USSR 1-4
Mexico 0-1

1982
Argentina 1-0
El Salvador 1-0
Hungary 1-1
Poland 0-3
USSR 0-1

BOLIVIA

1930
Yugoslavia 0-4
Brazil 0-4

1950
Uruguay 0-8

BRAZIL

1930
Yugoslavia 1-2
Bolivia 4-0

1934
Spain 1-3

1938
Poland 6-5
Czechoslovakia 1-1
Czechoslovakia 2-1 (R)
Italy 1-2
Sweden 4-2 (T)

1950
Mexico 4-0
Switzerland 2-2
Yugoslavia 2-0
Sweden 7-1
Spain 6-1
Uruguay 1-2

1954
Mexico 5-0
Yugoslavia 1-1
Hungary 2-4

1958
Austria 3-0
England 0-0
USSR 2-0
Wales 1-0
France 5-2
Sweden 5-2 (W)

1962
Mexico 2-0
Czechoslovakia 0-0
Spain 2-1
England 3-1
Chile 4-2
Czechoslovakia 3-1 (W)

1966
Bulgaria 2-0

Hungary 1-3
Portugal 1-3

1970
Czechoslovakia 4-1
England 1-0
Rumania 3-2
Peru 4-2
Uruguay 3-1
Italy 4-1 (W)

1974
Yugoslavia 0-0
Scotland 0-0
Zaire 3-0
East Germany 1-0
Argentina 2-1
Netherlands 0-2
Poland 0-1 (F)

1978
Sweden 1-1
Spain 0-0
Austria 1-0
Peru 3-0
Argentina 0-0
Poland 3-1
Italy 2-1 (T)

1982
USSR 2-1
Scotland 4-1
New Zealand 4-0
Argentina 3-1
Italy 2-3

BULGARIA

1962
Argentina 0-1
Hungary 1-6
England 0-0

1966
Brazil 0-2
Portugal 0-3

Hungary 1-3

1970
Peru 2-3
West Germany 2-5
Morocco 1-1

1974
Sweden 0-0
Uruguay 1-1
Netherlands 1-4

CAMEROON

1982
Peru 0-0
Poland 0-0
Italy 1-1

CHILE

1930
Mexico 3-0
France 1-0
Argentina 1-3

1950
England 0-2
Spain 0-2
USA 5-2

1962
Switzerland 3-1
Italy 2-0
West Germany 0-2
USSR 2-1
Brazil 2-4
Yugoslavia 1-0 (T)

1966
Italy 0-2
North Korea 1-1
USSR 1-2

1974
West Germany 0-1
East Germany 1-1

Australia 0-0

1982
Austria 0-1
West Germany 1-4
Algeria 2-3

COLOMBIA

1962
Uruguay 1-2
USSR 4-4
Yugoslavia 0-5

CUBA

1938
Rumania 3-3
Rumania 2-1 (R)
Sweden 0-8

CZECHOSLOVAKIA

1934
Rumania 2-1
Switzerland 3-2
Germany 3-1
Italy 1-2 (L)

1938
Netherlands 3-0
Brazil 1-1
Brazil 1-2 (R)

1954
Uruguay 0-2
Austria 0-5

1958
Northern Ireland 0-1
West Germany 2-2
Argentina 6-1
Northern Ireland 1-2 (P)

1962
Spain 1-0
Brazil 0-0

Mexico 1-3
Hungary 1-0
Yugoslavia 3-1
Brazil 1-3 (L)

1970
Brazil 1-4
Rumania 1-2
England 0-1

1982
Kuwait 1-1
England 0-2
France 1-1

DUTCH EAST INDIES

1938
Hungary 0-6

EAST GERMANY

1974
Australia 2-0
Chile 1-1
West Germany 1-0
Brazil 0-1
Netherlands 0-2
Argentina 1-1

EGYPT

1934
Hungary 2-4

ENGLAND

1950
Chile 2-0
USA 0-1
Spain 0-1

1954
Belgium 4-4
Switzerland 2-0
Uruguay 2-4

1958
USSR 2-2
Brazil 0-0
Austria 2-2
USSR 0-1 (P)

1962
Hungary 1-2
Argentina 3-1
Bulgaria 0-0
Brazil 1-3

1966
Uruguay 0-0
Mexico 2-0
France 2-0
Argentina 1-0
Portugal 2-1
West Germany 4-2 (W)

1970
Rumania 1-0
Brazil 0-1
Czechoslovakia 1-0
West Germany 2-3

1982
France 3-1
Czechoslovakia 2-0
Kuwait 1-0
West Germany 0-0
Spain 0-0

EL SALVADOR

1970
Belgium 0-3
Mexico 0-4
USSR 0-2

1982
Hungary 1-10
Belgium 0-1
Argentina 0-2

FRANCE

1930
Mexico 4-1
Argentina 0-1
Chile 0-1

1934
Austria 2-3

1938
Belgium 3-1
Italy 1-3

1954
Yugoslavia 0-1
Mexico 3-2

1958
Paraguay 7-3
Yugoslavia 2-3
Scotland 2-1
Northern Ireland 4-0
Brazil 2-5
West Germany 6-3 (T)

1966
Mexico 1-1
Uruguay 1-2
England 0-2

1978
Italy 1-2
Argentina 1-2
Hungary 3-1

1982
England 1-3
Kuwait 4-1
Czechoslovakia 1-1
Austria 1-0
Northern Ireland 4-1
West Germany 3-3+
Poland 2-3 (F)

GERMANY

1934
Belgium 5-2
Sweden 2-1
Czechoslovakia 1-3
Austria 3-2 (T)

1938
Switzerland 1-1
Switzerland 2-4 (R)

HAITI

1974
Italy 1-3
Poland 0-7
Argentina 1-4

HONDURAS

1982
Spain 1-1
Northern Ireland 1-1
Yugoslavia 0-1

HUNGARY

1934
Egypt 4-2
Austria 1-2

1938
Dutch East Indies 6-0
Switzerland 2-0
Sweden 5-1
Italy 2-4 (L)

1954
South Korea 9-0
West Germany 8-3
Brazil 4-2
Uruguay 4-2
West Germany 2-3 (L)

1958
Wales 1-1
Sweden 1-2
Mexico 4-0
Wales 1-2 (P)

1962
England 2-1
Bulgaria 6-1
Argentina 0-0
Czechoslovakia 0-1

1966
Portugal 1-3
Brazil 3-1
Bulgaria 3-1
USSR 1-2

1978
Argentina 1-2
Italy 1-3
France 1-3

1982
El Salvador 10-1
Argentina 1-4
Belgium 1-1

IRAN

1978
Netherlands 0-3
Scotland 1-1
Peru 1-4

ISRAEL

1970
Uruguay 0-2
Sweden 1-1
Italy 0-0

ITALY

1934
USA 7-1

Spain 1-1
Spain 1-0 (R)
Austria 1-0
Czechoslovakia 2-1 (W)

1938
Norway 2-1
France 3-1
Brazil 2-1
Hungary 4-2 (W)

1950
Sweden 2-3
Paraguay 2-0

1954
Switzerland 1-2
Belgium 4-1
Switzerland 1-4 (P)

1962
West Germany 0-0
Chile 0-2
Switzerland 3-0

1966
Chile 2-0
USSR 0-1
North Korea 0-1

1970
Sweden 1-0
Uruguay 0-0
Israel 0-0
Mexico 4-1
West Germany 4-3
Brazil 1-4 (L)

1974
Haiti 3-1
Argentina 1-1
Poland 1-2

1978
France 2-1
Hungary 3-1
Argentina 1-0

West Germany 0-0
Austria 1-0
Netherlands 1-2
Brazil 1-2 (F)

1982
Poland 0-0
Peru 1-1
Cameroon 1-1
Argentina 2-1
Brazil 3-2
Poland 2-0
West Germany 3-1 (W)

SOUTH KOREA

1954
Hungary 0-9
Turkey 0-7

KUWAIT

1982
Czechoslovakia 1-1
France 1-4
England 0-1

MEXICO

1930
France 1-4
Chile 0-3
Argentina 3-6

1950
Brazil 0-4
Yugoslavia 1-4
Switzerland 1-2

1954
Brazil 0-5
France 2-3

1958
Sweden 0-3
Wales 1-1

Hungary 0-4

1962
Brazil 0-2
Spain 0-1
Czechoslovakia 3-1

1966
France 1-1
England 0-2
Uruguay 0-0

1970
USSR 0-0
El Salvador 4-0
Belgium 1-0
Italy 1-4

1978
Tunisia 1-3
West Germany 0-6
Poland 1-3

MOROCCO

1970
West Germany 1-2
Peru 0-3
Bulgaria 1-1

NETHERLANDS

1934
Switzerland 2-3

1938
Czechoslovakia 0-3

1974
Uruguay 2-0
Sweden 0-0
Bulgaria 4-1
Argentina 4-0
East Germany 2-0
Brazil 2-0
West Germany 1-2 (L)

1978
Iran 3-0
Peru 0-0
Scotland 2-3
Austria 5-1
West Germany 2-2
Italy 2-1
Argentina 1-3 (L)

NEW ZEALAND
1982
Scotland 2-5
USSR 0-3
Brazil 0-4

NORTHERN IRELAND
1958
Czechoslovakia 1-0
Argentina 1-3
West Germany 2-2
Czechoslovakia 2-1 (P)
France 0-4

1982
Yugoslavia 0-0
Honduras 1-1
Spain 1-0
Austria 2-2
France 1-4

NORTH KOREA
1966
USSR 0-3
Chile 1-1
Italy 1-0
Portugal 3-5

NORWAY
1938
Italy 1-2

PARAGUAY
1930
USA 0-3
Belgium 0-1

1950
Sweden 2-2
Italy 0-2

1958
France 3-7
Scotland 3-2
Yugoslavia 3-3

PERU
1930
Rumania 1-3
Uruguay 0-1

1970
Bulgaria 3-2
Morocco 3-0
West Germany 1-3
Brazil 2-4

1978
Scotland 3-1
Netherlands 0-0
Iran 4-1
Brazil 0-3
Poland 0-1
Argentina 0-6

1982
Cameroon 0-0
Italy 1-1
Poland 1-5

POLAND
1938
Brazil 5-6

1974
Argentina 3-2

Haiti 7-0
Italy 2-1
Sweden 1-0
Yugoslavia 2-1
West Germany 0-1
Brazil 1-0 (T)

1978
West Germany 0-0
Tunisia 1-0
Mexico 3-1
Argentina 0-2
Peru 1-0
Brazil 1-3

1982
Italy 0-0
Cameroon 0-0
Peru 5-1
Belgium 3-0
USSR 0-0
Italy 0-2
France 3-2 (T)

RUMANIA
1930
Peru 3-1
Uruguay 0-4

1934
Czechoslovakia 1-2

1938
Cuba 3-3
Cuba 1-2 (R)

1970
England 0-1
Czechoslovakia 2-1
Brazil 2-3

SCOTLAND
1954
Austria 0-1
Uruguay 0-7

1958
Yugoslavia 1-1
Paraguay 2-3
France 1-2

1974
Zaire 2-0
Brazil 0-0
Yugoslavia 1-1

1978
Peru 1-3
Iran 1-1
Netherlands 3-2

1982
New Zealand 5-2
Brazil 1-4
USSR 2-2

SPAIN
1934

Brazil 3-1
Italy 1-1
Italy 0-1 (R)

1950
USA 3-1
Chile 2-0
England 1-0
Uruguay 2-2
Brazil 1-6
Sweden 1-3 (F)

1962
Czechoslovakia 0-1
Mexico 1-0
Brazil 1-2

1966
Argentina 1-2
Switzerland 2-1
West Germany 1-2

1978
Austria 1-2

Brazil 0-0
Sweden 1-0

1982
Honduras 1-1
Yugoslavia 2-1
Northern Ireland 0-1
West Germany 1-2
England 0-0

SWEDEN

1934
Argentina 3-2
Germany 1-2

1938
Cuba 8-0
Hungary 1-5
Brazil 2-4 (F)

1950
Italy 3-2
Paraguay 2-2
Brazil 1-7
Uruguay 2-3
Spain 3-1 (T)

1958
Mexico 3-0
Hungary 2-1
Wales 0-0
USSR 2-0
West Germany 3-1
Brazil 2-5 (L)

1970
Italy 0-1
Israel 1-1
Uruguay 1-0

1974
Bulgaria 0-0
Netherlands 0-0
Uruguay 3-0
Poland 0-1

West Germany 2-4
Yugoslavia 2-1

1978
Brazil 1-1
Austria 0-1
Spain 0-1

SWITZERLAND

1934
Netherlands 3-2
Czechoslovakia 2-3

1938
Germany 1-1
Germany 4-2 (R)
Hungary 0-2

1950
Yugoslavia 0-3
Brazil 2-2
Mexico 2-1

1954
England 0-2
Italy 2-1
Italy 4-1 (P)
Austria 5-7

1962
Chile 1-3
West Germany 1-2
Italy 0-3

1966
West Germany 0-5
Spain 1-2
Argentina 0-2

TUNISIA

1978
Mexico 3-1
Poland 0-1
West Germany 0-0

TURKEY

1954
West Germany 1-4
South Korea 7-0
West Germany 2-7 (P)

USA

1930
Belgium 3-0
Paraguay 3-0
Argentina 1-6

1934
Italy 1-7

1950
Spain 1-3
England 1-0
Chile 2-5

URUGUAY

1930
Peru 1-0
Rumania 4-0
Yugoslavia 6-1
Argentina 4-2 (W)

1950
Bolivia 8-0
Spain 2-2
Sweden 3-2
Brazil 2-1 (W)

1954
Czechoslovakia 2-0
Scotland 7-0
England 4-2
Hungary 2-4
Austria 1-3 (F)

1962
Colombia 2-1
Yugoslavia 1-3
USSR 1-2

1966
England 0-0
France 2-1
Mexico 0-0
West Germany 0-4

1970
Israel 2-0
Italy 0-0
Sweden 0-1
USSR 1-0
Brazil 1-3
West Germany 0-1 (F)

1974
Netherlands 0-2
Bulgaria 1-1
Sweden 0-3

USSR

1958
England 2-2
Austria 2-0
Brazil 0-2
England 1-0 (P)
Sweden 0-2

1962
Yugoslavia 2-0
Colombia 4-4
Uruguay 2-1
Chile 1-2

1966
North Korea 3-0
Italy 1-0
Chile 2-1
Hungary 2-1
West Germany 1-2
Portugal 1-2 (F)

1970
Mexico 0-0
Belgium 4-1
El Salvador 2-0

Uruguay 0-1

1982
Brazil 1-2
New Zealand 3-0
Scotland 2-2
Belgium 1-0
Poland 0-0

WALES

1958
Hungary 1-1
Mexico 1-1
Sweden 0-0
Hungary 2-1 (P)
Brazil 0-1

WEST GERMANY

1954
Turkey 4-1
Hungary 3-8
Turkey 7-2 (P)
Yugoslavia 2-0
Austria 6-1
Hungary 3-2 (W)

1958
Argentina 3-1
Czechoslovakia 2-2
Northern Ireland 2-2
Yugoslavia 1-0
Sweden 1-3
France 3-6 (F)

1962
Italy 0-0
Switzerland 2-1
Chile 2-0
Yugoslavia 0-1

1966
Switzerland 5-0
Argentina 0-0
Spain 2-1

Uruguay 4-0
USSR 2-1
England 2-4 (L)

1970
Morocco 2-1
Bulgaria 5-2
Peru 3-1
England 3-2
Italy 3-4
Uruguay 1-0 (T)

1974
Chile 1-0
Australia 3-0
East Germany 0-1
Yugoslavia 2-0
Sweden 4-2
Poland 1-0
Netherlands 2-1 (W)

1978
Poland 0-0
Mexico 6-0
Tunisia 0-0
Italy 0-0
Netherlands 2-2
Austria 2-3

1982
Algeria 1-2
Chile 4-1
Austria 1-0
England 0-0
Spain 2-1
France 3-3*
Italy 1-3 (L)

YUGOSLAVIA

1930
Brazil 2-1
Bolivia 4-0
Uruguay 1-6

1950
Switzerland 3-0
Mexico 4-1
Brazil 0-2

1954
France 1-0
Brazil 1-1
West Germany 0-2

1958
Scotland 1-1
France 3-2
Paraguay 3-3
West Germany 0-1

1962
USSR 0-2
Uruguay 3-1
Colombia 5-0
West Germany 1-0
Czechoslovakia 1-3
Chile 0-1 (F)

1974
Brazil 0-0
Zaire 9-0
Scotland 1-1
West Germany 0-2
Poland 1-2
Sweden 1-2

1982
Northern Ireland 0-0
Spain 1-2
Honduras 1-0

ZAIRE

1974
Scotland 0-2
Yugoslavia 0-9
Brazil 0-3